The University College of
SWANSEA
AN ILLUSTRATED HISTORY

An engraving of Singleton Abbey from F.O. Morris, *The Country Seats of the Noblemen and Gentlemen of Great Britain and Ireland*, vol. 5 (1880). Built in the 'neo-Gothic' style by his father between 1827 and 1837, Sir Henry Hussey Vivian entertained Gladstone here on the occasion of the latter's visit to Swansea in June 1887, an event commemorated by Gamwell's verses

The University College of
SWANSEA
AN ILLUSTRATED HISTORY

DAVID DYKES

ALAN SUTTON

First published in the United Kingdom in 1992 by
Alan Sutton Publishing Limited
Phoenix Mill · Far Thrupp · Stroud · Gloucestershire

First published in the United States of America in 1992 by
Alan Sutton Publishing Inc · Wolfeboro Falls · NH 03896-0848

British Library Cataloguing in Publication Data

Dykes, David
University College of Swansea
I. Title
378.42982

ISBN 0-86299-904-9

Library of Congress Cataloging in Publication Data
applied for

Typeset in 11/12 Garamond.
Typesetting and origination by
Alan Sutton Publishing Limited.
Printed in Great Britain by
The Bath Press, Bath, Avon.

AT SINGLETON
A Memory of June 4th, 1887

The leafy park of sea-side Singleton
Lay in the sunlight of as fair a sky
As ever wooed the unreluctant earth
And won her answering smile. Below, the beach –
A semi-circle of some twenty miles
Of yellow sand dunes and grey limestone rocks,
Rugged and bold – with outstretched arms embraced
That beauteous Bay which not unfitly claims
To share the palm that favoured Naples holds . . .

Upon a central space, where terraced banks,
With flowers enamelled, rise to velvet lawns,
The pleasant mansion of the Vivians stands . . .
Not built for ostentation, but delight,
Not lifting up to heaven a Babel-tower,
Nor spreading over acres, like a town,
It stands a monument of happy art,
In harmony with nature's sweetest self,
The home and heirloom of a favoured race.

Samuel Clearstone Gamwell (1850–96)

CONTENTS

PREFACE AND ACKNOWLEDGEMENTS

The great Dr Arnold once defined the history of universities as having to do 'with that which the several members of each of these societies have in common: it is . . . the biography of their common life'. This work is an attempt to tell the story of the University College of Swansea, its genesis and growth, through the lives and work of some of those personalities who created the college as we know it today and, to quote Dr Arnold again, had a 'distinct notion of what this common life consisted'. Such an attempt, especially when contained within a relatively small compass, will be fairly open to the criticism that it is highly selective or sketchily superficial. This history is both. It lays no claim to being 'definitive'; it is purely 'an historical sketch', an 'overview' of the college's main phases of development set in the context of the institution's relationship with its local community and its place in the broader field of university development. And the former is as important as the latter for, as a prominent legal member of the college council put it in the heady expansionist days of the sixties, 'A university college is part of the community in which it is set, and must never be allowed to become an island, isolated from its surroundings.'

It has, not been thought necessary to encumber the text with a full apparatus of references. Sources should, without too much difficulty, be traced in the archives and publications listed in the bibliography.

It is in the nature of an undertaking of this kind that one is indebted to a large number of people. The late Sir Lewis Jones, the kindest of men, first encouraged me to tackle a history of the college and his reminiscences of its early days and personalities were not only invaluable but a delight, told in an inimitable way. I owed a great deal, too, to the friendship of the late Dr John Parry who was very supportive of the idea and to the late John McIntyre.

W.C. ('Bill') Rogers is a friend who has been unstinting in his generosity over his intimate knowledge of Swansea, its local government and its inhabitants and their foibles. Help has come, too, from Edward Wright whose knowledge of Singleton – and of Clyne – goes back before his own time at the college, Professor F. Llewellyn Jones on the department of physics and college developments generally, Professor W.G.V. Balchin on geography and the natural sciences, Professor Armel Diverres about the pre-war college, Dr Robson Davies with reminiscences of wartime days and the metallurgy department, Dr Vivian Phillips about the development of engineering, Robin Huws Jones and Andrew Lochhead about social administration and the former also about the Lower Swansea Valley Project.

The late Colonel Norman Thomas was a source of great assistance over his father's work and over the college's physical developments and I owe a particular debt in this context to Ivan Dale Owen and Keith Mainstone, successive senior partners of the Percy Thomas Partnership, the latter cutting his teeth as an architect on the developments at Singleton in the early sixties while I did so in university administration.

For kind help on particular points, for photographs, many of which, alas, it has not been possible to use, and for other material I am indebted to Dr John Alban of the City of Swansea Archives Office, Mrs D.A. Ambrose, Robert V. Barnes, the Revd Canon T.K. Brunsden, the late Professor J.E. Coates, Dr F.G. Cowley, D. Andrew Davies, the late Dr Elwyn Davies, the Principal of Dumbarton House School, Dr Neil Bingham, Robert Elwell and Leslie Pinfield of the British Architectural Library, Alun Evans, Ms Elizabeth Fraser of the Society for the Protection of Science and Learning, Colin Harris of the Bodleian Library, G.M. Holmes, John Vivian Hughes, Dr Michael Isaac, the late Elis Jenkins, the late Harold E. Jenkins, Mrs M.P. Jones of *The Cambrian* Indexing Project, Professor Roy Knight, George Little, Murray McLaggan, Dr Derek Maling, Neville Masterman, Donald Moore, Professor Colyn Grey Morgan, Ms J.W. Morris, the late Alderman Percy Morris, Miss Betty Nelmes, the late Professor Hugh O'Neill, Dr David Painting, Professor Howard Purnell, Professor Jack Richardson, R.O. Roberts, H.L. Smale, Stuart Thomas, David J. Thomas, the late Mrs Mary Vivian, the late Miss Isabel M. Westcott, Peter White, David Williams, Professor M.T. Williams and Professor O.C. Zienkiewicz.

Guy Lewis has been of great assistance over a number of issues but particular thanks are due to him for the graph and maps, drawn with his usual meticulous flair. Thanks are also due to Eric Broadbent, Bob Watkins and especially Roger Davies, for their expert photography. David Bevan has been assiduous in his help over the college archives and I am grateful to him and to Miss Mary Cooper and her other colleagues in the library. I am also grateful to John Vivian Hughes and the staff of the Swansea Central Library for their assistance, and similarly to John Kenyon, librarian of the National Museum of Wales, Douglas Matthews and the staff of the London Library, and the librarians and staff of the Bodleian Library, the Cardiff Central Library, the Royal Institution of South Wales, and the library of the Royal Institute of British Architects.

I owe much, too, to the helpfulness and expertise of Roger Thorp and Louise Kirby (and subsequently Simon Fletcher) of Alan Sutton Publishing.

Special thanks must go to Professor Ralph Griffiths and Professor Glanmor Williams. They have both read the text at various stages and the complete manuscript, and have greatly improved it. My discussions with them have been invaluable and not only in purely literary terms. I owe them both a great debt but in particular Professor Williams who (not for the first time) has been of immeasurable encouragement and support. With such formidable help the failings that remain are mine alone. As are any opinions expressed: they are not the opinions of the college which, while being unfailingly helpful, has in no way attempted to influence my judgement. This book has been a long time in the making, partly because of other responsibilities and partly because of indifferent health and I am truly indebted to those who have been so patient with me, most especially, my wife, Margaret.

Acknowledgement is gratefully made to the following institutions and individuals for so readily granting permission to reproduce illustrations included in this volume: the British Architectural Library, pp. 130 (top), 155 (left); the Trustees of the British Museum, p. 8; Dr Robson Davies, p. 144; the Principal, Dumbarton House School, Swansea, p. 88; Fotomas Index, p. 10; John V. Hughes, p. 76 (top); Hulton Deutsch Collection, pp. 122, 155 (right), 193; *Illustrated London News*, pp. 27 (bottom), 35, 39, 60; Dr Michael Isaac, p. 192 (left); Professor Roy Knight, p. 159; Murray Maclaggan,

p. 32 (bottom); National Museum of Wales, pp. 52 (top left), 137; National Portrait Gallery, p. 1; Ivan Dale Owen, pp. 168, 169; Dr David Painting, p. 27 (top); Professor Jack Richardson, p. 189 (top left); W.C. Rogers, p. 41 (right); Professor Robert Steel, p. 209; Swansea Central Library, pp. 5, 24, 30 (right), 34 (left), 41 (left), 46, 52 (bottom right and left), 57, 64, 67, 76 (bottom), 95 (bottom), 108; Swansea City Archives Office, pp. 48, 71; Swansea Museum, pp. 22 (bottom), 30 (left), 34 (right); the late Mrs Mary Vivian, p. 65; Professor Glanmor Williams, pp. 150, 187 (left); Professor Oleg Zienkiewicz, p. 187 (right).

INTRODUCTION:

'ENLIGHTENMENT OF THE DEMOCRACY'

O n the evening of 26 November 1921, the Viscount Haldane of Cloan addressed a crowded and enthusiastic audience in Swansea on the subject of the university and the Welsh democracy. For Haldane, the theme was well-tried and not unfamiliar; he had, after all, covered similar ground on countless occasions to equally rousing receptions. Whatever the weakness of his delivery – for despite his imposing physique he spoke in a piping tenor with 'few rich shades in his intonation' while his gestures reminded some people more of a penguin than of 'a man whose life has been lived in thinking out great abstractions' – it was strikingly redeemed by his evident intellectual power and his obvious passion for the topic in hand. The following morning the local newspaper waxed lyrical over the evening's performance. It was, said the *Cambria Daily Leader*,

one that will be long remembered for the immense field it covered, its prophetic note, its breadth of outlook, its calm belief in a great future for Welsh democracy attainable only through its higher education . . . [Lord Haldane's] arresting personality, his gentle, serene charm of manner, a smile never far from his face, captivated as really as his matter, and there were unforgettable moments when, 'Attired with sudden brightness as a man inspired,' he spoke of communion with the great spirits; of the task he, unquestioning, has set himself; and finally of his feeling that Swansea really cares for the highest education.

The 'midwife' at the birth of the college: Lord Haldane (1856–1928), sketched by Sir Francis Carruthers Gould. Haldane's gestures reminded some of a penguin

Richard Burdon Haldane was the son of a devout, if austerely 'fundamentalist', Scottish lawyer, and had been educated at the universities of Edinburgh and Göttingen, where he had studied philosophy before taking up the English legal career for which, from the first, he had been destined. Over the years, throwing off the extreme religious convictions of his parents, Haldane had developed four passions: philosophy – he was an eloquent, if obscure, exponent of a modernized Hegelianism, the fruit of his German experience – the law, the army, and education. But, in his own mind, even his epic reconstruction of the army as the most effective Secretary of State for War (1905–12) since Cardwell or his achievements at the summit of his politico-legal career as Lord Chancellor (1912–15 and later, in the first Labour government, in 1924) counted for less than his commitment to the promotion of higher education. For, to Haldane, the furtherance of education, and, especially, the cause of universities and their place in the broader community were what he lived for.

As a Member of Parliament – Haldane was Liberal Member for East Lothian from 1885 until his elevation to the House of Lords in 1911 – he had interested himself in the problems of the University of London. In 1898, in the teeth of strenuous political opposition, he had, with Arthur Balfour and Sidney Webb, achieved its transformation from being merely an examining machine into a federal teaching university. Very much in Haldane's mind, too, were the issue of technological education and his conviction, derived from his intimate knowledge of Germany and its technical colleges, that higher technical education in Britain lagged so far behind that of its continental rivals as to be totally inadequate for this country's scientific prospects and 'the industrial needs of the Empire'. He was, thus, the prime mover in securing the amalgamation of the resources of the existing science colleges in South Kensington into the new Imperial College of Science and Technology in 1907. Here, Haldane's ambition to see the creation of a British Imperial Physical-Technical Institute – a metropolitan Charlottenburg – could be realized.

Haldane's broader concern with the need to sustain the work of the provincial university colleges which had been created in the last quarter of the nineteenth century was demonstrated, too, in the instrumental role he played in the creation, in 1906, of a continuing Advisory Committee on Grants to University Colleges – the precursor of the University Grants Committee (UGC). Then, in 1909, he returned to university education in the metropolis with his appointment, following his own suggestion, to the chairmanship of a royal commission on university education in London. Although it was an exhaustive four-year exercise, the commission's proposals to reconstitute the university on the lines of a unitary provincial university, frustrated by the Great War and castigated as 'attempted Germanisation', never led to decisive results. By 1915, too, Haldane, never a popular personality, had been forced out of the Lord Chancellorship, the innocent victim of a vitriolic campaign by the gutter-press against what was put about as his pro-German sympathies. But his casting-out into the political wilderness gave Haldane more scope for his enthusiasm for educational reform. And in April 1916 he became a natural, if not an initial, choice by the Asquith government to chair another royal commission, this time on university education in Wales.

What Haldane sought in education was most clearly and convincingly set out for the wider public in the series of addresses, like that at Swansea, that he gave all over the country in the first two decades or so of the century and where his metaphysics did not stand in the way of understanding. It was basically that 'everyone should have a chance, and that there should be the nearest possible approach to equality of educational opportunity'. What Haldane saw as inhibiting the practical application of this ideal was the absence of any conception of the process of education as being a single co-ordinated unit, an indivisible whole. What was needed was 'the welding of the educational system . . . into one complete whole, in which elementary education, secondary education, and the University shall be indissoluble parts of one system'. The universities, established in centres of population and supported by their local communities – truly 'civic universities' in the description coined by Haldane himself – would be the dominating influence of the overall structure, shaping the spirit of the schools in their districts and carrying their message, too, through extra-mural teaching by their staffs to their local adult communities. As he put it in Swansea, this was his 'Cause' – 'the Cause of the systematic enlightenment of the democracy and the organization of methods by which that enlightenment could be systematically and scientifically brought about'.

Thus it was that his ambition to see a wider opportunity for university and higher education led Haldane to spend so much of his later life in promoting the cause of universities and of adult education. In this campaign he had no qualms, either, about drawing out to the full what he saw as the menace to Britain's industrial future from the systematic application of science to industry which he had experienced in Germany. But he was at pains to stress that the technological education he had in mind – and it must be remembered that most of the nascent English provincial universities of the time bore a closer resemblance to technical colleges than to universities as we know them – 'must not be merely technical or designed as a means to material ends . . . Applied science is in its best form only possible on a wide foundation of general science. And the fruitful scientific spirit is developed to-day on a basis of high intellectual training . . . which only the atmosphere of a fully developed University can completely provide.' Moreover, 'without danger of partial starvation' it was not possible to 'separate science from literature and philosophy. Each grows best in the presence of the other.' This was a lesson to be brought home to the full in the foundation of the new university college in Swansea.

Haldane came to Swansea in November 1921 to inaugurate the college's second session. The invitation had a certain piquancy because, in many people's minds, there were personal bonds linking audience to speaker. For it was not Haldane's reputation as statesman and politician alone, outstanding as that was, that attracted such a spirited and warm-hearted response from the college people and townsfolk who packed the Central Hall that Saturday evening. What mattered to them was the role Haldane had played in the creation of their college. Was he not, at the very least, the agent who had realized a dream that had been cherished for more than a quarter of a century? Although Haldane, publicly, would have dismissed any talk of himself as the college's *founder* – as he told his audience he was in no way the college's parent or its mother – he was willing to admit, jokingly, that he saw himself 'in the position of a midwife' at its birth.

The University College of Swansea had opened its doors to its first students little more than a year before on Tuesday 5 October 1920. As the youngest of what were then four constituent colleges of the University of Wales, its creation had flowed from a recommendation of that royal commission on university education in Wales set up four years earlier with Haldane, well-versed in the arcana of such bodies, as its genial,

The Lord Chancellor in 1913: Lord Haldane
at the height of his career. A cartoon by Owl
from *Vanity Fair*, 19 March 1913

searching and industrious chairman. The commission's appointment had been preci-
pitated by a variety of problems, not least a questioning of the adequacy of the
university's central machinery of government, but any notion that a new university
college might be established in Swansea had not been one of them. This had been very
much a side-issue that had forced its way on to the agenda only after the commission had
been appointed; but this side-issue – the elevation of the town's technical college into an
institution of university status – became a matter close to Haldane's heart and to his
educational philosophy.

With a wide-ranging brief, framed to embrace nothing less than a complete review of
the organization of university education in the principality, it was typical of Haldane
that he should throw himself into his work with energy and enthusiasm and that he
should imbue his team of commissioners with his own spirited and meticulous
approach. Their study and understanding of the university were painstaking to a degree
and their examination of witnesses, always courteous, was thorough and penetrating.
Their Final Report, published in March 1918, was greeted with general satisfaction and

its comprehensive proposals, which were to become the constitutional blueprint of the University of Wales for much of the twentieth century, were hailed as both 'sane and imaginative'. Sir Emrys Evans has called them 'epoch making', and for those in Swansea who had campaigned for a college of university standing for twenty years or more this description was amply justified. For the commission recommended that the Swansea Technical College should become a constituent college of the university. The news was a local relief from the increasingly grave communiqués coming from the Somme, where the German army had launched its spring offensive only two days after the publication of the Report. It seemed, at last, that a long-felt desire for a college of university standing might now be gratified and that the protracted, if fitful and at times acrid, campaign for its establishment might soon reach a satisfactory conclusion. Such hopes were quickly proved to be well founded: in its broad terms, the commission's advice was accepted with especially commendable speed in view of the larger preoccupations of the difficult final months of the War, and the foundation of the University College of Swansea was formally sanctioned by the grant of the necessary royal charter on 21 January 1920.

The Cambria Daily Leader's impression of Lord Haldane's inaugural address at the Central Hall, Swansea, on 26 November 1921

CHAPTER ONE

'SCIENTIFIC AND PRACTICAL WANTS'

I n its genesis, the new university college was distinct from its sister institutions at Aberystwyth and Bangor and, in some ways, even from that at Cardiff. It drew heavily upon that reservoir of Welsh cultural and patriotic sentiment that had brought the earlier colleges into being in the previous century and continued to sustain them. But its direct inspiration came from its own region and from what its promoters saw as the need to produce a technocratic élite to serve the major industries of the Swansea area. In this respect the University College of Swansea, both in its promotion and in its early development, was more akin to some of the budding civic universities founded in England in the latter half of the nineteenth century – though each of these had characteristics peculiar to itself – than to its sister colleges in Wales. As Percy Watkins pointed out in *The Times Educational Supplement*, 'Unlike most modern English universities, which were founded primarily to foster science and technology, the Welsh colleges were deliberately fashioned from the first as centres of a liberal education'.[1] This was a distinction not lost on the Haldane Commission. For while science was certainly not ignored in the other three colleges – Cardiff's first two principals were physicists and at Bangor the relevance of science to local agriculture was always stressed – the commission felt obliged to dwell upon the desirability of introducing into them a greater technological dimension, at the same time bringing home to the promoters of the Swansea scheme the need to humanize their proposals.

Nevertheless, despite the local concern for technology which was the key-stone of the college and central to its foundation, the development of higher education in Swansea can in no way be divorced from the wider context of the educational movement in Wales which, in the latter part of the nineteenth century, was virtually inseparable from articulate cultural opinion and its growing consciousness of nationhood. And no real sense can be made of the story of the college without something being said of the history of that movement within its broader British framework.

A century before the college's foundation, when the country was recovering from the long, weary wars with France, Britain could boast seven universities: Oxford and Cambridge, collegiate in structure, their beginnings lying in the mists of the twelfth century; the very different Scottish universities – St Andrews (1411), Glasgow (1451), Aberdeen (1495) and Edinburgh (1583) – owing more to continental models than to anything south of the Tweed; and, in Ireland, Trinity College, Dublin, founded in 1592 as a bastion of the Elizabethan protestant ascendancy.

For generations admission to Oxford and Cambridge, Anglican dominated and secure under the operation of the Clarendon Code, had been severely restricted. For a century or more, if not sunk in an aura of 'port and prejudice', the ancient universities had been unadventurous and torpescent in terms of scholarship; when not training men for the

Church, dwindling into places of 'polite learning', cultural polish and social resort for the aristocracy and gentry at large. Now, although a wind of change was already beginning to blow through Oxford and Cambridge, they were still shackled by their Anglican restrictions and tone, and remained socially remote and inaccessible. If one wanted an opportunity to grapple with a broader curriculum, to study new disciplines in an atmosphere free of religious tests and open to all classes, then it was to Scotland or above all to Germany, that one had to turn. Lord John Russell was sent to Edinburgh because his father was convinced that 'nothing was learned in the English universities'. In the latter years of the eighteenth century the contributions that university made to new knowledge through political economy, metaphysics and natural science constituted an irresistible lodestone. And, as the nineteenth century unfolded, for all their shortcomings – their Presbyterian ambience and their didactic, low-level undergraduate teaching – the non-sectarian and cheaper Scottish universities continued to draw students from England and Wales and did so in increasing numbers. In the new disciplines, especially, they still met with little competition from Oxford and Cambridge, although, paradoxically, the new studies derived largely from English sources. Their real rivals, with whom they had always enjoyed the most fruitful contacts, were the continental universities: those of Germany, especially, since the recrudescence of Prussia after the débâcle of 1806.

The new foundations of Berlin, Breslau and Bonn, in particular, attracted widespread attention for their philosophical and scientific studies. The impression the work of these German universities, their dedication to learning and their religious toleration, created on receptive minds like Thomas Campbell (1777–1844), the poet, and the Benthamite, Henry Brougham – both Scottish educated – eventually crystallized in the foundation, in 1826, of the 'University of London', built on an old rubbish dump at the end of Gower Street. Aptly said to have been conceived in Germany of Scottish parentage, the new institution imposed no religious tests on its members and the teaching of theology in any form was excluded from its curriculum. In the climate of the time its secular character – that 'sty of infidelity' as it was graphically described by the ultra-Tory *John Bull* – and its arrogation of the title of 'university', though it could take upon itself no power to confer degrees, were bound to provoke a passionate response. Yet, amid all the jeers and taunts of the cheap Tory press, the anguish of orthodox opinion was adroitly harnessed and energies were directed towards the creation of a rival institution which would provide the missing element of spiritual and moral instruction. Even before the new 'university' opened in 1828, therefore, measures were being set in train that, within the year, were to see King's 'College', Anglican and Tory from its inception, established next to Somerset House in the Strand.

Politic and deferential to customary practice as was the implication of the title and status of the new institution, it became clear before long that its inability to award degrees was a serious encumbrance, especially to its medical school. Gower Street was as shackled as the Strand. Thus, in 1836, a new 'University of London' was set up with the power to grant its own degrees, open not only to the students of King's College and 'University College' – as Gower Street now became – but to the students of any other recognized institution. The University was, however, essentially an external examining body and it had no authority over the policy or development of the institutions from which its examinees came. But it had broken the mould. The ancient universities were

The POLITICAL TOY-MAN.

Lord Brougham (1778–1868) hawking shares in the original 'University of London', founded as a joint-stock company, around Lincoln's Inn. He is shown in this 1825 cartoon by Robert Cruikshank as a toy-seller with a tray on his head supporting a 'neo-Gothic' university building (a vision of the 'red brick' to come!). Brougham was also a potent force in movements for popular education, including the mechanics' institutes and the Society for the Diffusion of Useful Knowledge (Thomas Love Peacock's 'Steam Intellect Society' in *Crotchet Castle*)

now no longer the only route to an English university degree and, in the future, the University of London was to ease the passage to other equally dramatic changes in the provinces and in Wales.

If the first step in widening university education had been taken by Benthamites and 'philosophic radicals' in London, it was the conservative establishment which now began to further its development outside the capital. In 1827 St David's College, Lampeter was founded for the express purpose of training Welsh clergy and, in 1831, at the height of the ferment over the Reform Bill, discussions began at Durham about the establishment of a college there. It was widely believed that the lands and revenues of the Church would be the next bastions to be attacked if the Reform Bill were passed, and the dean and chapter of Durham therefore strove to disarm criticism by alienating part of their very large revenues to set up such a college, one that would be under their own control and open only to Anglicans. To the considerable disadvantage of the Welsh college, as it turned out, the new *University* of Durham was opened in 1833 with the immediate power of conferring degrees, its reputation founded on theology, though it also offered degrees in arts and science.

Until the 1840s London and Durham remained the only university institutions outside Scotland, Oxford, Cambridge and Dublin. Little was otherwise available to offer even a modicum of a higher education – Lampeter was still a struggling theological college and was not empowered to grant degrees until 1852 and then only in divinity. Even the best of the English dissenting academies that still continued from the previous century had decayed; the expansive scope of study and the imaginative curricula that some of them had offered were but memories and they were now mere sectarian theological colleges. In a sense the kind of education that they had once provided had been taken over by voluntary societies of another kind: the literary and philosophical societies, the Athenaeums, the Royal Institutions, that, following the seminal example of the Society of Arts in London (1754), had been springing up from the late eighteenth century in almost every town with pretensions to importance in Britain. It was 'a busy age', said Jeremy Bentham, 'where everything teems with discovery and with improvement'. The new institutions stemmed from that flowering of scientific interest that, at this time, marked the cultural growth of society in the provinces where mining, industry and farming were being remodelled on progressive lines, and civility and urbanity were becoming fashionable. They were dedicated, with varying degrees of success, to the advancement and the transmission of 'useful knowledge'. In membership and outlook they were essentially 'middle class', though lectures and classes were frequently provided for 'operative mechanics'. Wales was late in this field, but by 1840 literary and scientific institutions had been established in a number of the thrusting commercial centres of south Wales: Neath in 1825; Swansea ten years later; Cardiff in 1837, and Carmarthen two years after that.

Parallel with them, but frequently possessing all too short an effective existence, were the mechanics' institutes. The earliest mechanics' institutes in Wales, perhaps naturally, appeared in the industrializing south in the 1820s (Cardiff 1826, Swansea 1826, Bridgend 1829); yet, although 'formed with great zeal and spirit', they had chequered and spasmodic careers and increasingly lacked working-class, or rather skilled-artisan, support. By mid-century, while the movement had spread to mid and north Wales, its original utilitarian object of systematic instruction for the mechanical classes had degenerated, all too often, into the provision of social clubs for the lower middle classes where lectures on phrenology, mesmerism and other popular subjects of the day held sway: 'play centres for serious clerks' was what G.M. Young was, rather ungenerously, to label them.

Systematic instruction was beginning to develop outside London, though, for the emergent professions. Growing in vigour, status and self-consciousness as it abandoned old-fashioned notions and practices, medicine is a case in point. Particularly noteworthy were the medical schools set up as feeders to hospitals in the wennish industrial cities of the north: Manchester, for example, in 1825; Sheffield in 1828; Leeds in 1831; and Liverpool and Newcastle in 1834. Although these medical schools had no power to confer degrees, they could prepare candidates for examinations of the Royal College of Surgeons and the Apothecaries' Society which gave to the successful students licences to practise medicine.

The aims of these schools, and their courses of study, were, by their very nature, limited and circumscribed. The atmosphere that gave rise to them, however, and to the literary and philosophical societies, in which, frequently, doctors were leading lights, also encouraged the growth of the idea in some of the greater towns that more broadly based educational institutions should be set up. In 1826, for example, an attempt was made to set up a university in Leeds. In 1829 and again in 1836 proposals to establish a university in Manchester were resurrected after an interval of two hundred years. Again, in Newcastle in 1831 a similar suggestion was mooted. But all these schemes foundered largely because, although there was much local enthusiasm, the capital necessary to establish the institutions on a sound financial basis was not forthcoming. At last,

'Calves Heads and Brains', an 1826 caricature of a lecture on phrenology – the pseudo-scientific craze of the age – to the gullible and fashion-conscious middle-class members of a provincial literary and philosophical society however, capital was provided for one such scheme, under the will of a Flintshire Welshman, John Owens, who died in 1846; this allowed 'Owens College' to begin its work in the former home of Richard Cobden in Manchester some five years later. Free of religious tests but permitting theological studies provided that they were not 'reasonably offensive to the conscience of any student . . .', the new college broadly leant upon the example of Scotland and London. It could not, however, grant degrees itself and to facilitate this the University of London took the unprecedented step of recognizing the first college outside London as an 'affiliated' institution on behalf of which London degrees could be awarded. It was an umbrella that was to help many provincial colleges to weather the storms and stresses of their early days.

Yet, Owens College was to have a chequered and uncertain career for many years. At more than one point it was almost closed or converted into a technical college. The college was essentially a private venture. It received no financial backing from central government funds until 1890; indeed, not for a further two years after that was it to receive any grant from the city corporation of Manchester itself. However, if the government was unwilling to give financial support to the private venture in Manchester, it was, on the other hand, concerned, on political grounds, to advance a similar project in Ireland from government funds. This was intended to ensure an indigenous higher education on a broader non-sectarian base than that provided by Trinity College and which would, at the same time, be acceptable to both Catholics and Presbyterians. In the year of Owens's death, the undenominational Queen's Colleges were set up in Cork, Galway and Belfast, followed in 1850 by the creation of the Queen's University as a federal umbrella for the colleges. However uneasy and difficult the practical application of the scheme was to be, from the outset it was firmly funded from the public purse, £10,000 being provided for buildings together with a recurrent grant of some £30,000.

What had happened in Ireland now concentrated some people's minds on the plight of Wales. Amid the storm of controversy surrounding the Report of the Welsh Education Commission there arose a loose flurry of debate which increasingly identified the provision of higher education in Wales as an aspiration of cultural nationhood. After a decade or more, however, it remained no more than an aspiration. It was left to Hugh Owen (1804–81), a civil servant who had spent many years immured in the utilitarian 'hot-house' atmosphere of the Poor Law Commission, to organize a practical campaign for higher education. Autocratic, obsessive and ubiquitous, Owen, a strong advocate of state-aid, had, since the thirties, campaigned vigorously for popular education in the principality. In 1854 he took his first faltering steps towards a 'university' for Wales based on the model of the Queen's Colleges, with government financial aid as its eventual keystone. His ideas, though, were premature and too ambitious and, in the face of Voluntaryist (Nonconformist anti-state-aid) objections, came to nothing.

It was to be another eight years before the movement for higher education in Wales seems to have been taken up again. Hugh Owen's enthusiasm was rekindled by the ideas of Dr Thomas Nicholas (1816–79), a Congregational minister and a professor at the Presbyterian College, Carmarthen. What was important about Nicholas's intervention was his emphasis on the need for what he called 'Middle' and 'High' schools in Wales. It was perhaps the earliest recognition of the fundamental point that no scheme of higher education in Wales could really succeed unless it was adequately underpinned by a supportive secondary system open generally to the middle class. This was his priority but he advocated, too, the creation of two colleges, one in north Wales and one in the south, which would come together to form a university for Wales, with either the University of London or the Queen's Colleges as the model. Moreover, he was adamant that whatever Voluntaryist objections there might be to accepting government financial aid, 'university education without it is totally impossible'.

The years 1862 and 1863 may be said to have seen the university movement in Wales beginning in earnest. Nevertheless, progress was not rapid. There were many stumbling blocks for Hugh Owen and his helpers to overcome but, narrowing their horizons to the more limited foundation of a single college, the opportunity arose, in 1867, of acquiring the bankrupt Castle Hotel at Aberystwyth and, there, in October 1872, their new University College of Wales opened.

For years the college was to face recurring financial crises. All of Owen's efforts to collect contributions, now a part of Welsh folklore, were insufficient to ward off financial embarrassment. Several attempts to secure state-aid met with firm refusals from governments of the day, an opposition based less on an entrenched dogmatism than on a concern that grant-aid for Aberystwyth – as indeed for the new university colleges that were multiplying over England at the time – would lead to 'the power of granting cheap degrees'. And it must be recognized that academic standards were low. A high proportion of the students at Aberystwyth, for instance, were very young, some mere schoolboys under sixteen years of age. The number of entrants, also, did not rise to expectation. In part this was due to the perennial problems of Welsh geography. Nearly half the college's students came from Cardiganshire and few from the populous industrial districts of south Wales. In part it was due to cost. More fundamental, however, was the lack of an adequate system of secondary education to bolster the college and provide a continuing supply of adequate university material.

Despite the heightened trauma and vicious animosity that had surrounded the activities of the two voluntary societies (the non-sectarian British and Foreign Schools Society and the ponderously entitled Anglican National Society for Promoting the Education of the Poor in the Principles of the Established Church) and government attempts at sponsorship and inspection in the face of Voluntaryist scruples earlier in the century, the provision of popular education – education at the elementary level – had improved considerably. It was to improve even more dramatically as the full effects of Forster's 1870 Education Act began to be felt, especially after the tightening of the attendance rules in 1876.

At secondary or intermediate level things were very different. Forster's Act was the capstone to the utilitarian urge to establish a national scheme of education specifically for the lower orders of society: what Brougham and his fellow 'philosophic radicals' had looked forward to at the beginning of the century. Such opinion did not see schooling as, in any sense, 'tiered' or with any natural progression from one grade of education to another. Each grade of schooling was self-contained and each grade was intended for a different social class. And, while elementary education might be systematized for the creation of more useful citizens in the face of the rise of democracy or for reasons of 'social control', the principles of *laissez-faire* and self-help conditioned attitudes to what was seen as 'middle-class' schooling. At intermediate level, therefore, there was no national system and, for the lower middle classes, there was still an immense dearth of schools. In

Wales, it was the gradual realization that this serious gap existed that was one of the several strands that helped to bring about the establishment of the Aberdare Committee in 1880.

For the more affluent of the middle classes, the pioneering activities of some great headmasters, from Thomas Arnold of Rugby and his disciples onwards, and the introduction of new foundation schemes through the Charity Commissioners had led to a reformation of the public schools and the grammar schools. But, despite the introduction of modern subjects like English, French, German and mathematics, their emphasis was still on the classics, as it had been since the sixteenth century, and those pupils who thought about university generally looked to Oxford and Cambridge. Otherwise – and this is one reason for the popularity of the urban private school in the eyes of Victorian middle-class parents, particularly the less affluent among them, who eschewed, or were daunted by, the 'irrelevancy' of a classical grammar school training – pupils left early and went into commerce or some equally 'useful' or necessary employment.

This attitude was not confined to schooling. G.M. Young remarks on 'how alien to the middle classes was the idea of higher education not connected with practical utility or social distinction'. Times, nevertheless, were changing. Insecure the college at Aberystwyth might have been, but at least it did not stand alone. Critical as its Welsh cultural background was as a formative force in its foundation and its very existence, the college cannot be isolated from a new atmosphere of enthusiasm for university expansion that was now pervading many parts of provincial England. In London, what had been dingy, poverty-stricken and unattractive institutions with no social cachet were at last emerging from their long years of stagnation. Both University College and King's College were building reputations for their science teaching. Durham, in 1850, had abandoned its engineering classes and seven years later had seriously thought of closing altogether. Now, with the foundation of a College of Physical Science at Newcastle in 1871 (later, Armstrong College and a nucleus of the University of Newcastle), it was injected with new blood though it took another decade for the new foundation to become viable. In Manchester, Owens College, from being dismissed as a 'mortifying failure', little more than a decade later was attracting staff of distinction. It had become a place to watch and to copy. And the copying began: once more the country embarked on a period of university expansion, but this time in a climate of growing anxiety.

The late 1860s introduced an element of 'future shock' into the complacency of a mid-Victorian generation that even the Crimean War and the Indian Mutiny had failed to shake. The widening of the franchise by the Reform Act of 1867 was unsettling to much of informed opinion: Robert Lowe was not just reflecting his own grim view of democracy when he announced that 'it will be absolutely necessary to compel our future masters to learn their letters'. There was a genuine concern about the inadequacy of the country's education made more urgent by the inevitability of further electoral reform. Already, this concern had manifested itself in two Royal Commissions on schools: the Clarendon Commission on the nine leading public schools in 1864, and the Taunton Commission on 'secondary' education in 1867. And Forster's Act was the ineluctable corollary to Disraeli's 'leap in the dark' and Lowe's apprehensions.

There were other issues besides the political which were giving rise to disquiet. A major factor starting to cause serious alarm in certain quarters of the business and industrial community was Britain's increasing failure to maintain its competitive position over its European rivals. By the more far-seeing this was attributed to the superiority of technological training and research on the Continent, and some of them had had forebodings of this since 1851. At the Great Exhibition, it is true, Britain had carried off most of the prizes in nearly all of the one hundred or so departments. But even then, perceptive minds like Lyon Playfair, at that time a professor in the School of Mines, and Henry Cole, both commissioners of the Exhibition and later the first secretaries of the Department of Science and Art, saw that this position could not be maintained unless there were a robust injection of new blood into the existing educational system.

Playfair hoped that some kind of 'Industrial University' to bear comparison with the industrial colleges of the Continent – Berlin, Karlsruhe, Munich and the École Centrale in Paris – would flow from their agitation. This 'competition of intellect', as he called it, was to happen but in the distant future. A much more pressing problem was 'the disadvantage of the want of preliminary education' in technology and the immediate gain was the establishment of the Department of Science and Art at South Kensington under the aegis of the Education Department of the Privy Council. Through the new department, a country-wide system of state-supported science schools was set up over the years which, in some instances, were eventually to blossom into technical colleges and universities. Nevertheless, despite the energetic enthusiasm at South Kensington and the dedication of many of the teachers on the spot, progress was slow, the work of the schools was comparatively low-level and, as we shall see in the case of Swansea, it was not altogether appreciated by local industrialists.

There was, however, further shock to come. The 1867 Paris Exhibition was a traumatic failure for Britain which confirmed in the minds of many commentators the prophecies of the Cassandras of half a generation before. To Lyon Playfair, 'the one cause upon which there was most unanimity of conviction is that France, Prussia, Austria, Belgium, and Switzerland possess good systems of industrial education for the masters and managers of factories and workshops, and that England possesses none'.

At the same time, the spectacular rise of Prussia and its rapid growth as a military and industrial power in Europe gave pause for solemn thought. In 1865 Matthew Arnold had been asked to report on the German universities for the Schools Inquiry (Taunton) Commission, and had pinpointed the challenge they presented. The crushing defeat of France in 1870 and the obvious military and industrial might of the newly united German state – even if, in Britain, it was not yet the menacing spectre it was to become – starkly pressed home the efficacy of Germany's educational system, particularly in the technical sphere, that seemed, self-evidently, to underlie its lightning success.

Already, in 1868, in the midst of the anguish following the débâcle of the Paris Exhibition, the Society of Arts had organized a conference to discuss the problem of technological education. From it had emerged a scheme for the establishment of a series of new colleges on the model of those already existing in London and Manchester specifically designed to provide training in the sciences. The proposal was never implemented because of a lack of money, but it was, in large measure, the atmosphere created by the debate surrounding it that brought forth a rash of development in higher education in the provinces over the next decade. Owing much to the enthusiasm and organizing energies of their local commercial and industrial communities, led in many

The spectre of continental industrial competition spurred Lyon Playfair (1818–98), later Britain's first scientific peer, *left*, to associate industrial advantage with technological education. In Britain, he complained that 'instruction in science terminates just where the Industrial Colleges of the Continent begin'. Matthew Arnold (1822–88), *right*, as an inspector of schools reported on the German universities for the Taunton Commission. An advocate of the 'civic university' providing a cheap, non-residential education, he concluded that 'It is in science that we have most need to borrow from the German universities. The French university has no liberty, and the English universities have no science; the German universities have both.' (Cartoons by Ape [Carlo Pellegrini] in *Vanity Fair*, 20 February 1875 and Coïdé [James Tissot], 11 November 1871)

instances by self-made men who had keenly felt the fiasco of Paris, university colleges began to be established in a number of English cities. Mention has been made of the setting-up of the Newcastle College of Physical Science in 1871. Three years later, the Yorkshire College of Science was established in Leeds; in 1876 the College of Science for the West of England in Bristol; Firth College, Sheffield, in 1879; and Mason College, Birmingham, in 1880. Though different and multi-disciplinary from the start, what these colleges had in common was that they were science- or technically-orientated, that, in their formative years, they operated under the degree-giving patronage and respectability of the University of London, and, above all, that they were non-residential and cheap.

Public opinion in the great urban centres of the nation was, at last, being stirred but it had taken events on the Continent to achieve this. Parliament, too, was taking notice of what was happening and, in 1868, it set up a Select Committee (the Samuelson Committee) 'to enquire into the Provisions for giving Instruction in Theoretical and Applied Science to the Industrial Classes'. Although, in Sir Eric Ashby's words, the committee's eventual Report was to 'set technical education on the course that led to twentieth century industrial Britain', it was to be more than half a century before all its advanced recommendations were put into effect and it is still quoted today as a not wholly heeded beacon. The essential implication of the committee's Report was state-aid for education, and especially for higher education in pure and applied science. The nation was not ready for such state direction but by 1872 the Gladstone government was at least persuaded to set up a Royal Commission (the Devonshire Commission) to enquire into the relationship of the state to science. The commission's thorough – almost Germanic – investigations and the Report that followed, with its stress on the 'primary duty' of research and the creation of scientific research laboratories, had a profound effect upon the direction that the new university colleges were to take.

Wales, to all intents and purposes, stood apart from the thrust of the university developments that were dynamizing provincial cities elsewhere, despite the intensity and the rapidity with which parts of the principality were being industrialized. For all the immense industrial changes which were to have profound demographic and geographic effects on Wales and to spawn a variety of industrial endeavours, it is remarkable how little impact they made on the university movement. Nicholas, it is true, emphasized the relationship between higher education and the industrial needs of Wales. It was a sobering fact that:

> The direction of our large and lucrative undertakings, the chief posts in the country which require superior skill and attainments, are monopolised by strangers. The Welshman has to struggle in an unequal race, and is necessarily left behind. Let Wales have 2,000 of her sons under daily University training (about the proportion found in Scotland), and a different result will certainly follow.

He had already emphasized the importance of a university being 'properly adapted to the scientific and practical wants of its chief centres of manufacture'. Yet, for all these pious sentiments, it is remarkable how little was done to cultivate any higher scientific or industrial training in Wales and how limited the support of industry itself was for the university movement. Aberystwyth, the town chosen for the eventual college, was not only lacking in industry itself but could hardly be located more remotely from the industries of both north and south Wales. There was little or no conception that the college had any role in contributing to industry. The industrialist David Davies of Llandinam, the most loyal of benefactors, expressed his deep dismay when he discovered that, because of a lack of students, there were suggestions that the college should concentrate more on the training of teachers and ministers. Davies himself was uncharacteristic in that he was one of the few industrialists actively to support the college. There was, indeed, little interest in technological education among Welsh industrial leaders although the growing national concern was beginning to make itself felt in the minds of a few in south Wales who were dimly realizing that the varied industries of that region required a trained scientific expertise if they were to develop effectively.

'The Western University of Great Britain', to have been established at the Gnoll House, Neath, in 1857. Its remarkable prospectus, from which the engraving is taken, shows an attitude to education much in advance of its time. If it had been successful the Gnoll College project might well have changed the course of the university movement in Wales

In 1857, it is true, a private venture scheme had been floated to establish a technological university at the Gnoll, Neath. The grandiosely entitled 'Western University of Great Britain', intended to 'complete the education of young gentlemen in the practical applications of science to the management of land manufactures and commerce, to the public service, the professions and other pursuits', seems to have collapsed even as it was being launched. To what extent its projectors saw it as a genuinely educative scheme or as a mere financial speculation must be open to doubt. It seems that the college was, at least in part, modelled on the École Centrale in Paris which had captured Playfair's imagination. Some of the 'resident professors' said to have been appointed were later to have distinguished scientific careers: Arthur Cayley, for instance, already an FRS, was to go on to become Sadlerian Professor of Pure Mathematics in Cambridge in 1863; and Thomas Spencer Cobbold, elected an FRS in 1864, was to have a special chair in helminthology created for him at the Royal Veterinary College. It is likely that, as *The Cambrian* (13 November 1857) darkly hinted, the projectors 'may have had self-aggrandizement for their object'. Certainly the fees were prohibitive enough but they needed to be to meet the high salaries offered as a lure to quality staff. But as *The Cambrian* also confessed, 'self interest and the interest of the public seemed most closely united'. Nobody could 'deny but that the nation does not possess such an establishment as it was hoped Gnoll College would be, and nobody can deny but that the nation requires it'. Whatever the motives, bearing in mind the doubtful experiences elsewhere, the enterprise was way ahead of its time. Had it been successful, though, it might have become the first full university college in Wales and the history of the university movement might have taken a different course.

While the Gnoll project seems to have had some influence on Nicholas's ideas, it was soon forgotten and its ghost was firmly laid to rest. Benjamin Jowett, the Master of Balliol, who took a keen interest in the affairs of Aberystwyth and was the inspiration behind the new university college in Bristol, had, in 1874, also been the driving force behind a scheme to set up a provincial college at Merthyr Tydfil, on the lines of Armstrong College and partially endowed from Oxford money, but this, too, was still-born.

Among those who had given some encouragement to the Gnoll scheme had been Henry Hussey Vivian, the Swansea copper magnate. In the very year of the flotation of the project he had been elected one of the two Liberal Members of Parliament for Glamorgan. It was in the context of the broader developments in higher education, the inadequacy of intermediate education in Wales to meet them and, most pressing, the critical financial state of the Aberystwyth college, that, on 1 July 1879, Vivian was persuaded to introduce a motion into the Commons urging the government 'to consider the best means of assisting any local effort which may be made for supplying the deficiency of Higher Education in Wales'. It was not unnatural that the motion should be lost, for, as the ever-hostile *Western Mail* (2 & 3 July 1879) pointed out, the idea of grant-aid for Aberystwyth was 'simply absurd': what government could grant a subsidy to Aberystwyth when it refused one 'to the infinitely more important undertaking at Manchester'? And it was not just Manchester: none of the new university colleges received an iota of government support.

Nevertheless, as Professor Kenneth Morgan has pointed out, the debate was an important landmark for 'it made Welsh higher education a political issue for the first time'. Higher education became a critical question in the electoral campaign of the early summer of 1880 in Wales and a number of candidates of both political persuasions committed themselves in their election addresses to state grant-aid for Aberystwyth. On the return of Gladstone to power in May 1880, Lord Aberdare was induced – the veteran Hugh Owen had a great part in this – to suggest an inquiry into the current state of higher and intermediate education in Wales. After much political manoeuvring, and in the face of the studied opposition of Vivian, who thought the 'case . . . too strong to need any further investigation', on 25 August 1880, a Departmental Committee was appointed, with Aberdare as its chairman, 'to enquire into the present condition of Intermediate and Higher Education in Wales and to recommend the measures which they may think advisable for improving and supplementing the provision that is now, or might be made, available for such education in the Principality'. Adroitly, Lewis Williams, the vice-chairman of the Cardiff School Board, on his own responsibility, secured through Sir Edward Reed, the Liberal MP for Cardiff, the inclusion of Monmouthshire in the scope of the inquiry. It was an action that was to have considerable consequences in the contentious days after the publication of the Aberdare Committee's Report.

The membership of the six-man committee was diverse but distinguished. Only one member – the radical MP Henry Richard – was a Nonconformist. He had been returned to Parliament for Merthyr – defeating the future Lord Aberdare himself – in the celebrated election of 1868 and his reputation as 'the Member for Wales' made him an

Two of the authors of the 'educational charter of modern Wales'. Henry Austin Bruce, Lord Aberdare (1815–95), *left*, for four years Gladstone's 'heaven born' Home Secretary in the reforming Liberal government of 1868–74. After his retirement from active politics Aberdare devoted himself to the advancement of education, especially in Wales. It was on his suggestion that the departmental committee bearing his name was set up in 1881, but its proposals regarding intermediate education – the essential linchpin of the whole educational strategy – were not given serious attention by the government until 1889. An advanced Liberal, Henry Richard (1812–88), *right*, was the sole Nonconformist on the committee. Pugnacious and passionate, his parliamentary prominence as 'the Member for Wales' made him an obvious choice for the committee. (Cartoons by Ape [Carlo Pellegrini] in *Vanity Fair*, 21 August 1869, and Spy [Leslie Ward], 4 September 1880)

inevitable choice for the committee. The others, Lord Emlyn (1847–1911), later, as earl of Cawdor, chairman of the Great Western Railway and, as First Lord of the Admiralty, a powerful ally of Admiral Fisher in his naval reforms; Professor John Rhys (1840–1915), scholar, university teacher – he had been appointed the first professor of Celtic at Oxford three years before – and former inspector of schools; Lewis Morris (1833–1907), lawyer, poet and patriot; and Prebendary Hugh Robinson (1820–82), a former principal of York and Ripon Diocesan Training College, a Charity Commissioner and an acknowledged authority on endowed schools – to Aberdare, 'one of the ablest men I ever knew' and the man on whom the brunt of the exercise fell – were all Anglicans. However, suspicion that they might see Welsh education problems through English eyes was submerged in the anticipation that perhaps at long last serious attention would be paid to the educational needs of Wales. To many concerned with Aberystwyth there was the hope that, with four of the committee's members connected with the college, grant-aid would be forthcoming, while to some few others, not least in Swansea, there was the possibility of other collegiate institutions being established in the principality to meet the needs of higher technological study in an industrial age.

By the autumn of 1880, twelve universities or university colleges had been established in England and Wales. Six of these had been set up within the previous ten years. Only the April before, the status of Owens College had been secured by the creation of the federal 'Victoria University'. Although Owens College was to be its only constituent until the new university college in Liverpool joined it two years later, the principle of a full degree-giving university education in the provinces was now firmly established. There was even talk of University College, London, coming into the new federation. This did not happen, but the Yorkshire College at Leeds did join in 1887. That was for the future: but already Wales was alive with possibilities. In 1880, with a royal charter at Manchester and the buzz of developments at Liverpool, the appointment of the Aberdare Committee seemed to suggest that some positive action might at last be taken to consolidate and even extend higher education in the principality. It could not go unnoticed that five of the six largest provincial towns in England now boasted their own university colleges: towns which were all thrusting industrial communities possessing both a considerable civic pride and a denominational thirst for higher education which, despite the abolition of religious tests at Oxford and Cambridge in 1871, could not be adequately satisfied elsewhere. In Wales, by contrast, some sort of higher education was to be found only at the decidedly rural centres of Lampeter – which was given a restricted right to award Bachelor of Arts degrees in 1865 – and Aberystwyth. Still, in both colleges it was directed primarily to the instruction of future men of the cloth or teachers and, in practice, they provided for the needs of a strictly limited geographical area. With an eye to what had been happening in England, it was only natural that the Aberdare enquiry should be looked upon as an opportunity of advancing the notion of a university college to cater for the particular requirements of south Wales, with its spreading industries and burgeoning population.

It was an aspiration that was eventually realized but only after the most intense rivalry between Swansea and Cardiff. These were the two towns with the clearest technological claims for such an institution and they were unyielding in their opposition to each other. Already major industrial ports, they had developed very different characteristics. Swansea, with a measured municipal history as a trading port and with a long-established reputation as a social and cultural resort of some importance, was recognized through its copper smelting and tinplate industries, as the 'metallurgical centre of the world'. Cardiff, while it possessed equally ancient antecedents acknowledged in its position as the county town, had mushroomed from little more than an overgrown village to a coal-handling metropolis of international importance in hardly a generation or so. Even to the soberest citizens of Swansea, their own town already being rapidly outstripped commercially, Cardiff was a brash boom-town, lacking a middle class of any social or intellectual substance, dominated by the Catholic influence of the Bute interest and a large Irish community, and Welsh neither in its heterogeneous population nor in spirit.

By 1880, although copper smelting was already on the brink of decline, Swansea was still predominant in the industry and over two-thirds of the copper ore imported into Britain continued to be smelted in the six large works of the area. At the same time, seventy per cent of British tinplate was being manufactured along the south Wales coastal strip from Kidwelly to Port Talbot, and Swansea was regarded as the business centre for the tinplate trade in the United Kingdom. In the Swansea Valley alone, four steelworks and thirteen tinplate works were in operation and production was to expand greatly over the next decade.

With the advance of industry had come an unparalleled increase in population. In 1801 the population of the area of the later municipal borough numbered some ten thousand. Thirty years later the population of the municipal borough – which included the populous industrial settlements of the Swansea Valley – had more than doubled to over 24,500. By 1881 it exceeded 65,000. This explosive growth of population was directly linked to the development of industry; an expansion seen most dramatically in those previously rural districts where the traditional pattern of dispersed hamlets and individual farmsteads had been normal, and where now industrial development and the associated immigration of workers were at their greatest. By the census of 1881 Swansea was, as it had been since mid-century, essentially a lower-middle and working-class town.[2] This social pattern, and the Nonconformist ethos that characterized it, were to be of great significance in the development of Swansea's educational facilities in the later nineteenth century. For local government became an increasingly middle-class and Nonconformist affair, more sensible of 'self help' and the burden of rates than of what a more socially sensitive age might consider as the collective common good.

In the early years of the nineteenth century, with the Napoleonic wars inhibiting continental travel and with sea-bathing becoming popular, Swansea achieved something of a reputation as a fashionable watering place. For a long time it was not clear whether its future lay in the direction of the more sordid ways of trade and manufacture or in that of a pleasure resort. Yet, while the town could continue to be regarded by tourists as a healthy resort with an equable, relaxing climate, industry and commerce were swiftly gaining the upper hand, and with industry came associated social problems. Whatever improvements were taking place in central Swansea and however much, after the reform of the Corporation in 1834, civic pride might be reflected in new public buildings, for much of the nineteenth century many of its resident working-class population lived out crowded and insanitary lives in harsh and squalid social conditions. It was a stark contrast to the elegant villas rising in the western parts of the town and along the road to Mumbles, where over the decade 1827–37 John Henry Vivian, the copper-master, was building his neo-Gothic 'abbey' at Singleton. Even in the centre of the town itself a high proportion of the inhabitants were obliged to rely on a water supply that was both inefficient and suspect while the small burial grounds were becoming dangerously overcrowded.

This state of affairs was not the result of any deliberate negligence or callous absence of social conscience; rather was it due to the prevailing 'entrepreneurial ideal', a general reluctance to accept a collective responsibility for the town and, underlying this, an evangelical thrift and self-dependence that induced a fear of introducing any novelties

Wealth, its display and making. *Above*, a view of Singleton Abbey, soon after its completion in 1837, by the architect Peter Frederick Robinson (1776–1858). The figures on horseback are likely to be John Henry Vivian (1785–1855) and his wife Sarah. *Below*, the Vivians' copper works at Hafod, after a photograph by Sir Henry Hussey Vivian

VIEW OF THE HAFOD COPPER WORKS.
ON THE SWANSEA RIVER, TAWE.
CONSTRUCTED BY MESSRS VIVIAN & SONS.
A.D. 1810.
Photographed by H. Hussey Vivian

that would impose a greater fiscal burden on the town's citizens. It also reflected a considerable body of local opinion, ever vigilant to curb authority's all too obvious wanton proclivity 'of picking the ratepayers' pockets'. More often than not the inspiration and dynamic for change came from a single forward-looking individual who had the temerity and energy to challenge the *status quo*. Henry Sockett (1765–1847), a local barrister, had been one such hero in the early part of the nineteenth century but it was in the nature of things that he should be applauded less for the actual improvements he instigated than for bringing them about without adding 'one penny to the ordinary amount of the paving rate'.

Sockett had been a controversial figure in his day but every major scheme of forward development that was introduced in the council chamber later in the nineteenth century was the subject of the most acrimonious debate. The establishment of a local Board of Health in the town after the creation of the General Board of Health in 1848 was a case in point. It was, too, only after much heart-searching, that new schemes for the supply of water were undertaken and, during the 1860s, that the first adequate drainage scheme for the town was completed, to be followed by new measures for paving and scavenging the streets. By 1858 a new municipal cemetery had been opened at Danygraig and, in the face of considerable opposition from vested interests, some success had been achieved in improving the housing conditions of many of the poor of the town, although it was not until the late 1870s that the first slum-clearance schemes were introduced, to be followed in the succeeding decade by municipal rehousing projects. Only at this time, too, in an atmosphere of the utmost acrimony, did measures begin to be taken, largely through the initiative and single-mindedness of William Thomas of Lan (1816–1909), a Morriston tinplate manufacturer and colliery owner, to provide public open spaces in the more densely populated districts of the town. It was a very self-righteous Corporation which, in 1881, with its sights set on the establishment of a south Wales college, could congratulate itself with the thought that 'the Borough of Swansea is very healthy'.

Equally passionate was the campaign for a town library. Vitiated by personal antipathies, it again illustrated the Corporation's obsession with public 'thrift', the grudging attitude of 'informed' opinion and the enterprise and drive of a minority of the town council against the entrenched 'old men'. Although an enabling act of 1850 had empowered boroughs like Swansea to levy a rate to establish a library, Swansea was not a pioneering authority. As with the provision of a museum and art gallery, such public facilities were left as the responsibility of a private society, the stolidly middle-class Royal Institution of South Wales, which, while it recognized that it had an obligation beyond its membership, had no intention of being cast into the role of a *municipal* 'Library and Reading-room'.

The establishment, in 1865, of a public library in Cardiff, interpreted as yet another instance of that town's growing ascendancy, acted as an incentive locally. Still, it was not for another three years that any serious attempt to provide public library facilities was made in Swansea and the attempt was soon wrecked by the opposition of outlying ratepayers, particularly those of Morriston. Led by the acerbic John Glasbrook, the town's most prominent colliery owner, a tinplate manufacturer and a local alderman, they objected to the imposition of a special rate which they saw as benefiting primarily the central parts of the town. Glasbrook took upon himself the mantle of 'economic thrift' of those who, in the past, had opposed public expenditure on town developments.

THE SWANSEA BOY.—Oct. 8, 1880.   9

The Coming Struggle.

See page 7.

John Glasbrook (1816–87), the Goliath-like
defender of 'economic thrift' in municipal affairs.
Glasbrook was 6 ft 6 in tall and weighed 29
stone. At his funeral his coffin required the
support of thirty-two bearers working in relays of
eight at a time

The waterworks schemes, the campaign for open spaces, even, in the year of his death, the new Swansea market all felt the lash of his tongue. His watchword was 'economy with efficiency'. Of an almost Sibthorpian mould, he did not believe in 'newfangled educational notions' and saw real danger in the purpose of a public library – the diffusion of knowledge among the working classes who (he said) 'have too much knowledge already; it was much easier to manage them twenty years ago; the more education people get the more difficult they are to manage'. As he bluntly told Deffett Francis, 'it was better to put "bread and cheese" into the hands of working people than any number of "books"' (*The Cambrian*, 7 October 1870 & 29 April 1887).

In 1870 a fresh opportunity presented itself with Swansea's acceptance of a bequest of 6,000 volumes, the library of Dr Rowland Williams,[3] to form the nucleus of a town library. Even then, it was only by virtual sleight of hand on the part of the forward-looking mayor, John Jones Jenkins, himself one of the town's foremost industrialists, that the principle of a special library rate was agreed; and it was a further six years before a municipal library was eventually established in scarcely suitable premises in Goat Street. The atmosphere of controversy and the personal antipathy between Glasbrook and Jenkins was to dog the library movement for nearly twenty years until eventually, through the persistent efforts of Jenkins, permanent buildings were erected in Alexandra Road in 1887. Underlying all these schemes of wider collective responsibility – public health, open spaces and library facilities – were the recurring themes of cost and, because of Swansea's municipal financial weakness, its impact on the private individual, through either the rates or voluntary contributions.

None of this suggests there was much in the character of the town to promote the foundation of a university college; indeed, rather the opposite. In some minds there might be a sense of an overpowering need for such an institution; but what cultural tradition or intellectual foci were there to foster a project of this kind?

Ivy Lodge (the white house with veranda), a former Swansea home of the Moggridge family, was, with the adjoining properties, the premises of Evan Davies's Normal College from 1851 to 1867 and of the Swansea Training College from 1872 until the college moved to Town Hill in 1913. The college, for women, was sited in Swansea partly because of Swansea's 'moral and political atmosphere in which [it] was likely to thrive'

The only institution providing any form of advanced instruction in the town was the Swansea Training College for women teachers. The Voluntaryist 'Normal College', which had been established at Brecon for the training of men teachers in 1846, had been transferred to Swansea in 1849, but the impossibility of maintaining it on the basis of voluntary financial contributions led to its closure as a training college in 1851. The 'Normal College' continued as a reputable private middle-class school until 1895, when its pupils were absorbed into the grammar school under the terms of the Welsh Intermediate Education Act. Forster's Education Act, in the meantime, while providing for the creation of new elementary schools, did nothing for the training of additional teachers; the British Society therefore decided in 1871 to establish two training colleges for women teachers, one in the north of England and the other in Wales. The following year, the Society acquired the former premises of the old 'Normal College' and developed them into the first training college for women teachers in Wales. The venture was begun as an experiment, but its evident success secured its permanent establishment in 1875. Its prestige grew rapidly and by 1880 one hundred and ninety-nine teachers had been trained, and there were then fifty-six students taking the two-year training course.

Grammar-school education dated back at least to 1682 when Hugh Gore, Bishop of Waterford and Lismore and a former rector of Oxwich, endowed a school for the education in Greek and Latin of 'twenty poore children and youthes, sons of the poorer sort of Burgesses', to prepare them for 'Trade or the University'. The early history of the school is obscure. By the middle of the eighteenth century, however, it was experiencing the decline which was afflicting many other similar schools. Its continuing existence as a grammar school depended less on pupils from the town than on private fee-paying boarders from outside the district among its sixty or seventy pupils and when the Charity Commissioners visited Swansea in 1836 they found that there had been no foundation scholars for many years for 'the poorer burgesses, finding that Greek and Latin only were to be taught, did not send their sons to the school'.

The headmaster at this time, the Revd Evan Griffith, was an accomplished scholar and teacher and was responsible, as a private tutor, for the early education of a number of pupils who later attained great distinction: among them Henry Austin Bruce, the first Lord Aberdare, Howel Gwyn, MP, and Sir William Grove, the scientist and jurist. But by 1842 his school had become moribund and, for all practical purposes, it ceased to exist during the next eight years. In 1850, mainly through the efforts of George Grant Francis, a local businessman and antiquary and, again, a former private pupil of Griffith, the foundation was revived and three years later the school was reopened amid great civic pomp in new buildings on Mount Pleasant. Although designed to provide an education fitting for 'Trade or the Universities', the refounded school never effectively combined its essentially classical curriculum with 'those other branches of education which fit men for the everyday business of life' until after its further reorganization in 1895 under the terms of the Welsh Intermediate Education Act (Francis, p. 41; *Swansea and Glamorgan Herald*, 23 August 1848).

In his evidence to the Aberdare Committee, the Revd John Young, headmaster from 1877 to 1895, admitted that a leavening of modern subjects would make the school 'very much more popular and would meet the wants of the place [Swansea] very much more', since so many of the pupils were the sons of professional or business men who subsequently went into commercial life. It was a shift of emphasis supported by most of the witnesses, especially by John Jones Jenkins who, starting as a tinplate boy himself, had risen by his own efforts to become one of the most influential industrialists of the area. He acknowledged that the special needs of the district, in particular the large metallurgical and chemical works, made the study of scientific subjects particularly important. It was a conclusion that Mr Bompas, the examining assistant commissioner of the Taunton Commission, had come to thirteen years earlier.

The grammar school was plagued by yet other problems. The Revd Charles Heartley, headmaster from 1862 to 1877, inherited a school which, racked by a ten-year history of antagonism between governors and headmasters, and already unpopular in its locality, had been reduced to some forty pupils. Influenced by the contemporary advance of the English public schools, Heartley saw the grammar school's salvation more as a first-class classical/modern school with a significant boarding element than as an institution directed to the immediate needs of its locality. His attempts to shake off local obligations and to achieve in Swansea the distinction of an English public school being attained at Llandovery by its warden, A.G. Edwards,[4] not only put a hopeless financial halter round its neck but also successfully alienated it even further from its locality.

George Grant Francis (1814–82), as Mayor of Swansea in 1853–4. A man of vision who ceaselessly engaged in schemes for local improvements from dock developments to the provision of open spaces, tramways and gracious public buildings, his ideas, according to Glasbrook, were 'somewhat in advance of his time, and being always financially weak, met with an imperfect appreciation'. Francis is thus better known as an antiquary but, among his successes, was the refoundation of the local grammar school in 1850. The engraving of the opening of the school three years later is taken from the architect's perspective drawing and is shown as he envisaged it and not as it was finally built

Most Swansea parents seeking a middle-class education for their sons sent them to private schools in the town. John Jones Jenkins, in his evidence to the Aberdare Committee, suggested that the level of tuition fees at the grammar school deterred many parents. The fees were, however, comparatively low and that they were not an overriding consideration is borne out by the fact that the fees at the best of the private schools were much the same. How many such private schools there were is not known, but few of them were of high calibre although, on paper, their claims might appear to be large. Only Evan Davies's Normal College – 'one of the best secondary schools for boys in the country' – and three other private schools for boys – the Cambridge Collegiate School, Arnold College and St Andrew's College – achieved any success in the Oxford Local Examinations during the eleven years between 1869 and 1880. The majority of the schools were indifferent in the standard and range of their curricula, indulging in a superficial 'liberal' or 'finishing' education – like those of the Benvenutis in Gore Terrace or Madam Amelia D'Austeins in St Helens Road – or specializing in elementary commercial subjects for a career in the counting house rather than in the rigour of academic subjects. It was an education that was 'very much below the mark and very much below the need of the district'.

For girls the facilities for secondary education were even more limited. There were, it is true, a number of self-styled 'superior' private establishments 'at which the accomplishments are taught', but the education provided by these schools was far from satisfactory either in terms of tuition or curriculum. Mrs Emily Higginson, the widow of one of the town's most eminent Unitarian ministers, who came before the Aberdare Committee to press the claims of Swansea girls for secondary education, was brief and to the point: 'There are very numerous private adventure schools, but none which can bring up girls to the point of passing the London Matriculation Examination.'

The provision of elementary education in the town was dramatically changed by the 1870 Education Act. The defective state of such education in Swansea a generation earlier, so graphically catalogued by Ralph Lingen in the 1847 'Blue Books', had gradually been improved and the best of the voluntary schools were doing good educational work. The limited number of such schools,[5] however, could cope only with a fraction of the population, while their work was vitiated by absenteeism and the early withdrawal of children: to the majority of parents and children the schools were a not altogether relevant interval between infancy and employment. In 1871, it was estimated by the new Board for the United School District of Swansea that there was a deficiency of 4,035 places in the borough alone. With the exception of the National schools, the existing public voluntary schools within the board area were taken over by the school board, which also set about establishing a number of new schools in both the borough and the adjacent industrial areas. Yet, it was to be some time before the 'educational destitution' inherited by the board could be completely eradicated. It still faced the seemingly endless task of providing a sufficient number of schools, and even by 1881 there was still a deficiency of 1,269 places in the district. Gradually, however, the effect of tightening the attendance rules in 1876 began to bear fruit and parents were 'encouraged' – a palpable euphemism – to see their children's education not so much as 'a matter of choice but of necessity'. By the early 1880s some ten thousand children were attending board schools and voluntary schools in the Swansea district. A working class was beginning to emerge which, broadly educated, would permit the development of the first vestiges of a modern universal system of education, a system which departed – in theory at least – from the traditional compartmentalized Victorian educational principles and which would eventually generate, through the tiered schooling set up by the close of the century, a degree of social and intellectual mobility that had not existed before.

This was still a generation in the future. The absence of a working class with such a sufficiently broad educational base is brought home by the fate of the various movements for adult improvement which were launched in the town during the century. Little is known of the shadowy activities of either the Swansea People's Institute in Oxford Street, the Literary and Working Men's Improvement Society in Fisher Street, or the Swansea Society for Acquiring Useful Knowledge which used the premises of the Royal Institution of South Wales for a few years about the middle of the century. The lectures of these 'mutual improvement' societies seem to have been of a generalized kind typical of their period – 'The Advantages arising from the Cultivation of a Flower Garden' was the title of one given to the Swansea Society for Acquiring Useful Knowledge in 1845.

That perennial problems of adequate finance and sustained organization and the low educational level of their members were critical to the effectiveness of these societies is borne out by the longer-term but even more chequered history of the Swansea Tradesman's and Mechanic's Institution. The first mechanics' institute in Wales had been established in Cardiff in March 1826 and this led to a somewhat desultory campaign to create a similar society in Swansea. The formation, by John Francis, the coach-builder father of George Grant Francis, of a Commercial, News and Reading Society 'for the commercial part of the inhabitants of Swansea' early in November was the necessary spur. With the active encouragement of John Hodder Moggridge,[6] the president of the Cardiff Mechanics' Institute, and, significantly, with the support of a few local Nonconformist ministers, the 'Swansea Tradesman's and Mechanic's Institution' was established later that month (29 November 1826). It managed to maintain a precarious existence for a few years in its attempt to instruct its 'members in the principles of the trades they practise, and in the various branches of science and useful knowledge' and, for a short time, even succeeded in providing lectures and demonstrations in mechanics and hydrostatics. But, like so many other mechanics' institutes, it failed to capture the long-term interest of the very section of society – mechanics and artisans, the élite of the working class – at which it was primarily directed. No person of real influence in the town nor any leading industrialist seems to have lent it support and when its chief enthusiast left the district it soon became moribund. By 1831 it had collapsed altogether, part of its library being absorbed into that of the Royal Institution of South Wales. But by then it had already lost much of its original purpose.

The causes of the demise of the Mechanic's Institution went deeper than any loss of inspiration occasioned by the removal of its most prominent supporter. A correspondent to *The Cambrian* eight years later (31 August 1839), when efforts were being made to revive the Institution, explained some of the fundamental problems. The scattered nature of their employment meant that the 'workmen employed in the mines and works . . . could not easily be brought together, for instruction, or for the purpose of consulting books of reference in the library, or of exchanging such as circulate'. At a time when cheap public transport was non-existent – and the bicycle not yet invented – it was natural that workers from even the nearest outlying industrial districts should

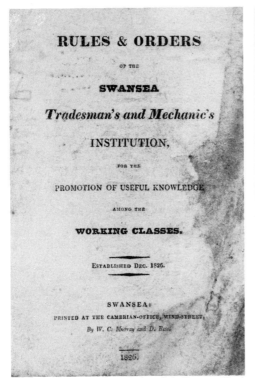
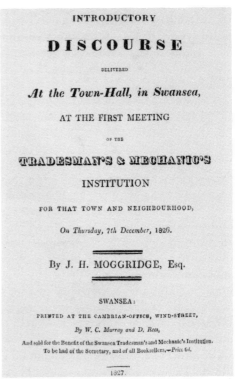

The cover of the *Rules & Orders of the Swansea Tradesman's and Mechanic's Institution*, and the title page of John Hodder Moggridge's inaugural address on 7 December 1826

have the greatest difficulty in getting into town for instruction after a day's work, and not less so after exhaustive labour in the heavy local industries.

Perhaps even more fundamental was the fact that even the most paternalistic of local industrialists displayed little desire to support the Institution. Critical financial help was not forthcoming and with no permanent headquarters it was forced into a nomadic existence. No workshop or laboratory facilities were available and such science classes as were given were theoretical, bearing little practical relationship to the members' employment. Our correspondent noted that 'many, perhaps most, of the workmen' were 'mere "routine operators", and have the usual prejudices against a scientific prosecution of their trades or arts'. There was, though, little practical incentive to study because of the absence of any material reward or promotion at the works. Few employers regarded the function of the institutes as more than an intellectual diversion and generally they did not see them as a means of disseminating greater technical knowledge or producing a more technically adept workforce. While our correspondent's assessment that some workmen were discouraged from attending the Institution because there was a general view abroad that 'many of the middle classes are hostile to a more thorough enlightenment of the people, believing that it leads to political discontent and mischief' many of the middle classes, in fact, saw its real value lying in what Sir Arthur Lewis has called 'social investment education' rather than 'productive investment education', a civilizing element of 'social control'. As *The Cambrian* (24 June 1843) put it, through the efforts of the Mechanic's Institution,

A well informed labouring population would grow up, happy in their own condition, free from the liability of being acted upon for political purposes by designing men, obeying the laws, and conducing in various other ways to the peace of the empire.

In some quarters it was a view that took an unconscionably long time dying, especially in the tinplate industry: even as late as 1915 it could still be said that what were needed were 'practical men who were in sympathy with their rolls [*sic*]'.

The Mechanic's Institution was revived in September 1838, and, through a fruitful co-operation with the Royal Institution of South Wales where it held its meetings, it was able to do good work for a few years until 1847. In 1839–40, for example, classes in English language and composition, chemistry, arithmetic and algebra, geometry, French, and Welsh, and also instruction in writing and instrumental music, attracted some seventy-three active members. Such a low degree of active participation, however, was in marked contrast to the numbers who had thronged the Institution's inaugural meeting in 1826. *The Cambrian* (18 July 1840) pinpointed the underlying cause:

The early education of mechanics is not carried sufficiently far, to enable them to engage in the business of the classes. The time which might be devoted to these pursuits is, from the deficiency of their early instruction, necessarily given to preliminary studies – to reading, writing, and becoming acquainted with their own language. The business of the *school* [my italics] is thrown on the Mechanic's Institution.

In part it was a problem of language. As our correspondent had argued, one third of the inhabitants of Swansea, at least, are ignorant of the English language'. This handicap most affected the industrial workers intended to benefit from the Institution. Many of them may have been literate in the sense that they had been taught to read the Scriptures in Welsh in Sunday school, but they suffered from the absence of a basic secular education and a crippling inability to read the English scientific literature provided for them. That this was still a salient problem over a generation later is brought home by the fact that it exercised the Newcastle Commission (1861) during its enquiries in south Wales into popular education.

The Institution had the positive support of Lewis Llewelyn Dillwyn of Hendrefoilan, an industrialist of wide-ranging interests and, in the tradition of his family, an amateur scientist of no mean attainment. But Dillwyn was not typical: although warmly regarded personally, he was something of an eccentric, in both his 'advanced Liberal' politics – he succeeded his father Lewis Weston Dillwyn as MP for Swansea in 1855 and represented the newly formed Swansea Town division from 1885 to 1892 – and in his behaviour. Other industrialists remained aloof, and the lack of industrial incentive and encouragement that had beset the Institution in its earlier incarnation equally affected its successor. Despite exhortations in the local press, the lack of basic primary education discouraged the artisan class from attending the Institution, which became more the cultural preserve of middle-class clerks and shopmen from the town who, anxious to repair the deficiencies of their own educational background, could also more easily attend for instruction. The earlier courses of specific instruction degenerated into general addresses on popular subjects, such as bump-by-bump disquisitions on phrenology, the pseudo-scientific craze of the age that consumed the attention of even the most rational. This was a clear departure from the original objects of the Institution and a situation

Lewis Llewelyn Dillwyn (1814–92), an 'advanced Liberal', eccentric in character, shared the scientific and scholarly interests of his father, Lewis Weston Dillwyn. Committed to the improvement of popular education, he was staunch in his support of the Mechanic's Institution in its various guises. In 1853 he built Hendrefoilan House, illustrated here from a contemporary photograph, and laid out the grounds at a cost of £14,000

which the artisan, seriously bent on improving himself, found of little comfort. Yet systematic instruction after a hard day's work would not readily appeal to a weary mechanic intellectually unequipped to appreciate a droning technical lecture delivered, perhaps, under the beneficent eye of his employer as patron of the institute. By 1847 the revived Mechanic's Institution had gone the way of its predecessor. A further attempt to re-establish it was made in March 1848 but, again, without success and within the year it seems to have been consigned utterly to the lumber-room of history.

The very failure of the Mechanic's Institution provided an impetus to the Royal Institution of South Wales to arrange a series of Wednesday courses in 1848 on 'a great variety of subjects in general literature and popular science' for the public, who paid a token fee for admission. Unhappily, 'the attendance was so scanty that . . . unlimited free admissions were authorised to persons to whom the admission fee might be a consideration'. At the end of the first year, the Royal Institution council was forced to question whether 'it would be expedient again to organise a series of lectures with which the taste of the public does not harmonise, and their own resources are not commensurate'.

The Royal Institution of South Wales catered primarily for the cultural appetite of Swansea's middle classes. It had arisen phoenix-like from the ashes of an earlier society, the Cambrian Institution for the Encouragement of Pursuits in Geology, Mineralogy and Natural History which had been founded in 1821. By the early 1830s this rather exclusive organization was *in extremis* largely, it was said, because of 'the non-residence of most of the members, and a want of energy in the others'. However, thanks to the enthusiasm of a rising young lawyer and amateur conchologist, John Gwyn Jeffreys, and the powerful support of his mentor, Lewis Weston Dillwyn, a local industrialist, Member of Parliament, Swansea alderman and, above all, a botanist of considerable distinction, the Royal Institution had been founded (as the Swansea Philosophical and Literary Institution) with rooms in Castle Square in 1835.

The new body was very much part and parcel of the movement to promote 'useful knowledge' that had been a mark of cultured industrial society in the provinces since the middle of the eighteenth century. The establishment of the British Association for the Advancement of Science in 1831 and the creation of similar local organizations at Bristol and Neath provided an immediate stimulus. Jeffreys, too, was especially fortunate in the existence in Swansea at this period of a remarkable group of forward-looking industrialists and professional men, some of whom, like Dillwyn, wielded great influence in local public affairs and all of whom shared Jeffreys's own interest in serious scientific study.

There was, too, a coterie of young local intellectuals who joined him in the enterprise: all of independent means and all products, like Jeffreys, of Evan Griffith's schooling. Chief among these was the twenty-one-year-old George Grant Francis, already a difficult young man who, a year or two later, had hurriedly to leave a post at the Liverpool Royal Institution because of his brashness. Ever the enthusiast, if often lacking in discretion and sensibility, he threw himself whole-heartedly into promoting the Swansea scheme. His hard work was to prove invaluable and, whatever his personal failings, it was the start of an untiring enthusiasm for the cultural and physical improvement of his birthplace. The most noteworthy of the group was William Grove (1811–96). He was a young lawyer of indifferent health who devoted his leisure time to scientific experiment. In the years to come he was to be both an eminent judge and a distinguished man of

Lewis Weston Dillwyn (1778–1855) *left* and John Gwyn Jeffreys (1809–85), *right*. Their joint interest
in conchology led to the foundation of the Royal Institution of South Wales in 1835

science, both a privy councillor and a professor of the Royal Institution in London.
Within a few years, too, he was to be the 'young Turk' who secured the professional
reorganization of the Royal Society to admit only 'cultivators of science'. And there were
other young supporters like William Logan (1798–1875), later to earn the title of 'the
father of Canadian science', John Dillwyn Llewelyn (1810–82), Lewis Weston Dillwyn's
elder son who earned a prominent place in the early development of photography, and
Matthew Moggridge (1804–82), a son of J.H. Moggridge and, as befitted Dillwyn's
son-in-law, an 'ardent votary of science' but as erratic and 'advanced' a Liberal as Lewis
Llewelyn Dillwyn. Without the active support of this veritable galaxy of talent the Royal
Institution is unlikely to have been established and certainly would not have achieved
rapid scientific recognition.

Notable among the Royal Institution's original officers and committee were three
Fellows of the Royal Society – Lewis Weston Dillwyn, John Henry Vivian and C.R.M.
Talbot of Margam and Penrice – and four future Fellows – John Dillwyn Llewelyn,
Logan, Jeffreys, and Grove. Although the Royal Society had not yet cast off its
reputation of being a grand gentlemen's club – this was Grove's task ten years later –
these founder members of the Swansea society were not merely rich dilettanti but were
also themselves distinguished scholars concerned to promote serious scientific research
through the Royal Institution. Their industrial connections ensured that such studies
would, in the like traditions of earlier societies in similar districts, be of practical
application. John Henry Vivian and Lewis Weston Dillwyn, for instance, were men
deeply involved in scientific enquiry, absorbed in the creation of new industrial processes

The new building of the Royal Institution of South Wales opened in 1841. Seven years later the
Institution was host to the British Association when it visited Wales for the first time

and actively engaged in political life. After 1841, with its new museum, library and
laboratory, the Royal Institution sought to be the natural focal point for the cultural
activities of the locality, and in its early days, through the like of Grove, it captured the
interest and support of scientists of international standing such as Michael Faraday. Its
founders hoped that, like other provincial societies, it would fulfil some of the functions
expected of an embryo university, but this period of scientific endeavour, marked,
characteristically again, by a series of important statistical reports on subjects such as
vaccination, climate and the town's imports and exports, was short-lived. Indeed, one
must guard against overstating the Royal Institution's scientific role.

By 1848, when the Royal Institution acted as host to the annual meeting of the
British Association, which was venturing into Wales for the first time, it had already
passed its zenith as a society involved directly in primary scientific research. This aspect
of its work depended on a few outstanding individuals and young enthusiasts. After
their departure from the town or their greater involvement in other, weightier matters
of public concern, it rapidly declined. A proposal by Jeffreys in 1847, in the flush of
enthusiasm before the British Association visit, that the Institution should seek
incorporation as the 'Royal College of Wales' was seen to be pitching its aims far beyond
its capabilities. Thereafter, it was not unnatural that the Royal Institution should
subside into the comfortable backwater of an average provincial society providing
popular lectures on literary, historical and scientific subjects to its essentially upper and
middling middle-class membership; such limited scientific work as it carried out was
undertaken through specialist offshoot groups like the Swansea Geological Society.
When the British Association paid its second visit to Swansea in 1880, the Royal
Institution had effectively ceased to be the systematic educational force for which its

founders had yearned. No longer could it play the intimate role of substantive host as it had done in 1848.

Nevertheless, even if it failed in its objective of advancing the boundaries of knowledge, it did try to continue to make serious efforts to sponsor science classes for the public at large. The local schools provided virtually no scientific education for their pupils. If it was vestigial in the grammar school, it was almost totally absent from even the best of the private schools. Under the provisions of Forster's Act of 1870, science became one of the specific subjects that might be taught in the senior classes of elementary schools. A number of towns introduced some elementary science in this way but Swansea was not one of them. Classes in physiography, magnetism and electricity were conducted at the Kilvey copperworks school, it is true, but this was an isolated episode that lasted for a short four-year period between 1879 and 1883 and then faded away. Technical instruction of a sort, it has been suggested, was provided at the Hafod copperworks schools but, in reality, this seems to have amounted to no more than classes in elementary art.

It was perhaps not unnatural, given the scientific ferment of the age, that the absence of any public provision for scientific education in the town should prompt private enterprise to take some initiative. In 1873 the South Wales School of Chemistry was established by William Morgan, the public analyst, in Orange Street. Little is known about his venture but in 1880 the laboratory was described by Samuel Gamwell (1850–96), later the editor of *The Cambrian*, in his Swansea *Guide* as 'a large airy and well fitted room with all kinds of apparatus required for chemical investigations and sufficient space for the experimental work of twenty five students . . . the Library is a handsomely fitted room containing well filled bookshelves and a fine assortment of the more remarkable scientific instruments such as spectroscopes, microscopes, telephones, microphones, electrical apparatus, balances of great delicacy etc'. Gamwell's *Guide* was prepared for the British Association visit of that year and perhaps, in puffing up the town, the author's poetic imagination got the better of him. There is certainly no information as to the success or otherwise of Morgan's students at this time.

The Royal Institution's early ventures in the field of sustained scientific education met with little success. A genuine enthusiasm pervaded its council but its plans were dogged by totally inadequate funds. There was a defeatist lack of public interest and great difficulty in securing competent teachers. In the late 1840s, under Jeffreys's influence, it became the avowed intention of the Royal Institution to establish 'a school of science, and to organise a more advanced and systematised form of instruction' so that a 'popular college for the higher departments of useful knowledge' could be developed. Little came of this and, eight years later, efforts to foster classes 'for the rudimentary and progressive study of some of the sciences more directly applicable to the arts, manufactures and inventive genius of the country' met with equal failure. The ever-present problem of finance and the impossibility of obtaining for 'the teachers, if but for the short time of an experiment, a certain and adequate remuneration' stood in the way. As an alternative, special lectures on scientific subjects, in addition to the usual lecture programme by members, were given from time to time, but it was not until 1867 that a regular series of science classes was successfully established in the Royal Institution under the aegis of the Department of Science and Art.

It was the personal initiative of a local certificated art teacher, an Irishman named

Frederick Hosford, that led to the opening of a school of art in Swansea in 1853 after the creation of the Department of Science and Art. In its early years, the school – the first in Wales – had an uncertain career, largely due to a lack of public support owing to the absence of any significant demand for design skills from the primary industries of the locality. After a number of false starts, however, the school was eventually established as a School of Science and Art under Hosford's direction in 1868.[7] Its practical evening classes proved especially popular with 'students, chiefly of the artizan class, who go through a course of geometry, building construction, machine drawing and other subjects connected with their daily avocations' (Gamwell, p. 87). Hosford was also responsible for promoting drawing as a subject in some of the town's elementary schools at this time through the instruction of pupil-teachers attending the School's classes. However, popular as these classes may have been, examination results both at the School of Art and at the local elementary schools were far from satisfactory.

The establishment of the 'South Kensington Centre' at the Royal Institution in 1867 was again due to the personal enthusism of one individual, A.R. Molison. His science classes became increasingly popular and within three years of their inception over one hundred students were receiving instruction in mechanics, magnetism and electricity, and chemistry. Unhappily, much of the practical work in chemistry, in particular, was hampered by a serious lack of facilities and by 1874 the laboratory at the Royal Institution was in a deplorable condition, its apparatus being condemned as more suitable for the collections of 'a museum of antiquities'. By 1880 the laboratory was closed, having been condemned by the visiting inspector of the Department of Science and Art. The major problem was still a crippling lack of money. In 1873 one of the class teachers, W.G. Bell, by day a full-time employee of the Landore Siemens Steel Company, complained in *The Cambrian* (28 February) that the teaching of science in Swansea was 'left to support itself, and received no encouragement from the wealthy employers of labour in the vicinity'. Nevertheless, local demand for science instruction increased and in 1877 the classes were extended to other parts of the town. Yet, popular though these courses were, the continuing absence of funds meant that the accommodation remained inadequate, with little provision for practical instruction, while all too often the aptitude of the teachers left a great deal to be desired. The low level of their remuneration and the necessarily poor academic standard of their students conspired to make instruction unrewarding; and, all too often dependent upon the personal initiative of an individual, it was haphazard and ill-organized.

The old problems that had plagued the Mechanic's Institution and its fellows in south Wales thirty or more years before still existed: poverty, the low educational base of members and the absence of sufficient influential support. Furthermore, as John Jones Jenkins was to explain to the Aberdare Committee,

> Frequently young men after they have been working hard all day do not care afterwards to have their minds taxed in the evening, with the exception of a very few of them indeed. There is but a very small percentage of the working men that attend night schools.

This lack of vitality – in contrast to that of Cardiff – was to deny any success to the university extension movement in Swansea which, elsewhere, provided much impetus to the development of provincial universities. Cambridge University Extension lectures were begun, in association with Cardiff and Newport, in 1875–6. But the lectures were 'so far below the expectations of its promoters' that the experiment was abandoned. The lectures were renewed in 1878 and struggled on into the 1880s, but with variable success and mainly on popular arts subjects. In the 1890s a similar fate befell the Oxford University Extension lectures held in Swansea.

Swansea was almost entirely bereft of any higher scientific training, though William Morgan was beginning to build something of a reputation for his South Wales School of Chemistry. While one might not expect much from the like of Glasbrook – popular as he was among his own workforce – local industrialists, on the whole, continued to show little interest in such developments. There were, thus, few technically or scientifically qualified men available locally. Vivian, the town's major industrial employer and richest citizen, would have been able to provide substantial financial support which others, like Sir William Siemens who had brought his steel-making process to Landore in 1868, might have followed. But Vivian, it was claimed, was obliged to get his technical assistants from among the products of the School of Mines at Freiburg in Saxony where he had been trained himself. It was not unnatural, therefore, to find that numbers of foreign workers, 'chiefly Belgians and Germans, are, in consequence of their skill, to a large extent employed as refiners and assayers in the copper works'.

Some of the larger copper and steel concerns did, it is true, send a privileged few of their key technologists to the Royal College of Chemistry and the Royal School of Mines to undertake research and to qualify in mining and mineralogy, but the same liberal attitude was not apparent among the majority of the smaller local employers, especially in the tinplate industry. Here, engineering and analytical staff were regarded, all too often, as a luxury and a waste of money. What was wanted by the tinplate owners – in the main local men who had themselves risen through the industry – was 'tradition and experience' rather than 'scientifically developed technique'. Suspicious of new methods and especially of the scientific metallurgist, it was not surprising that employers like Glasbrook were averse to supporting advanced technical education in the town, especially when the bulk of the cost would have to be borne by themselves and the local public purse.

For some years the need of a scientific or technical school to serve the metallurgical industries of the Swansea Valley had been talked about. The idea was revived during the hearings of the Devonshire Commission in 1870. Nothing came of this, however. Nor did the exhortation of Dr Hugo Harper, the principal of Jesus College, at the somewhat bizarre forum of the Church Congress in Swansea nine years later, that 'Swansea might become the Science School of South Wales', stir the imagination of many of the leading industrialists of the district. Experience had shown that their coolness to technical instruction in the past, in respect of both the old Mechanic's Institution and, more latterly, the local 'South Kensington' science classes, was unlikely to bring forth readily the financial support necessary to sustain a technical school or college. While there might be those, both locally and far beyond the district, who saw the need for such an institution to serve industrial south Wales, it was left to an enlightened minority to press this need before the Aberdare Committee when it visited Swansea in December 1880.

'The Metallurgical Centre of the World.' Swansea's industry and commerce depicted by the *Illustrated London News* in August 1880 to mark the visit of the British Association for the Advancement of Science. In spite of the smoke and the fumes of the works in Hafod and Landore, and the squalor and grime of much of the town, the Corporation could still represent it as being 'very healthy'

Notes

1. Percy Watkins (1871–1946), was later Permanent Secretary of the Welsh Department of the Board of Education (knighted in 1930), and was at this time contributor of the regular 'Wales' column to *The Times Educational Supplement*.
2. Over 41 per cent of Swansea's male labour force were returned as being engaged in industry or industry-related activities, and nearly 22 per cent as belonging to the 'commercial class'. The various gradations of upper- and upper-middle classes, gentry, professional and business, were only a tiny proportion of the whole, perhaps at their widest amounting to only two per cent.
3. Rowland Williams (1817–70), vice-principal of St David's College, Lampeter (1850–62), achieved notoriety in 1860 as a contributor to *Essays and Reviews*, one of the 'Seven Men against Christ'.
4. Alfred George Edwards (1848–1937) was Warden of Llandovery College from 1875 to 1885, Bishop of St Asaph from 1889 and the first Archbishop of Wales (1920–34).
5. In addition to three voluntary schools established early in the century and supervised by the British Society, three national schools had been set up in the aftermath of the 1847 Report, while at Hafod John Henry Vivian provided a model works school on British lines to complement those of the Grenfell family at Kilvey and St Thomas.
6. John Hodder Moggridge (1771–1834) came of a west-country woollen-manufacturing family. He acquired the Woodfield estate in the Sirhowy Valley about 1810, and, with industrial interests in Monmouthshire and Glamorgan, was the paternalistic founder of Blackwood. In politics a 'Reform' Whig, he unsuccessfully contested Monmouth boroughs in 1820.
7. Hosford was to remain Headmaster of the School of Art for forty years until he was retired in 1908. By then the school was in a sorry state with 'no specially organised courses for trades and manufactures', and it was reconstituted under the local education authority with Grant Murray combining the headmastership with the curatorship of the 'Swansea Museum and Gallery of Art'.

CHAPTER TWO

'A NIGHT-CAP ON . . . A BRILLIANT INTELLECTUAL LUMINARY FOR SOUTH WALES'

T he Aberdare Committee lost little time in setting about its task following its appointment on 25 August 1880. Evidence was first taken in London early in October and then the committee embarked on an exhaustive tour of Wales during the late autumn. Witnesses were examined at a number of centres in the principality and the committee eventually arrived in Swansea on 9 December.

Represented at the two-day hearing in the town hall was a variety of interests in the district, including the local school board, the Swansea Training College, grammar school, and local industry, and there were lengthy exchanges about the educational requirements of the locality and of Wales generally. All the witnesses were agreed on the critical need for substantially increased and improved facilities for intermediate education. Stressed repeatedly was the limited local appeal of the grammar school owing to the almost exclusive classical nature of its curriculum and the general distrust of what was seen to be its 'Church character'.

On the whole, the witnesses were agreed as to the steps that should be taken to improve the provision of intermediate education in Swansea. It was thought, for example, that the traditional control of appointments to the governors of the grammar school should, in some form, be transferred from the school's patron to an authority reflecting a more popular and locally-based system of choice, and that the school should also be freed 'from all sectarian and religious restrictions'. Furthermore, there was considerable support for long-standing proposals that the appeal of the school should be widened by introducing 'modern and scientific subjects' into its curriculum.

With regard to the provision of an adequate secondary education for girls, the positive demand was made that there should be a clear departure from the traditional concept of inculcating 'accomplishments'. 'When middle class schools for boys are set on foot we should have the same for girls with as strong a staff of teachers, and with facilities for taking the most promising pupils from the Board schools . . . so that they may rise higher and higher', argued Mrs Emily Higginson. Two 'superior' day schools were, therefore, suggested, one in Landore and one in the town, organized on non-sectarian principles with graduate teachers in the arts and sciences to ensure that the teaching was 'of the highest possible character'.

Captive as they were to the educational thought of their time, both committee and witnesses saw these changes as having an essentially 'middle-class' application. Separate proposals were advanced for the lower classes and the view was put that, subject to the important qualification of the ratepayers' agreement – 'since people are not willing to pay the existing school rate' – the school board should look at the possibility of creating one or two advanced elementary schools. At the same time, consideration should be given to the introduction of a scholarship system to facilitate the transfer of able pupils from the lower elementary schools to these advanced schools. The demand for skilled labour in the district, too, called for the establishment of a technical or trade school of a 'cheap and practical character' on the lines of the trade school at Bristol.

Expansion of the grammar school's teaching to include a significant emphasis on science subjects and the creation of a cheap trade school were seen by the industrialists present as but a partial solution, a first step. What was ultimately required, in their view, was a 'technical school apart from, and in addition to, the Grammar School, . . . a school' [commented John Jones Jenkins, echoing Nicholas a generation earlier] 'from which people in the neighbourhood and Welshmen in general could take leading positions in the different works in the neighbourhood, because up to very recently indeed all the principal posts that require special knowledge have been filled up by foreigners and not by natives; and I attribute that greatly to the want of the means of technical education in Wales'.

JOHN JONES JENKINS, ESQ., MAYOR OF SWANSEA.

John Jones Jenkins (1835–1915), *left*, and Richard Martin (1843–1922), *right*. Both self-made industrialists, Jenkins and Martin were in the forefront of the movement for higher technological education in Swansea in the nineteenth century. Jenkins, Mayor of Swansea on three occasions, was knighted in 1882 and became Lord Glantawe in 1906. Martin, an educational schemer of the first water, founder of the Swansea Technical College and 'father' of the University College, was knighted in 1920

Jenkins's views were echoed by Richard Martin, part-owner of the Llansamlet zincworks. Like Jenkins and many of his fellow industrialists in the Swansea Valley, he had risen to his commanding position in local industry by his own efforts. But, unlike so many of their colleagues, both Jenkins and Martin believed that the future development of their industries depended on the availability, locally, of scientifically-educated staff. It was a viewpoint for which the Aberdare Committee was well prepared. Already, on numerous occasions during their hearings, witnesses had pressed the need for a college in Glamorgan to meet the needs of the populous areas of south Wales. Mostly the case had been made in general terms. The principal of the university college at Aberystwyth, however, acknowledging the deficiencies of his own institution and, having regard to possible future competition, suggested that any 'Glamorganshire College should be a science college, and the Aberystwith College should be the only one dealing with general subjects of instruction'. Frederick Rudler, who until recently had been a lecturer in the natural sciences at Aberystwyth, considered it important that there should be a science college 'in any great town in Glamorganshire . . . it ought to be a great success' for 'there is in Glamorganshire a splendid collecting ground for just the right sort of men'.

Although there were dissentient voices at the Swansea hearing, local support for a science college in south Wales was not confined to the industrialists. One witness, speaking for the Nonconformist element of the town, was emphatic in the view that not only should there be such a college but that it should be situated in Swansea. John Jones Jenkins, also, challenged as to the comparative advantages of Swansea and Cardiff for such an institution, was of like mind. 'I am not prepared to say that the advantages are not great at Cardiff', he answered, 'but the works are not so varied as they are here. Here we have steel works, copper works, tin works, arsenic works, and so on', a range of industry which would 'give students the opportunity of practically applying the knowledge they obtain at the time that they are instructed'. It was an argument that was to form an important element in the eventual debate as to the site of the south Wales college.

In discussions with the committee, witnesses agreed that any college established at Swansea should, like the emergent university college at Bristol, offer, in addition to daytime instruction, evening classes in a far wider range of subjects and to a higher standard than those already organized locally for the Department of Science and Art. But prodded by Lord Aberdare, John Jones Jenkins agreed that the college should be one where 'all the elements of a liberal education' should be provided with 'technical education in conjunction with it'. Aberystwyth, Jenkins conceded, was doing good work but it took a long time to get there: 'it is out of the way, and I think that militates very much against it, however efficient the teaching may be . . . if that college had been established in some centre of population I have no doubt that a very much larger number of students would have attended from Glamorganshire'. Already, Rudler had impressed on the committee his anxiety to get students for Aberystwyth from the mining and metallurgical areas of Glamorgan who would have benefited from his courses in mineralogy and chemistry, but 'very few agreed to it, I had only two or three'. Humpidge, his successor at the Cardiganshire college, found only one student from the industrial regions of south Wales, and he was a medical student. As well as teaching arts subjects, the Swansea college might also cater for medical studies, Jenkins added.

Swansea possessed an 'excellent infirmary' so that there would be 'a very fair field . . . for medical students' undertaking initial studies at the college before completing their degrees at one of the great medical schools.

Although Jenkins was Mayor of Swansea, it must be emphasized that both he and Charles Henry Glascodine, the other town council witness, were expressing personal views to the Aberdare Committee. Jenkins had no clear remit from the Corporation to press for a college at Swansea and the town council had not examined the implications of such a foundation. Indeed, Glascodine, an élitist and an ardent churchman, at this time was not in favour of either a special, state-aided south Wales college or the establishment of a University of Wales, the degrees of which, he considered, would be devalued rather than the character of the students raised. He wished, rather, to see existing *schools* improved, 'raising the course of education in those, and affiliating them in some way to the existing universities'. As far as the local problem of science teaching was concerned, he saw this more effectively dealt with through the enlargement of the grammar school than by the creation of a separate college. To Glascodine the root-and-branch deficiency of intermediate education had to be taken first and higher education could then be adequately covered by the existing universities.

Neither was the foundation of a technical college at Swansea a question that had been given much public consideration locally. *The Cambrian* (17 December 1880), giving a résumé of the evidence submitted by the witnesses – direct reporting was forbidden by the committee – faithfully retailed John Jones Jenkins's statements but without comment. The newspaper was much more exercised by the fate of the grammar school and by the idea of setting up an advanced elementary school. All it could say about the latter was that:

> We hope it will pay its way. . . . Otherwise we think Government should come forward to help, for as it is Swansea is about the most heavily rated borough in the United Kingdom. . . [T]he object of these schools is to give the sons of working men advanced education. What security is there that when so educated they will not leave the neighbourhood? . . . and thus we shall out of our rates be educating skilled workmen for the general benefit of the Kingdom, and surely this is an imperial and not altogether a local matter.

If the conceptual problem of dealing with the deficiencies of scientific and technical instruction in the town had not been adequately thought through, neither had the practical question of finance. Throughout the discussions with the committee, there was an underlying *naïveté* and parochialism in financial matters. To promote the extension of elementary and secondary education, for example, the extremists present saw a solution in stripping the grammar school of its endowment, not realizing that the foundation was financially embarrassed to a degree that was beyond the comprehension of religious controversy. With regard to a south Wales college, John Jones Jenkins was of the view that substantial government grant-aid should be provided to set it up. But, taxed as to whether Swansea itself would help, his characteristic optimism clearly outran his personal experience of local attitudes to past cultural innovations such as the town library scheme. While the foundation of a college, in his view, was a question that the government should take up since Wales, unlike Ireland and Scotland, received nothing from central funds for higher education, he thought that 'Swansea has the name of being very liberal towards things of that kind'.

After two days at Swansea, the Aberdare Committee moved on, first, to Merthyr and, then, to Brecon, Cardiff and Newport, before completing its tour of the principality by Christmas 1880. It was natural that when the committee came to Cardiff there should be strong representation that the town itself should be the site of a south Wales college. Lewis Williams, originally from Swansea, a Wesleyan, and now a prosperous local iron-merchant, thought that, on balance, Cardiff, 'the metropolis of Wales', should be the site of any college, both on grounds of population and also because he believed that the people of Cardiff were prepared to contribute substantially towards the cost of its establishment. Williams, the radical vice-chairman of the Cardiff School Board who had been instrumental in enlarging the geographical remit of the Aberdare Committee, was later to play a crucial part in the arbitration campaign. At Newport, the committee heard the redoubtable Alfred Marshall, principal of the university college at Bristol, who was later to acquire an international reputation as a political economist. Marshall was positive in his view that colleges should be established in Wales, and, protective of his own college, he felt that Swansea would probably be the best site for one. He emphasized, however, that the expenditure on such a college would probably be as large as at Bristol and, allowing for receipts from fees, that a subvention of nearly £4,000 a year might have to be sought. Back in London the committee completed taking oral evidence on 10 February 1881.

Although there were many witnesses who were adamant in their opposition to the proliferation of colleges of higher education in Wales – churchmen like the warden of Llandovery, A.G. Edwards, and the majority of Welsh grammar school headmasters who gave evidence – the balance of opinion expressed to the Aberdare Committee as it went on its round of visits was that provincial colleges such as that at Aberystwyth were necessary for the principality. By and large, opinion was in favour of having two colleges, one for north Wales and one for south Wales. The future of the existing college at Aberystwyth was much more open to question. Some of the most influential witnesses before the committee were in favour of removing it either north or south and the committee acknowledged that 'if the difficulty connected with the expenditure incurred on the College buildings could be obviated, there would probably be a much greater harmony of opinion in favour of removal'.

The Report of the Aberdare Committee, submitted on 18 August 1881, has been hailed as 'the educational charter of modern Wales'. It was the first comprehensive survey of Welsh intermediate and higher education and it set out proposals for a reformed educational system in advance of the pattern in England at that time. The defective nature of Welsh intermediate education was re-emphasized. Throughout the whole of Wales only some 4,000 pupils were enjoying such education while, on the basis of the calculations of the Taunton Commission, it was estimated that there should have been provision for 15,700. As in Swansea, so elsewhere, the majority of these pupils were in private schools, for the grammar schools, shunned by many because of their classical emphasis and alleged 'Church character', took only 1,540.

The solutions prescribed by the committee were, as might be expected, wholly in accord with current educational thinking, envisaging different types of schools for different sectors of society. The committee's major recommendations accordingly included the development of some half-dozen of the existing grammar schools as first-grade classical schools preparing pupils for the ancient universities, with the grammar school at Swansea reconstituted as a first-grade science school. These schools would be stripped of any denominational influences, but, on grounds of cost, would be available primarily only to the middle classes. 'Those who cannot afford to pay at this rate [a minimum tuition fee of £10 per annum was thought to be necessary], or cannot gain a scholarship or exhibition to meet the cost, must be content with a school of a lower type providing a less costly type of education.' Thus was suggested the creation of a new revolutionary system of intermediate schools administered by elected governing bodies, a radical redistribution of endowments to widen the scope of existing schools, the institution of rate and government grant-aid to support the new schools, and the provision of scholarships to facilitate movement of the ablest pupils from the elementary system to the intermediate.

These were ideas that had been canvassed throughout the hearings and many of them were discussed at the meetings at Swansea. It was to be another decade or more before they were implemented in some form. Although the essential linchpin of the proposed educational system was the intermediate schools and, despite the agonizing of A.J. Mundella, Gladstone's Vice-President of the Committee of Council on Education – and the driving force behind the government's educational policy – over the introduction of appropriate legislation for them, it was the establishment of provincial colleges that was the first recommendation of the committee to be put into effect. The committee was emphatic that 'colleges of this kind which have recently been founded in many of the larger towns of England are desirable in the circumstances of Wales'. Nevertheless, while the committee was concerned that the experience of Aberystwyth, 'where various adverse causes have operated', should not be taken as an inhibiting example, it was clear in its mind that until intermediate education was put on a better footing it would be premature to set up any considerable number of colleges. It, therefore, recommended that, for the present, only one additional college should be established:

> [This] new college should be placed in Glamorganshire though there might be some difference of opinion as to the rival claims of Cardiff and Swansea, to be regarded as the most suitable site.
>
> Cardiff, and the places within reach of it, supply, within a given area, the larger population, while Swansea and its neighbourhood are the seats of more varied industries.
>
> The Glamorganshire college may be expected for some time, at all events, to meet the requirements of South Wales, and the college at Aberystwith, whether retained on its present site or removed to Carnarvon or Bangor, must be accepted as the college for North Wales.

'Science', the Report went on, 'especially in its application to arts and manufactures, should occupy a prominent place in the curriculum of the colleges, and, while classical studies are not overlooked, a leading position must be given to English literature and to those modern languages, the knowledge of which, in places like Cardiff and Swansea, is found most conducive to commercial success.'

In Swansea, the apathy which had hitherto been almost the sole reaction to the spasmodic and individual suggestions for the establishment of a higher technical college in the town was dissipated virtually overnight. The possibility of outbidding Cardiff added a piquant urgency to traditional regional jealousies. Some of the more conservative elements in the town, including the indecisive but opinionated new mayor, Thomas Davies, were, it is true, unconvinced of the desirability of such a college in Swansea, believing that it would be wiser to strengthen the traditional grammar school

SUPPLEMENT TO THE "SWANSEA BOY" NOV. 8TH 1870.   No 66.   VOL. V.

COUNCIL CHAMBER

MARKING THE LAMBS.   See page 7.

Charles Henry Glascodine (1841–1928), shown in this cartoon (*extreme right*) with William Williams, Maesygwernen (1840–1904), and Thomas Freeman (1842–1902) as new members of the town council, waiting to be tarred by the devil. Freeman has been described as 'cold and calculating' and the one-legged Williams as a 'natural villain'. Glascodine was the one gentleman among them. After retiring from public affairs, Glascodine qualified as a barrister, and for many years was the much respected deputy clerk of arraigns at the Swansea assizes

or even to do nothing until the government showed its hand over the Report in its entirety. But there were many others who in the past had been lukewarm or had even been critical of the idea of local colleges, who now changed their position. John Jones Jenkins, its most vocal supporter so far, had other weightier personal considerations to occupy his mind for he was cultivating the Carmarthen Boroughs to which he was returned as Liberal Member in January 1882. Jenkins's leadership of the movement on the town council was therefore, perhaps surprisingly, initially assumed by Glascodine, who at the quarterly meeting of the Corporation on 9 November 1881 successfully secured formal support for a bid for the college.

Glascodine, a local solicitor, had, in a very short time on the town council, gained a considerable reputation as a thorn in the flesh of the old guard. Within three years he was to become disillusioned with what he saw as the duplicity of local politics and retired from public life: but, for the present, with all the fervour of a convert, he entered the fray for the south Wales college with spirit. When Charles Wilkins [*Catwg*] was soliciting articles voicing the rival claims for the college for *The Red Dragon*, Glascodine was an obvious contributor for Swansea. As originally the most active member of the town council group – which also included Jenkins, Alderman Frank Ash Yeo, a colliery owner and later a Liberal MP, and the town clerk, John Thomas – appointed to draw up a *Memorial* in support of Swansea's case to Earl Spencer, the Lord President of the Council, Glascodine was well placed to provide an essay. Swansea's geographical centrality in south Wales, the variety of its industries, the cultural foundations of the

Royal Institution of South Wales and the newly established town library, the 'charming variety of its Dissent, and the absence of any high or active element in its Churchmanship' – here a jibe at the growth of Anglo-Catholicism in Cardiff – all contributed to make Swansea the obvious site for the college. Moreover, its central position, accessibility, healthy air and beautiful surroundings, meant that Swansea was 'unsurpassed, nay unequalled, by any other place in South Wales'.

Amid all this hyperbole, there was a hesitant note. The Aberdare Committee had made it clear that while it recommended an annual government grant of £4,000 to each of the proposed Welsh colleges for 'the efficient maintenance of each institution', it considered that any capital contribution to the establishment of the colleges should be made locally. In south Wales, particularly, the resources were 'considerable', and the 'expense of providing the necessary buildings, apparatus, and plant will only have to be incurred once for all and will not be very great, if, as is the case in the colleges established in the English towns, and as we strongly recommend in this case, no provision is made at the cost of the foundation for boarding and lodging the students'.

Henry Richard told Glascodine that the south Wales college 'would, in all probability, go to the place willing to make the greatest concessions in favour of it' (*The Cambrian*, 11 November 1881). Bearing in mind past responses to cultural ventures in Swansea, this was a matter of some concern. As Glascodine had to confess, 'No amount of promises of voluntary local effort should be deemed to give any place a claim. *Timeo Danaos*,' but he ended on a more hopeful note: 'no doubt the people will give of their ability towards the erection of the college there'. It might be expected, too, that the Corporation, 'under the influence and advice of Alderman J.J. Jenkins, MP, who has his heart in this scheme, and is Chairman of the Property Committee', would 'offer as a free gift a freehold site for the college buildings, able to bear comparison with any likely to be given elsewhere'.

Early in 1882 it became known that Cardiff was already well advanced in the preparation of a *Memorial* to the Lord President, and a new degree of urgency entered the contest. Swansea, though, seemed to be dragging its feet and the Corporation was heavily criticized for not doing enough to publicize the local case. Approaches were quickly made to other town councils and public bodies to enlist support, and on 3 February, at an enthusiastic public meeting, Lewis Llewelyn Dillwyn and John Jones Jenkins had no difficulty in securing unanimous popular support for a Swansea bid.

In the meantime, the Corporation had decided in principle to offer a freehold site for the college but, despite all the enthusiasm, the question of actually finding one was more intractable than anyone had thought. Nothing suitable had materialized by the autumn of 1882, and having in mind the Aberdare Committee's recommendation that the grammar school should be reconstituted as a first grade science school, the town council, by no means wholeheartedly – the mayor himself, Thomas Davies, was wilfully cool – approached the governors and headmaster to see whether they were prepared to transfer the school's buildings, together with its 'surplus funds and endowments', to the Corporation as a nucleus for the college. The governors were themselves powerless to alter the scheme of the Court of Chancery under which the school operated, and in any case they had no 'surplus funds' – financially the school was still 'under water'. George Strick, one of the most influential of the governors, and the Revd John Young, in

THE TOWN CLERK ON "GAS."

John Thomas (1840–1914), Swansea's far from brilliant but exceptionally astute town clerk from 1875 to 1911

particular, had little stomach for either the town council's proposal or the college; it was all a damp squib and nothing came of the approach.

Other sites in the ownership of the Corporation were canvassed and dismissed. Town Hill was 'too exposed. It is highly healthy, but slightly inaccessible'. So was the Hill House estate on the road to Cockett. St Helen's Field, although it was 'near at once to the west end of the town, the beach and the cricket grounds', was too low. The Rhyddings – Thomas Bowdler's former home – seemed the best suggestion. To *The Cambrian* (30 December 1881): 'This site possesses unusual beauty of aspect, is alike free from the ruggedness and exposure of the Hill and from the damps of the lower slopes. It is at once sufficiently near the town for the convenience of the collegians, and far enough off to prevent the too frequent participation in the vices and dissipations of the town.' In the event, despite its 'lowness', the Corporation decided to make available twenty acres of undeveloped land in St Helen's Field on the road to Mumbles, about one hundred yards west of the hospital, as a site for the college. It was a wilderness of refuse heaps and the resort of strayed cattle and donkeys. There were more serious problems, though, because the area concerned was currently leased to Col. Evan Morgan of St Helen's House and it took some months of legal wrangling before the lease could be surrendered to the Corporation.

The ultimate question of the comparative claims of Cardiff and Swansea had still to be settled. Cardiff submitted its *Memorial* to the Lord President of the Council on 13 February 1882. It was to be another seven months before Swansea's *Memorial* was ready, ostensibly because of the difficulties of finding a suitable site and a curious misconception locally that it should be delayed until the government brought in a Welsh Education Bill. John Thomas, Swansea's wily town clerk, too, was anxious first to determine the degree of backing which Cardiff had succeeded in obtaining from other public bodies. Both town councils had been active in canvassing support throughout south Wales, and Carmarthen, Neath and Llanelli had come forward readily in favour of Swansea. The position of other authorities was more doubtful but an attempt by Thomas to extract from the Privy Council details of the allegiance of such bodies was not unnaturally turned down, the Privy Council Office advising the Lord President that they doubted 'the expediency of giving such information – the object of which is not quite apparent – seeing that *Swansea* from which this letter comes is "nowhere" in the running so far as memorials are concerned'.

At last, by early September, Swansea's *Memorial*, drafted by Thomas, was ready and printed but, inexplicably, it was not forwarded to Earl Spencer until 25 October 1882, just a week before the contending parties were to appear before Mundella. Accompanied by 102 petitions from public bodies in south-west Wales, the *Memorial* treated every facet of the town which could be taken to its advantage. Its healthfulness, its central location in south Wales both in terms of communications and size of population, the importance and variety of its industries together with the significance of its trading activities and the development of its port, and yet also its continuing Welsh character, its educational and cultural institutions, its hospital which could provide the basis of a medical school, all of which suggested that Swansea was 'in every way adapted as the site for a Welsh and Scientific College'.

Locally, the case seemed unassailable. Cardiff was hardly a Welsh town; it was on the periphery of south Wales, to Glascodine the *'ultima Thule'* of the principality, for Monmouthshire, whatever the remit of the Aberdare Committee, could not be regarded as a truly Welsh county; Cardiff's population was heterogeneous, migratory and of suspect morality and religion, 'among whom cursing and coarse ribaldry are as common as the breath of their nostrils' (*The Cambrian*, 16 March 1883); and its economy was based entirely on coal, an industry, in any case, to which the best authorities gave a life-expectancy of little more than thirty years. Whatever the obloquy, and even for Victorian times it was unsparing, Cardiff's campaign was characterized by a thoroughness, expedition and flair that Swansea could not match. Neither could Swansea mirror the breadth of local support that Cardiff's promoters secured. The business of organizing the Cardiff case was undertaken by a widely representative committee of some two hundred, but, under the eye of the mayor – the outstandingly able Alfred Thomas,[1] it was co-ordinated by a small group of vigour and determination led by Lewis Williams, with Joseph Wheatley, the Cardiff town clerk (1879–1919), as honorary secretary. In Swansea most of the work had been thrust upon the town clerk alone and, dedicated to the task as Thomas was, he himself possessed neither the influence nor the time to project Swansea's argument effectively. On the other hand, personal antipathies and dissension on the town council ensured that no one else of prominence would take the necessary lead in co-ordinating the campaign properly. Even the enthusiasm of Glascodine soon waned and by November 1882 he had left the town council.

It was all in stark contrast to the zeal, determination and administrative acumen of Cardiff. On 3 November, Mundella formally received the two *Memorials*. The difference

The Arbitrators: A.J. Mundella (1825–97), *top left*, Lord
Carlingford (1823–98), *bottom left*, and Lord Bramwell (1808–
92), *bottom right*. The cartoons are by Tissot (unsigned), Ape,
and Spy from *Vanity Fair*, 9 December 1871, 14 August
1869 and 29 January 1876

of approach of the two towns was graphically demonstrated by the different methods of presentation. Swansea's *Memorial* was presented by a small group of thirteen representing the town council and the local Members of Parliament – to Cardiff's unconcealed glee an almost exclusively 'official' deputation, although Mundella had made it clear to John Thomas that he expected the Swansea representation to be confined as far as possible to MPs. Cardiff's *Memorial*, on the other hand, was accompanied by a large gathering of seventy-eight individuals, calculated, by the breadth of its representation of civic, religious, literary, artistic and commercial interests, to impress Mundella.

Mundella, having failed to convince the two towns to agree on a joint scheme and faced by their unyielding hostility, suggested that the site of the college could be determined only by arbitration, a device for settling disputes that he had himself introduced into the British hosiery industry twenty years before. The Swansea Corporation proposed that the matter should be settled either by a tribunal of the Lord President and Mundella sitting with other privy councillors or by two justices of assize who were familiar with the south Wales circuit. Such ideas were not acceptable to Cardiff, which wanted Mundella himself to adjudicate. To Swansea, however, such an arrangement was patently suspect because Mundella had already, 'in his published remarks', been perceived to have 'manifested a partiality for Cardiff' (*The Cambrian*, 8 December 1882). Besides, he had already made it clear that he would not act alone in a matter of such gravity. After a lot of hard bargaining Mundella, eventually, secured a compromise agreement to the appointment of a three-man arbitration panel under Lord Carlingford, the Lord Privy Seal (Earl Spencer, Lord Lieutenant of Ireland since April, being unable to serve because of the heightened political situation in Ireland following the Phoenix Park murders), with Mundella himself and, on the suggestion of Swansea, Lord Bramwell, a former Lord Justice of Appeal.

Although the arbitration was formally restricted to a consideration of the claims of Cardiff and Swansea, other towns attempted to enter the fray and cases were submitted by Neath and Bridgend. John Howells of St Athan in the Vale of Glamorgan, a retired businessman of some literary flair and a ready pen – he contributed regularly on a variety of topics to the early issues of *The Red Dragon* – ignoring the Aberdare Committee's recommendation, cast his own pebble into an already turbulent pool by imploring the arbitrators 'to prevent the calamity of the South Wales College being fixed in either of the two big towns that are in rivalry for it. They are about the last places that should be thought about. In either of them the College would sink into merely a high school for the sons of merchants and traders and its high purpose will be complitely [*sic*] defeated.' This was a view shared wholeheartedly by the immensely rich lord lieutenant of the county, C.R.M. Talbot, who was totally opposed to the college being established in a seaport-town and favoured the rural location of Bridgend. Despite Howells's plea, Talbot's political influence – the latter had already been Whig/Liberal MP for Glamorgan for fifty-two years – and the intervention of the other towns, the arbitration went ahead on the basis of the claims of Cardiff and Swansea to be the site of the south Wales college. The arbitrators met representatives of the two towns together on 7 March 1883, Cardiff's case being put by Dean Vaughan of Llandaff and Lewis Williams, and that of Swansea by Sir Hussey Vivian and John Coke Fowler, the town's stipendiary magistrate, and, like Vaughan, a product of Arnold's Rugby and a distinguished educationist.

The arbitration witnesses: Dean Vaughan (1816–97), *top left*, Lewis Williams (1844–1909), *top right*, Sir Henry Hussey Vivian (1821–94), *bottom left*, and John Coke Fowler (1815–99), *bottom right*. The cartoon of Vaughan is by Montbard (Charles Auguste Loye) from *Vanity Fair*, 24 August 1872

In the meantime, both towns made strenuous efforts to obtain local financial backing for the project. On 24 July 1882 Mundella announced that grants of £4,000 each would be made available for a north Wales and a south Wales college for 1883–4. The grant, however, would not be continued beyond 31 March 1884 unless satisfactory progress had been made by then towards the firm establishment of the colleges and schemes had been approved for their management and maintenance. Government support for the colleges, moreover, would be assured only 'if the liberality of the Government meets with an adequate response from the inhabitants of the Principality' (*The Cambrian*, 28 July 1882).

At last the Gladstone administration had confirmed what many had feared, that Wales would not be treated with anything like the liberality shown to Ireland and that substantial financial support locally would be an essential ingredient in the establishment of the colleges. Mundella, who was the prime educational influence in the administration, had shown his hand. Vital as provincial colleges were, in his mind, especially to the industrial health of Britain, local financial initiative was essential to their foundation. As MP for Sheffield, he had seen what could be done locally for Firth College and his intimate involvement in the hosiery industry demonstrated to him that an important development like the technical college at Chemnitz depended upon the financial involvement of the locality. *The Cambrian* (28 July 1882) responded querulously:

> The people of Swansea were led to believe that the site of the proposed College for South Wales was not to depend upon the amount of money subscribed, but on the fitness and the requirement of the immediate district. The good folks of Cardiff, feeling that they were so far away on the borderland of Wales as to have no claim to the College on grounds of centrality, made the most they possibly could of the money argument, and they have subscribed in the most handsome manner. . . . It now remains, therefore, for Swansea to face the financial question.

Already, Lord Bute had drawn Earl Spencer's attention to the endeavours that Cardiff had made in this direction: the townsmen had evinced, in practical terms, 'an appreciation of the advantages which the establishment of the University College would confer upon that town – an appreciation', he added snidely, 'which I understand that the people of Swansea have not shown in anything like an equal degree'.

Bute's derisive judgement appeared to be too near the mark for Swansea to take any comfort by the time of the arbitration. For all its apparent enthusiasm, the town could not tap anything like the same degree of wealth available among the thrusting shipowners and coalowners of Cardiff and the noble marquess himself, who had made a conditional promise of £10,000. To the *Saturday Review* there could be no argument: 'Cardiff is by far the richer and the more enterprising of the two towns'. Despite the euphoria of the public meeting in Swansea on 3 February 1882, little of value in practical financial terms had emerged. 'There was no lack of pronunciation in favour of Swansea as the most suitable site for the new educational institution', agonized *The Cambrian* (10 February 1882), 'there was more than enough denunciation of the claims of Cardiff; the resolutions arrived at were long and strong enough; and the speeches were quite up to the average of local eloquence; but yet so little was done!' The offer by the shipowner and current high sheriff, John Crow Richardson, of £1,000 was the solitary gesture of the occasion, a sorry match to the £7,800 promised in a single night in

Cardiff the previous winter. Still, others followed and similar promises were made in due course by the Earl of Jersey, Frank Ash Yeo, Councillor James Jones and Sir John Dillwyn-Llewelyn. Sir Hussey Vivian, on the other hand, perhaps the one man who might have been foremost in supporting the scheme, held back. He was, in fact, so concerned about the problem of raising sufficient financial support through individual subscriptions that he suggested the levying of a county rate. While this would have been a device calculated to assure a positive and long-term basis for the college, the suggestion was both unpopular and at the same time served to delay further the contribution of private donations. In the event, although Vivian himself did come forward with a donation of £1,000, the college fund was never effectively established.

Local attitudes to personal thrift and public economy, and, most importantly, the failure of local industrialists once more to demonstrate their practical support, conspired to limit the resources available. The land made available by the Corporation had been valued at between £24,300 and £28,548, while Cardiff had agreed to provide a site worth £10,000. But while, by the time of the arbitration, it was understood that Cardiff had succeeded in raising promises of some £40,000 (including, it was said, the absolute use of a charitable endowment which, capitalized, would be worth £15,000), Swansea had been able to gather together something in the region of only £15,000, over half of which had been promised by eight subscribers. Even *The Cambrian*'s efforts to stress the advantages the college's coming would bring to Swansea's economy and local trade made little impression. On the other hand, Swansea had been able to achieve grass-roots support that Cardiff had not attempted. No fewer than 6,500 workmen in the Swansea Valley had undertaken to subscribe ¼d. per week, or 1s. per year for ten years, to secure an endowment fund of £325 per year to provide scholarships or for any other purpose.

Such support, however, even if legally practicable – and there was considerable doubt about that – could not disguise the fact that Cardiff had raised promises for a much larger endowment fund. In the event, the actual donations to the Cardiff fund were to fall far below what was promised. By the end of the college's first session (1883–4), subscriptions amounted to only £12,217, while immediate and absolute support from the Wells Charity proved to be illusory because of local political infighting. In March 1883, however, Lewis Williams's forceful advocacy of Cardiff's case conveyed no hint of such difficulties.

The arguments used before the arbitrators were, in their nature, essentially elaborations of the statements that formed the basis of the *Memorials* and must have already exhausted the patience of many by their constant repetition in the local press. The geographical centrality of Swansea in south Wales, the variety of its industries, the Welsh character of the town and its associations with the south-western counties, the preponderance of Nonconformity were all persuasively argued as salient features to support Swansea's case for the south Wales college. For Cardiff, its greater size and its wealth – signified by its total rateable value, bolstered by a recent widening of its municipal boundaries, and the trading capacity of its port lately expanded to deal with its deluging coal exports – the larger population of the eastern half of Glamorgan and the accessibility of the town, through its railway network, to the vast industrial conurbations of the valleys were emphasized as critical factors in the decision.

Many of the issues in what, at times, became a heated discussion now seem trivial – the distance of St Helen's Field from Swansea's High Street railway station, for example

– and too many questions seem to have been raised by the remarkably captious Lewis Williams merely as interruptive debating points. The 'narrow, petty, and unworthy behaviour' of this 'itinerant local preacher and partizan of the first water' contrasted vividly with the 'judicial clearness, lucidity and freedom from exaggeration' of the Swansea deputation (*The Cambrian*, 10 November 1882). Although little insight into the minds of the arbitrators is immediately apparent from the nature of their questions, the very flatness of Carlingford's and Mundella's interest and their almost abstracted approach suggest that their minds were already made up. It is only the probings of the independent arbitrator, Bramwell, which give life to the record of otherwise uninterested proceedings and suggest that there was, perhaps, more than a grain of truth in Swansea's suspicions of Mundella's partiality to Cardiff. The public stance of the government over the question of the Welsh colleges was to obtain the utmost return from its investment: it was only natural, therefore, that such utilitarian considerations should attach most weight to questions of population and the extent of local financial support.

At the last minute, it was left to the volatile Lewis Morris to suggest a compromise plan to the arbitrators. Resigned, as he was at this time, to the closure of his own Aberystwyth, he was worried not least about the problems of the geographical accessibility of a single south Wales college. There was but one satisfactory solution 'if the object be to educate the greatest number of young men in South Wales', and that was 'to establish one college . . . with *branches* at Cardiff and Swansea respectively'. As far as buildings were concerned, all that would be necessary would be a college library, laboratories and classrooms in each town. No college building to lodge students would either be possible, or, in view of the religious condition of Wales, desirable, for 'residence in college at once brings in the Religious difficulty, is costly and unsuited to the habits of young men who might be expected to come mainly from the humbler classes'. 'Costly Façades and Quadrangles', too, would be 'out of place and mischievous. Money should be spent on attracting the best possible staff of teachers by offering adequate salaries'. The essence of Morris's scheme was that there should be a core of peripatetic professors and lecturers who would spend time at each centre, living, perhaps, 'at places half-way between Swansea and Cardiff so as to reduce the time expended in travelling ($1\frac{1}{4}$ hours by express) to half an hour, or little more'.

However attractive Morris's views may have been to Mundella in his anxiety to seek conciliation, they were totally unacceptable to both towns, each of which remained fixed to its objective of securing a single undivided college. In Swansea Morris's intervention was seen as 'the merest drivel'. There were enough 'small colleges' already: the 'certificates' of two more would be no better than a 'Ph.D. from Germany in the hands of a smart shopman, when compared with the "hallmark" which certifies the genuine article in London or Edinburgh' (*The Cambrian*, 17 November 1882). When it came, a week after the hearing, the arbitrators' decision was curt and to the point: it offered no explanations. Cardiff had won.

The first historians of the University of Wales tell us that, on the whole, Swansea accepted its defeat with good grace. This may well be true of sponsors of the Swansea project like Hussey Vivian and Dillwyn-Llewelyn, whose financial contributions to a south Wales college had been made without respect to site and who now threw their weight totally behind the new Cardiff college, Vivian becoming its first treasurer. Such a magnanimous approach did not apply in general to their fellow townsmen. Some doubtless shared the relief of the Revd John Young, who now showed his true colours on the issue in reporting to his governors: 'The School is to be congratulated that the new College was not placed in *this* town. Whatever may be said of the injustice of selecting Cardiff as the site, the injustice of planting a highly endowed place of education for youth in the same town as your own foundation would have been great'. But, for the most part, the award in favour of Cardiff was greeted with dismay in Swansea and, in Dean Vaughan's words, the town underwent 'a trying mortification' not, explained the *Western Mail*, with sly irony later, because of any 'petty jealousy of a beaten opponent' but rather owing to 'the paining of a disappointed but most laudable desire on the part of the people to have in their midst a great seat of learning'.

Lewis Llewelyn Dillwyn was certainly pained. 'The decision of the Arbitrators', he thundered, 'has put a night-cap on what might have been a brilliant intellectual luminary for South Wales . . . the Arbitrators have sacrificed the claims of the greater portion of South Wales to the pecuniosity and the push of one town, which is itself more than four fifths English, and which is situated quite on the English border.' It was all a dark plot. Were there not 'whisperings' that the 'incompetent' Mundella was 'a Roman Catholic by profession' and did not Carlingford have 'Catholic predilections'? The meaning obviously was that 'the influence of the wealthy Catholic house of Bute has been used against the just rights of loyal Welsh Nonconformity' and that a college in Cardiff 'under distinctly English, if not also Roman Catholic influence, can never do for the education of the real "people of Wales" what would have been effected by a College at Swansea.' Others saw it less in terms of a Catholic plot than as a simple matter of politics, for if Mundella had declared against Cardiff 'a Tory candidate will stand a very good chance of displacing Sir Edward Reed at the next election'. (*The Cambrian*, 16 March 1883, 25 January 1884, 23 and 30 March 1883.)

Thomas Davies, the former mayor, was made the scapegoat for the whole disappointment. To Glasbrook, who always personalized issues, the débâcle was entirely due to Davies's 'lack of direction of the campaign'. Lewis Llewelyn Dillwyn appreciated that it was easy to be wise after the event but he felt that the delay and indecision at the outset had been crucial. 'If Swansea's claim had been formulated and issued broadcast as Cardiff's was at the commencement of the agitation, many communities and public bodies that petitioned for Cardiff would have petitioned for Swansea. First come first served.' If Vivian, publicly, had not set so much store on a county rate, private individuals might have been less ready to believe that their subscriptions were unnecessary (*The Cambrian*, 16 March 1883).

Despite the righteous anger, the bewildered frustration and the abuse hurled at the unfortunate Davies, the matter seemed closed. Nevertheless, within a few months, a fresh opportunity suddenly presented itself when the future of the college at Aberystwyth came under review. In August 1883 the three arbitrators chose Bangor as the site of the north Wales college and under the terms of both the Aberdare Report and the government's declared policy towards the Welsh colleges this should have meant that the college at Aberystwyth would be closed. The original campaign, however, which had led to the establishment of the Aberdare Committee had been based on an attempt to secure government aid for Aberystwyth. A new campaign was now mounted to continue the Aberystwyth college and secure as a permanent grant the temporary aid

Thomas Davies, the former sea captain who was Mayor of Swansea in 1881–2. In the nineteenth century the mayor was more active in public issues than he subsequently became. Davies, an opinionated man, who wished to preserve and strengthen the grammar school, was lukewarm in the campaign for a south Wales college and was the target for attack over his perceived lack of leadership and indecision when the campaign failed

that was given to the college pending decisions on the north and south Wales institutions.

The Swansea town council, pinning its hopes on the criticism that had been made during the Aberdare hearings of the lack of success of the college at Aberystwyth – what Harper had described as 'an ill-advised effort of great patriotism' – forwarded a plea to Gladstone, Carlingford and Mundella that the Aberystwyth grant should be transferred to Swansea. It was an extraordinary approach which succeeded in conveying all the bitterness of defeat. Not unnaturally the new initiative was well supported in Swansea but, despite local enthusiasm, it received no encouragement from the Gladstone government, beset as it was by mounting political pressure from Aberystwyth's friends.

Nothing having been decided in the confused situation of the next few months, a public meeting was held in Swansea in April 1884 and, as a result, a fresh overture was made to the government by the town council. This time, however, the approach was less brash and was couched in deliberately general terms to give less offence to the supporters of the existing Welsh colleges. By suppressing any reference to Aberystwyth it was hoped that Swansea's plea would be less counter-productive in political terms and would stand on the declared need for technical education in Wales. Nevertheless, the Swansea town council was not so naïve as not to appreciate that any government grant for a college in the town would depend on the fate of the Cardiganshire college. Nearly a year went by before any meaningful reply was received and then it was in terms hardly calculated to raise great hopes, for it made it clear that the government was not prepared to consider the suggestion until Parliament had had an opportunity of considering the long deferred bill on intermediate education in Wales.

Within four months, however, it seemed as if events were playing into Swansea's hands and that the Aberystwyth college could be removed south. In July 1885 the college buildings were destroyed by fire. According to the *Western Mail* (11 July 1885), which had never shown any love for the Cardiganshire college, this marked 'the end of Aberystwith'. Now the paper, which had never evinced much sympathy for Swansea's case either, urged the townspeople that 'a long pull, a strong pull, and a pull together and the College is theirs'. If Frank Ash Yeo, then contesting the new Gower constituency, Richardson, Vivian and James Jones each made good their original promises of financial support, 'only a little effort', the paper pontificated, 'would be needed to get up a fund of fifty or sixty thousand pounds for the building and endowment of a College'. For 'no centre in the country, possibly in the world', the *Western Mail* had discovered, was 'so well adapted for the formation of a chemical, metallurgical, and mineral school'. If Swansea did not act positively now, its earlier 'zeal in behalf of Higher Education was all bunkum, selfish, a flash in the pan, something got up by a few of its citizens who were bent upon obtaining a cheap advertisement for a liberality which they knew they would never have the chance of carrying into effect . . . Aberystwith's difficulty is their opportunity.' The fire, in fact, proved to be Aberystwyth's own opportunity. Sufficient emotional reaction was generated by the disaster that before the end of August 1885 Aberystwyth's grant had been assured by the new Conservative government of Lord Salisbury and the future of the college guaranteed.

Justice had been done to Aberystwyth but, at the same time, hopes that Swansea might still become the seat of a university college had not been completely dashed. In April 1886 the town council addressed the returned Gladstone government on the subject of the establishment of a technical college, expressing the hope that, because of the continued delays in introducing legislation on Welsh intermediate education, the government would be prepared to reconsider the question of a local college. The indignation of 1883 was giving way to a realization that the chances of securing grant-aid were becoming more remote. Yet a noncommital reply from the Privy Council Office merely served to build up local enthusiasm and the town council warmed to the idea of dispatching a deputation to Lord Spencer.

The response was not encouraging, for the government held to its view that there should be no further commitments to higher education in Wales until the question of intermediate education had been settled by parliament. Now, for the first time since the arbitration, was thought given to local initiative. Hitherto, attention had been concentrated on government grant-aid and minds had been dazzled by the support given to the other Welsh colleges. In May 1886 a conference of representatives of the town council, the school board, the Chamber of Commerce, the Royal Institution of South Wales, and the Free Library Committee decided that, without waiting for a government decision, steps should be taken locally to set up a technical college. Since the college was intended to be 'not only of local but also of national advantage', pressure would be maintained for government grant-aid, but in the meantime, a scheme for a college should be drawn up to 'allow of extension hereafter as occasion may require' and an appeal for private financial support should be launched since it was recognized all too well that government aid would 'depend upon the amount of assistance that will locally be forthcoming'.

Despite the initial enthusiasm, the resulting campaign was a desultory one and local financial support was not readily forthcoming. In desperation, in March 1887, Gamwell, now editor of *The Cambrian*, which had always been positive in its approach to the issue, stressed the need for his fellow townsmen to persist in the effort to create an intermediate school and a technical college in Swansea, but nothing practical resulted, largely because of the difficulties of finance and the intractable problem of persuading townspeople that the rates should be used for such a purpose. For, as ever, there was a powerful lobby on the town council vociferously assertive that ratepayers should not be 'called upon to pay for the little whims of educationalists' (*The Cambrian*, 25 March 1887).

The truth was that the Corporation was still divided by arguments over the public library which, it had been agreed in April 1882, should be erected, together with an art gallery and a school of science and art, on a site in the new Alexandra Road. The new buildings were not opened – by Mr Gladstone – until 1887 and by the time of their completion had cost nearly double the original estimate of £10,000. Moreover, in their enthusiasm, the promoters had given little consideration to the maintenance of the magnificent edifice. Many townspeople viewed with lugubrious anticipation a further increase in the rates to meet the extra costs involved. The incorporation in the building of accommodation for the South Kensington Science and Art classes also presented problems, not only because of the administrative difficulties of duality of control but because there were many on the Corporation who considered that there were already sufficient science classes in the town and that the use of the new municipal building for such a purpose was both unnecessary and improper.

It was in this atmosphere of controversy and complacency that William Morgan, the public analyst, expanded his South Wales School of Chemistry in 1887, moving it from its original quarters in Orange Street to larger premises in Nelson Terrace. Additions to the existing buildings, 'designed in accordance with the requirements of the Science and Art Department, South Kensington, for instruction in practical Chemistry and Metallurgy . . . will be sufficiently large to accommodate 60 students', commented Samuel Gamwell for his newspaper. 'It is said to be Dr Morgan's intention later to extend the list of his subjects so as to include mechanics, mathematics, physics, mineralogy – in fact to start on a moderate scale – if he receives adequate support – a fully equipped technical college with all the varied departments conducted by efficient and competent teachers' (*The Cambrian*, 25 September 1886). By 1889 it appears that the school had become the 'The Technical Institute', most of its students coming from the School of Science and Art. Locally, at least, the Institute had developed a remarkable reputation by the 1890s although it is unlikely that the encomiums it attracted were altogether wholly deserved.

Successful as this venture may have been, Morgan's attempt to set up a complementary 'South Wales College of Practical Engineering' met with failure. An echo, perhaps, of the ill-fated 'Gnoll College', Morgan's new scheme was intended to be more than a local institution. The college would offer courses in 'Workshop Experience combined with theoretical training for any branch of engineering', and its classes were 'designed to secure to students intending to become Engineers, a thorough Scientific Education, and to provide Systematic theoretical training with practical demonstration of the principles involved'. Mining and civil engineering, machine-drawing, architec-

Mr Gladstone's visit to Swansea in June 1887 as seen by the *Illustrated London News*. Ostensibly Gladstone had come to open the new library buildings but the visit was turned into a political jamboree. While staying at Singleton he received political addresses from a throng of nearly 50,000 over an exhausting four-and-a-half hours

ture, surveying, mathematics, geology and mineralogy, French and German were to form the subjects of instruction in this grandiose undertaking. But it never got off the ground. The very magnitude of the project required more than the organizing genius of one man. Its financial foundations were shaky and the high level at which the fees were necessarily pitched combined with local apathy and municipal complacency to ensure its failure.

In 1889 the first Technical Instruction Act empowered the county councils and county boroughs, brought into existence the year before, to raise a rate of a penny in the pound to establish technical schools for teaching 'the principles of Science and Art applicable to industries' and 'the application of special branches of Science and Art to specific industries and employments'. The same year saw the passing of the Welsh Intermediate Education Act which authorized the local authorities to raise a half-penny rate towards the establishment of intermediate schools. In 1890, Goschen's Local Taxation Act placed at the disposal of the local authorities monies received from customs and excise duties. Difficult as it was in practice, it was natural that the implementation of the Intermediate Education Act should be given priority over the Technical Instruction Act. And even five years later only a relatively small proportion of the money received under the Local Taxation Act was devoted to technical education in Wales.

Under the terms of the Welsh Intermediate Education Act, a Joint Education Committee was set up in April 1890 to introduce intermediate education in Swansea. In August 1890 the members of this same committee were also charged, as the Technical Instruction Committee, to undertake consideration of the provision of technical instruction in the town. The most influential member of the new Technical Instruction Committee was Richard Martin, a town councillor since 1884. Martin, who was later described by Owen M. Edwards as the 'honoured leader of all educational movements in Swansea', was, with the firm support of Hussey Vivian (created Lord Swansea in 1893), the driving force behind the development of municipal technical education. During its first year the committee, at Martin's suggestion, sought the advice of a number of individuals who had played an active part in the provision of technical education in the town or had views about it, including William Morgan, Hosford, Molison, and Glascodine. In October 1891 the committee visited some of the principal provincial technical schools in Birmingham, Bristol, Cardiff, Liverpool, Manchester, Sheffield and also the City and Guilds of London Institute at Finsbury.

As a result of these enquiries and discussions, the committee took the view, in the report it eventually submitted to the Corporation in January 1893, that it was 'emphatically important to bring Technical Instruction, if it is to be of practical value, into the very closest connection with the local industries and in as many ways as possible'. It was an echo of the advice given by John Jones Jenkins to the Aberdare Committee over a decade before. Swansea, moreover, should be conceived of as 'the seat of a National Metallurgical School, occupying the same relative position to the education and industries of England, that Freiburg and Clausthal occupy in Germany'.

But there were considerable financial constraints on the Corporation, which was in no position to expend a large capital sum on the proposed technical school. As a result, the committee was obliged to tailor its proposals to more realistic local dimensions and to confine the proposal to a few rooms in the library. In financial terms, all that the Corporation could do was to earmark two-thirds of the 'Whisky Money' it received after 1893 under the Local Taxation Act for technical education.

Six months later, the committee, driven by the persistence of Martin, came back with further concrete proposals. Even if there were no bricks and mortar to *build* a technical school, the nucleus of a specialist staff should be appointed: 'a Specialist in Metallurgy as Principal of the proposed school and two Demonstrators – one for gold, silver, lead, etc., and the other for iron and steel; also a Professor of Engineering and an Assistant Demonstrator'. The committee thought that teaching should be provided by day classes and, during the winter months, by evening classes, each course of study being accompanied by laboratory practice or manual instruction but that until the principal was appointed and his views ascertained, 'it would be inexpedient to provide any plant or apparatus or to attempt the preparation of any syllabus for the working of the proposed school'. To provide a financial basis for the school, a special rate of one penny in the pound should be raised and an appeal made to 'the wealthier classes living in and around Swansea'. Finally, in a repeated echo from the past, the committee urged the council to set up a special committee to steer the whole project and to include among its members some of the locality's leading industrialists.

Although both reports were adopted by the Corporation, little emerged in practical terms. On the other hand, during these years active consideration was given to the implementation of the Welsh Intermediate Education Act. The year 1895 saw control of the grammar school, its property and endowments being taken over by the Joint Education Committee. At the same time the Girls Public Day School Trust school, established seven years earlier at Llwyn y Bryn in Walter Road largely due to the energies of John Coke Fowler, became a girls' intermediate school while, out of the higher grade elementary school in Trinity Place, two municipal secondary schools were created, one for boys (in new buildings, complete with laboratories and workshops, at Dynevor Place) and one for girls. Secondary education was at last being put on a sound footing in the town and the teaching of science was beginning to receive the attention it deserved. The Revd John Young accepted a living in Lincolnshire and the new governing body decided that in appointing his successor the duties of headmaster of the grammar school should be joined to those of the principal of the proposed technical school. Dr George Sherbrooke Turpin, Principal of Huddersfield Technical College, was appointed to the dual post later in the year. Educated at Cambridge and Berlin and of no mean reputation as a research fellow at Manchester, he had acquired notable experience in technical education and it was with this primarily in mind that he was encouraged to apply for the Swansea post by Hussey Vivian shortly before the latter's death. By January 1896 evening classes in science and commercial subjects had been started in the grammar school and in the immediately succeeding years Heartley's 'public-school' additions were adapted for instructional and recreational use.

Gradually the increasing number of school pupils, together with a growing demand for technical education in the locality, meant that these additional facilities became insufficient. As a consequence, in 1898 the Technical Instruction Committee acquired a site adjoining the grammar school and adopted a development scheme for a new technical school, estimated to cost £50,000. Unfortunately Martin's 'lawless audacity' outran the competence of the Corporation and the resulting legal difficulties over access to the site effectively stifled the plan. All that could be embarked upon was the construction of temporary chemical and metallurgical laboratories to which engineering workshops were added later. Despite these unpromising and constricting conditions, day technical classes were begun in mathematics, physics, chemistry, metallurgy, mining and engineering, with four specialist lecturers assisting Turpin, the principal. The success of these classes was such that, in 1901, the title of the school was changed to 'The Swansea Technical College' and serious thought began to be given to securing its recognition as a degree-awarding institution.

Turpin's resignation later in 1901 to take up the headship of Nottingham High School delayed this development, but within two years Richard Martin had succeeded in convincing the Corporation that the work of the technical college had advanced to such an extent that an application should be made to the University of Wales for its recognition as a constituent college in science and applied science. It was a premature approach and the resulting *Memorial* that the Corporation submitted to the university court in April 1903 met with a rebuff. The court was rightly unconvinced that the technical college was yet of the standard of a full constituent college and was thus not prepared to accept Martin's proposals. During the previous year, £3,000 had been spent on a new engineering workshop but the other facilities were still housed in temporary buildings and, while some successes had been obtained in the B.Sc. examinations of the University of London, both admission standards and the general level of students' abilities were low.

The university court was only prepared to recognize the technical college as an 'affiliated' college, and on the basis of stringent conditions which would have resulted in the conferment of a distinctly lower status than that of a constituent college, it obtained a Supplemental Charter three years later in 1906. This was a solution unacceptable to either Martin or the Corporation, who feared that even the lower status offered by the Supplemental Charter would be difficult to secure from a court safeguarding, with conservative eyes, the vested interests of the existing colleges. Accordingly, no further steps were taken to obtain 'affiliation', but the Technical Instruction Committee strove to develop the technical college into an institution of university standard, preparing students for external degrees of the University of London, in the hope that its work would eventually justify the University of Wales in accepting candidates from Swansea for Welsh degrees.

The close administrative connection between the technical college and the grammar school may have had advantages in terms of economy and possibly facilitated a degree of correlation of schemes of study, but the long-term development of both institutions was seriously inhibited by the practical problems of sharing the same buildings and using the same laboratories. Moreover, John Trevor Owen, Turpin's successor as headmaster and principal, able as he was, was more attuned to the 'quiet pursuit of the main functions of a school' rather than of a technical college. Clearly, an arrangement that had been devised as a temporary expedient mainly on grounds of cost could not be continued indefinitely. There is some suggestion that Turpin's somewhat precipitate departure in 1901 had been occasioned by frustration over the lack of progress towards the separation of the two institutions and the long drawn-out failure to erect the new permanent buildings he had conceived. These buildings were completed, to provide accommodation for physics, mathematics and engineering, only in 1909, and it was not until then that the first real step was taken towards separation.

A year later (1910) Martin achieved this aim with the appointment of an independent principal, Dr W. Mansergh Varley, Director of Technical Instruction for Devonport.

William Mansergh Varley (b. 1879), first
principal of the Swansea Technical College after
its separation from the grammar school

When Varley took over, the college was still a very small institution. There were fewer than a score of full-time students and only a few hundred who attended evening classes two or three times a week. Surprisingly, bearing in mind the emphasis that had repeatedly been put on the needs of local industries, there was still little or no co-operation or consultation between them and the college, especially over day classes. Varley, who had been for five years an assistant professor at the Heriot-Watt College in Edinburgh, brought a new vigour to the technical college. Its higher technological work grew rapidly and by 1913 complete three-year courses leading to the B.Sc. degree of London University in both pure science and engineering were running. By the autumn of 1916, 139 students had passed through the college's day courses although, naturally, they were dislocated considerably by the Great War. During this time the number of part-time evening students also increased beyond the available accommodation. Such a large and rapid increase was largely due to the fact that, through Varley's energetic exploitation of contacts with industrial firms, the interest of local employers was at last successfully enlisted in the development of the college, and success was breeding success. The curriculum was broadened to include marine and mining engineering and by January 1915 the college had been recognized by the coalowners' association and the county council as the centre for advanced mining instruction in the western area of the coalfield.

Since 1902, following the Balfour Education Act, the management of the technical college and the grammar school had been in the hands of the education committee of the Corporation. Martin had been its first chairman and had served in this capacity until his retirement as a town councillor in 1910, when he had finally achieved his ambition of creating an independent technical college. He was succeeded as chairman by Ivor Gwynne (1867–1934), a town councillor of long standing and secretary of the Tin and Sheet Millmen's Association since 1904, 'a self-educated student of great power and influence in the Labour world, who believes strongly in education', as Owen M. Edwards described him. Gwynne was as dedicated as Martin to the cause of the technical college, and as his deputy chairman he had David Matthews (1868–1960), a tinplate manufacturer and Liberal councillor. Together these two made a redoubtable team, all the more effective because it transcended the bounds of politics.

In 1916, in the wake of the appointment of Lord Haldane's royal commission,[2] Matthews was successful in persuading the Corporation to establish a new technical college sub-committee to serve as the active governing body of the college. This sub-committee was given wide powers and, subject only to confirmation by the education committee and the town council, a considerable measure of autonomy. Matthews was also able to enlist the support of many industrialists who had previously looked askance at Martin's educational endeavours and, resurrecting the latter's ideas of almost two decades earlier, devised a scheme for a considerable industrial representation on the sub-committee. Thus, while eleven members of the Corporation served on the sub-committee there were, in addition, twenty-two co-opted members, representative of the chamber of commerce, the manufacturing and industrial concerns of the district and others interested in the development of higher scientific and commercial education. Furthermore, an advisory committee for metallurgy was formed to assist specifically in the applied chemistry work of the college, and through this body Frank W. Gilbertson, the managing director of W. Gilbertson & Co., the family tinplate firm, was brought into the counsels of the college. As someone who only three years before had been among those who had condemned 'the luxury of an engineering and analytical staff' in the tinplate industry, Gilbertson was to become the acknowledged leader of the movement to create a university college in Swansea.

Although suffering from the dislocations of the Great War, Swansea appeared to be on the flood tide of its prosperity. It was still the major centre of the tinplate industry and

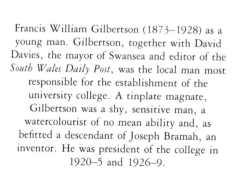

Francis William Gilbertson (1873–1928) as a young man. Gilbertson, together with David Davies, the mayor of Swansea and editor of the *South Wales Daily Post*, was the local man most responsible for the establishment of the university college. A tinplate magnate, Gilbertson was a shy, sensitive man, a watercolourist of no mean ability and, as befitted a descendant of Joseph Bramah, an inventor. He was president of the college in 1920–5 and 1926–9.

boasted, within eighteen miles of the town, sixty-five of the eighty-two works in Britain. There was little hint as yet of the real difficulties that the industry would have to face after the war and, despite the current crisis, the local tinplate manufacturers could bask happily in the thought that in 1913 they had produced 468,000 tons of plate. Furthermore, while the old copper industry, admittedly, had virtually disappeared, other non-ferrous metal production in the Swansea region was expanding. There were six distinct zinc spelter works in active operation in Landore and Llansamlet and, in addition, two firms were engaged in tin-smelting and three in arsenic refining on some scale. The most significant and technologically advanced development, however, was the arrival at Clydach in 1902 of The Mond Nickel Company Limited which established there the largest nickel works in the world. Swansea was, moreover, the commercial and shipping centre for what, in pre-war days, had been the rapidly-expanding south Wales anthracite industry and had seen over 4,530,000 tons of coal shipped through the port in the peak year of 1913. Docks facilities had been repeatedly expanded since the Prince of Wales Dock had been opened during the third mayoralty of John Jones Jenkins in 1881. Between 1896 and 1898 the dock was extended, and in 1909 the new King's Dock was completed. The peak turnover of 1913 (7,250,000 tons) saw even these facilities fully stretched.

The news of the appointment of the Haldane Commission on 12 April 1916 injected fresh enthusiasm into the movement for establishing a university college of full constituent status in Swansea and the technical college sub-committee immediately set about preparing a strong *Representation* to convince the commission of the justice of this ambition. Optimistically detailing the industrial activity of the district, especially where 'scientific control' was demanded, and setting out a full conspectus of the technical college, its history and development, the *Representation* was agreed by the town council, as the local education authority, on 21 June, just in time for it to meet the commission, which paid a flying and informal visit to Swansea two days later. The commission saw something of the college buildings at Mount Pleasant and made it clear to the council that, in the words of the mayor, Alderman David Davies (1862–1932), 'they could not dream of getting a college in Swansea of university rank unless they were in a position to pay its professors adequate salaries, and not merely the salaries of ordinary teachers, and they would not believe Swansea was in earnest unless it was prepared to raise an endowment fund of from £30,000 to £40,000 so that they would have the revenue to pay those highly skilled, highly trained men' (*South Wales Daily Post*, 30 November 1916).

Davies, in his dual capacity as mayor and editor/proprietor of the *South Wales Daily Post*, embarked on a lightning campaign to raise this 'colossal sum'. The 'task seemed appalling, but the Technical Committee put their backs into it and they started on the impossible task'. What *had* proved impossible in the 1880s was now achieved with a rapidity that startled even Davies, thanks almost entirely to the commitment of the industrialists associated with the technical college sub-committee. By 29 November 1916, when an enthusistic promotion meeting was held at the Albert Hall, the mayor could announce that £71,000 had been promised for the endowment fund. The critical factor, however, as Davies was at pains to stress, was that 'the manufacturers were going to make a success of the College'. For that was certainly their intention. Theirs was a generation that had been brought up on the spectre of German inventiveness, industry and success, all founded on the sound basis of an educational system, the virtues of which had been preached for half a century or more. Now, in the autumn of a year in which the 'zest and idealism with which nearly three million Englishmen had marched forth to war' (Taylor, p. 61) found a graveyard in the mud of the Somme, the shadow had become all too real. To men like Gilbertson the impact of the Great War and the realization of the extent to which Britain was dependent on the manufacturing capacity of the continent, future industrial strength demanded a workforce educated to high standards of technical accomplishment.

Thanks to Gilbertson, the steel and tinplate manufacturers came to the immediate support of the appeal: Baldwins, the South Wales Siemens Steel Association and the Welsh Plate and Sheet Manufacturers' Association gave £10,000 apiece; the Briton Ferry Steel Company £5,000 and its chairman, Herbert Eccles, a personal £2,500; and Sir Alfred Mond the same amount matched by an equal amount from his company. Glasbrooks gave £2,000, as did a number of other companies, including Vivians. The eighty-year-old Sir John Dillwyn-Llewelyn honoured his commitment to the college of forty years earlier as did Dulcie Vivian her brother's and Frank Cory Yeo his father's. The majority of the donations, though, were £1,000 or less and it cannot be said that, even in the state of euphoria generated by Davies, local industry and commerce reacted as handsomely as they might have. Before his mayoralty ended in 1918 Davies increased the endowment target to £150,000 and received further substantial promises from the coal exporter W.T. Farr, in due course to be the college's first treasurer, and from Yeo, but the fund never, in fact, reached the original £70,000.

T.J. Rees (1875–1957), the director of education for Swansea who coordinated the campaign for the college. A man of the utmost influence locally, 'Tee Jay' was treasurer of the college from 1950 to 1955

To what extent the industrialists had been cultivated by the local education authority as a means to an end must remain an open question. It cannot be doubted that a number of those actively engaged in the campaign for the creation of a university college were adept politicians, and the skill of David Davies and T.J. Rees, the superintendent (later redesignated 'director') of education for the borough since 1908, in prosecuting their aims and mobilizing support for their cause should not be minimized. The case, as presented, was that the college should provide only faculties of pure and applied science. When, however, the witnesses from Swansea were formally interviewed by the royal commission on 1 December 1916, they were subjected to a very searching cross-examination to discover how far Swansea was prepared to go in the direction of establishing a faculty of arts. Davies took up an ambivalent position on this question. In answer to Sir Henry Hadow, he immediately said 'yes' but went on: 'I want to guard myself against that. We are not asking for it now, unless we can do so without danger. We want to open the door; and then, when the door is open, we will do all that we can do.' Clearly, he had in mind both a long-term plan and the reactions of the other colleges: for the moment, however, 'we are aiming . . . to produce a first class technical college as good as that of Sheffield or Birmingham'.

Later, T.J. Rees was to justify this 'lopsided scheme' to a correspondent who had been sharply critical of the original proposals:

> To most Welshmen . . . the application of Swansea to become a fourth constituent College appealed very strongly as a set-off against what was regarded as the anglicising influence of Cardiff but many of those who favoured Swansea's claim to be recognised in the departments of pure and applied science and technology would have been hostile to a complete University College which might damage both Aberystwyth and Cardiff. We considered this matter at length. We . . . decided to go whole-heartedly for the smaller scheme leaving the future to take care of itself. By emphasising the technological side of the scheme, we secured the interest of the local commercial and industrial magnates and the lightning campaign of the then-Mayor, Alderman David Davies (the editor of the 'Daily Post') succeeded in collecting a sum of nearly £70,000 as a preliminary endowment fund for the proposed technological University College. Living as you do in a business area like Johannesburg, you will appreciate how much easier it was to get financial assistance for such a scheme than it would have been for one in which they were going to teach Latin and Greek.

Perhaps there was more than a degree of hindsight and self-justification in T.J. Rees's words for, however much they had to tailor their original proposals, the concept of the promoters remained one of an essentially technological institution and, until a late stage in the run-up to the foundation of the university college, it was one based firmly on the existing technical college.

The limitations of the concept were not received with enthusiasm even in Swansea. After the commission met the official representatives of the town, they were approached by a local consultant cardiologist, George Arbour Stephens, professing to speak for university graduates resident in Swansea. Stephens, a self-important man of short patience, had been incensed by the failure of the promoters of the Swansea college to consult anyone of academic pretensions outside the industrial world. Stephens's attitude was an importunate one but he did help to convince the commission that there was a local demand for a 'fuller basis' for a university college than technology would provide.

From Cardiff came both opposition and support. Principal Griffiths, raising the spectre of the 1880s, accepted the idea of a new constituent college with some

George Arbour Stephens (1870–1945). Stephens was one of the group of founders of the university college and a member of its original council. He later married Professor Mary Williams.

reluctance. 'I think already Wales has too many Colleges. The difficulty is, it has three instead of two; and I cannot believe that the population and wealth of Wales ought to be supporting three, four, five, or six Colleges of that kind. They ought to concentrate rather than become more diffuse.' Sibly, Professor of Geology at Cardiff, was also at first opposed to the creation of a new constituent college at Swansea and saw the natural development of the technical college lying in a scheme of affiliation with his own college.

While these discussions were taking place, a complex scheme was unfolding for the development and co-ordination of technological studies in south Wales. It was not until the summer of 1917, however, that the project became sufficiently firm for its promoters to submit it to the commission. The scheme was prepared by a small group of members of the South Wales and Monmouthshire Business Committee on Scientific Research and Technology, formed only in 1916 and representative of the university college at Cardiff, the technical colleges at Newport, Cardiff and Swansea, certain of the south Wales education authorities, and local industry. The committee had been set up to assist 'the Educational Institutions in the duty of Scientific Research and Technological Instruction as applicable to the different Industries of the District'. The industrialists, who were the driving force behind the new project, had a profound feeling of distrust of the University of Wales and its centralized control, and they were far from satisfied with the level of industrial linkage which the university college at Cardiff either professed or practised. As Sibly, one of the academic members of the committee, confessed to the commission, the college would never get the standing that it should unless it turned out original work, 'partly of a purely scientific character, and partly in relation to the industries of the area'. The mining department at Cardiff, started there in 1891 under Sir William Galloway, should have become a scientific centre for the south Wales coalfield. It had nowhere near achieved this distinction and it was an unpalatable fact that the largest coalfield in Britain was very badly served by its local university college. The coalowners, therefore, seeking to supply themselves with what the university and the college could not provide, had set up their own rival school of mines at Treforest in 1913 to the detriment of the mining department at Cardiff, which in 1914 had only one student.[3]

None of the other scientific departments in the university college had made the impact that comparable disciplines in university institutions like Sheffield and Newcastle had achieved and their applied research contribution was negligible. The development of metallurgy, chemistry, and engineering had been severely curtailed for lack of finance and these departments had never achieved the measure of success that they should, taking account of their industrial environment. This was partly due to the sceptical, if not openly hostile, attitude of the industrialists towards science and research despite the blandishments of Principal Griffiths. To an even greater degree, though, the fault lay with the college itself which, because of an over-diversification of subjects, failed to develop any areas of excellence attractive enough to gain the sponsorship of industry. Even the great Powell Duffryn Coal Company, faced with electrical problems in its mines, turned to Berlin and not to Cardiff.

The academic and local authority members of the committee, formulating the new and elaborate scheme for the development and organization of technological studies in south Wales, had no mandate from their respective authorities although it is clear that it had their tacit blessing. It was thus a powerful lobby. Both Principal Griffiths and Sibly, through their contact with the Business Committee, became converted to the idea of the establishment of a university college at Swansea, and the scheme assumed the existence of such a college so that any faculty of technology that might be set up would, in practice, be a joint faculty of Swansea and Cardiff.

This assumption and the underlying acceptance of the academic respectability of the Swansea Technical College were more than encouraging to the Swansea promoters because, as they emphasized in their *Representation*, the 'growing tendency to associate all higher scientific and technological training with the Universities' had led to the absorption or affiliation of 'almost all our larger Technical Institutes, at least so far as instruction in day courses is concerned'. Without university recognition, the promoters knew only too well that the full development of the technical college would be virtually unattainable. Academic acceptance and respectability for the college, as well as the sheer practical convenience of the availability of a Welsh degree and a still-rankling emotional urge for civic status following the débâcle of 1883, dictated an association with the University of Wales. To be unaccepted and remain outside, like Lampeter, would be second-rate in the eyes of the Swansea promoters. Although the word 'affiliation' might still be loosely used, nothing less than association with the University of Wales as a constituent college was acceptable.

The powerful support that was now coming from within the university and from the industrial interests of south Wales, together with the growing realization that there was no serious opposition to the Swansea case for constituent college status, persuaded the Swansea town council to submit to the Privy Council in July 1917 a petition and draft charter for the incorporation of the technical college as a constituent college of the university. The reaction of both the Privy Council Office, and of the Board of Education whose advice it sought, was all that could be expected: consideration of the application would be deferred until the report of the royal commission had been issued. Nevertheless, Swansea had pleaded its case, there seemed to be a groundswell in favour of it and the promoters could sit back and wait.

The Swansea Grammar School, c. 1903. In the foreground are the Heartley 'public school' additions of chapel, dining hall and dormitories, which were converted into gymnasium, laboratories and art-room when the school was taken over by the local authority in 1895. Under the original proposals for the university college, the school would have become a nucleus of the new institution

Notes

1. Alfred Thomas (1840–1927), knighted in 1902 and raised to the peerage as Lord Pontypridd in 1912.
2. In addition to Lord Haldane the members of the commission were Sir William Bragg (1862–1942), Quain Professor of Physics at University College, London; the Hon. W.N. Bruce (1858–1936), son of the first Lord Aberdare, and then Principal Assistant Secretary to the Board of Education; Sir Owen Edwards (1858–1920), then Chief Inspector of the Welsh Department of the Board of Education; Sir Henry Hadow (1859–1937), Principal of Armstrong College and later Vice-chancellor of Sheffield; Sir Daniel Hall (1864–1942), permanent adviser of the Development Commission; Sir Henry Jones (1852–1922), Professor of Moral Philosophy at Glasgow; Sir William Osler (1849–1919), Regius Professor of Medicine at Oxford; and Miss (later Dame) Emily Penrose (1858–1942), Principal of Somerville College, Oxford.
3. The South Wales and Monmouthshire School of Mines passed to the control of the former Glamorgan County Council in 1928, and, progressing from technical college, to college of technology and subsequently to regional college of technology it became a polytechnic in 1970. It is now poised on the brink of becoming the 'University of Glamorgan'. As such it will be independent of the University of Wales, with major implications for the future of the latter institution and its constituent colleges.

CHAPTER THREE

'HIGH IDEALS AND LOFTY PURPOSE'

The Final Report of the Haldane Commission was published on 19 March 1918. Permeated with Haldane's philosophical concepts about universities, it recommended that, while there should continue to be a single national university 'in the interests of the Welsh people as a whole', its existing organization should be remodelled to allow the constituent colleges an increased degree of local autonomy under the university's overall supervision and co-ordination. As Haldane, characteristically, put it later, 'we conceived the idea of a living spiritual life for the University of Wales – a life which should constitute that University, which should consist in constituent Colleges which were to live in it as it lived in them'.

The overall government of the university, the commission argued, should rest on a broad popular basis. It had been borne in upon them that a suspicion was growing that the university and the colleges were drifting away from their distinctive cultural roots. There should, therefore, be a deliberative, legislative and ceremonial court of some two hundred members with a greatly increased representation of local authorities; 'a Parliament of higher education . . .' where 'great projects of reform and development might be discussed . . .' so that 'the university will gain a new footing as a national institution and awaken interest in numbers of people it has never yet reached'. A university council of eighteen members should be the financial and administrative authority acting as the executive of the court, while an academic board, replacing the old senate, 'should represent the academic knowledge and experience of the University and . . . give the University Council the expert advice it needs'. There were at the same time specific recommendations for the creation of university boards to stimulate, direct and organize effort, on a national basis, in music, Celtic studies and extra-mural studies, and for a university press.

The government of the constituent colleges by court, council and senate was to remain untouched, but the standard of admission for students, the period of residence and study for degree were to be matters for the university. The appointment of professors and heads of departments was to rest with the colleges but, no longer the sole responsibility of their councils, was henceforward to be made on the recommendation of expert committees appointed jointly by the college concerned and the university – a change of procedure that was soon to be a cause of dissension in Swansea. On the question of finance, the commission took the view that an addition of almost £100,000 to the available recurrent income of the university and the colleges was necessary and that this augmentation should be provided partly by local authority contributions and partly by state-aid on a matching-grant basis. To colleges that had been plagued by poverty for nearly forty years such a recommendation must have been comforting, while the suggestion that in certain circumstances the state should also provide grants to assist approved capital projects must have seemed well-nigh revolutionary. On the vexed question of medical education, the commission proposed the creation of a national medical school, organized as an independent constituent college of the university and governed by a council and senate of its own. With regard to the problem of technological studies, the commission recommended the establishment of a board and faculty of technology, constituted generally on the lines suggested in the south Wales scheme, and the introduction of a distinct technological degree.

The transformation of the Swansea Technical College into a constituent college of the university had received support from the South Wales Business Committee and the commission had been impressed by Swansea's case. At the same time it had been concerned that in Swansea, as distinct from Cardiff where the single faculty medical school was recommended, there was 'no University tradition, no University atmosphere, very little even of pioneer work in the field of higher education and scientific research'. As Haldane was later to explain:

> Our problem was that in Swansea an old College existed; that it was in large measure a Technical College directed to purposes of importance and utility, but still purposes which did not embrace all the aspects of the humanities or bring out that humanism without which man is not complete. Well, we laid great stress on the necessity of Swansea's developing a faculty of arts not less than those other adjuncts which go to make a real University College, a College permeated by the University atmosphere in which knowledge is no longer taken to be an aggregation of disconnected fragments, but an entirety in which each branch has an intimate relation to the other, and has the wide-sidedness which can arise from no narrow view of knowledge, but only from the view that regards it as a whole.
>
> . . . [E]very constituent College – every College that was worthy of the dignity of being a constituent College and was allowed to become so – should be a place where the whole man should be developed by the stimulating presence of the University atmosphere. No atmosphere short of the University atmosphere could be adequate for the work, and therefore it was essential for the development of the whole man that an atmosphere that included humanism should be developed in each College.

This all may sound like the high-flown notions of a man of action more at home as a philosopher but it *was* what conditioned the approach of the commission and had to be impressed upon the college promoters. The transition of 'technical college' to 'university college' implied far more than a mere change in title. Thus the commission dwelt upon the need for any application for a royal charter to be entertained by the Privy Council only if it were submitted through the university and with the approval of the university court. In view of the unwelcome delay that would be likely because of the restructuring of the university's governmental machine, however, the commission suggested that the Privy Council itself should establish the fitness of the college to undertake university work, either, and preferably, on the advice of a committee of the existing university court composed of expert scientific and technological assessors or, alternatively, of the standing Advisory Committee on University Grants.

With such considerations in mind, the commission took the view that the Swansea representation should be allowed because 'the much needed provision of higher education in that part of South Wales is more likely to be made within a reasonable time and with a suitable range and standard if the institution in question is given the rank of a Constituent College and brought into the inner life of the university, than if it is restricted constitutionally by some partial recognition to a narrower field'. It was the death-knell of the proposal for the *affiliation* of the technical college, but the commission was at pains to stress that the college's admission to *constituent* membership of the university should be dependent upon certain stipulations being met. These included general requirements relating to the constitution of the college's council and senate, and the adequacy and the employment conditions of its teaching staff. Satisfactory provision also had to be made for full initial degree courses in pure science, applied science and technology; for higher education in arts subjects pending the establishment of a 'complete' faculty of arts; for buildings and equipment; and, financially, for the maintenance of the college.

The decisions of the commission were received with unalloyed pleasure in Swansea but, as David Davies was at pains to point out in his newspaper, 'the fact must nevertheless be recognised that this is not the time for taking off armour as if the fighting is done, but for putting it on'. He emphasized that much of the £70,000 endowment had been pledged

> on the faith of the assurance that it would be applied directly to the realisation of the promise of creating a Technical College equal to the best in this or any other Country, and that the administration of the College should be delegated to a body upon which practical business men in touch with our chief industries would predominate.

It was clear that if the promises of money were to be kept and that if the status of the new college upheld then 'the right type of member for the governing body had to be secured'. Continuing the old arrangement by which the governing body was a subsidiary of the education committee was undesirable 'and anything savouring of a reversion to the old system of control on narrow partisan lines would be calamitous'.

> We want more than the money of the leaders in local industries [Davies concluded]; we want their continuous sympathy and active co-operation in shaping the destinies of an instrument capable of doing untold good in West Wales.
> (*South Wales Daily Post*, 21 March 1918)

Davies's concern was not so much with the long-term instruments of the proposed university college's government. He was as well aware as anyone that these would be specified in detail by the new institution's charter and statutes in the light of the Haldane Report and current university practice. Indeed, as mayor – and as publisher – he had a close hand in the preparation of the draft documents submitted to the Privy Council the previous year. His concern was rather with the immediate decisions that would be taken on the college prior to any court and council being established, decisions which would shape the destinies of the college in many material ways and for many years to come. His plea, fortunately, did not fall on deaf ears and he received the immediate and powerful support of Ivor Gwynne. Although a political opponent of Davies and a dedicated leader of labour, Gwynne recognized only too clearly that the university college would have little or no chance of success without the active goodwill and practical encouragement of local industry, the absence of which had been so damaging to the development of technical education in Swansea in the past. In the political arena, Gwynne, as chairman of the education committee, was instrumental, therefore, in securing the gradual detachment of the technical college sub-committee from its parent authority and ensuring that in practical terms, if not in theory, it had considerable discretion of decision. With Gilbertson, who had played a critical role for Davies in extracting money or promises of money from his fellow industrialists, taking over the chair of the sub-committee from Gwynne there was also a greater degree of assurance of the continued interest of industry, especially in the all-important areas of steel and tinplate.

From the autumn of 1918, Gilbertson, as the new chairman of the sub-committee and, even more critically, as the chairman of its influential steering sub-committee for the university college, now came to dominate the gestation of the new institution. Personally shy and reserved – he would very rarely allow himself to be photographed and had refused any honour for his invaluable industrial work for the Ministry of Munitions during the war – through his remarkable powers as a conciliator he was yet able to impress his character upon individuals equally strong and emphatic in their views on the establishment of the college – men like Martin, Gwynne, Arbour Stephens, A.W.E. Wynn, the coal exporter, and T.J. Rees who formed his 'inner cabinet'. It was to Gilbertson, ably aided and abetted by 'Tee Jay', a master of political manoeuvre and a 'man who knew everyone', more than anyone else at this time that the formative decisions on the foundation of the college were due.

The petition of 1917 for a royal charter for a 'University College of Swansea and West Wales' had been framed in the context of 'technical instruction'. And Gilbertson himself was always to talk publicly of the new college as a 'school of metallurgy' and this not merely as a political ploy to win financial support from his fellow industrialists. The recommendation of the commission, however, that there should eventually be a 'complete' faculty of arts and that, pending this, 'satisfactory provision should be made for higher education in subjects belonging to that Faculty' made Gilbertson and his fellow promoters reconsider their original proposals. In particular, it led to a conviction that unless some provision was made for developments in the humanities and arts teaching was introduced at an early date the whole college scheme might be wrecked, if not irrevocably, then at least for a generation.

An earlier suggestion that the Swansea Training College for Women should be incorporated into the proposed university college was therefore revived, the training college being seen as forming the nucleus of an arts faculty. It was envisaged that men as well as women would be admitted to a more prolonged and advanced course of training of university standard, for it was argued that the requirements of the Education Act of 1918, necessitating the foundation of a large number of schools of a new type, would create a demand for highly qualified teachers trained in more specialized courses. This proposal was put to the Board of Education with the added intention that, if the board agreed the scheme, departments of classics, English, modern languages, Celtic studies and economics should be established in the combined colleges.

As far as the site of the proposed college was concerned, the promoters had it in mind to provide for the teaching of arts subjects in the training college on Town Hill until such time as it had been possible to develop and extend the site of the existing technical college at Mount Pleasant. For this they hoped to take over and adapt the adjacent grammar school buildings, together with an adjoining house – Brynsifi – as soon as alternative provision could be made for the school elsewhere. The total area of land available would thus have amounted to some six acres; but, as Gilbertson himself

The Swansea Training College (built in 1913 on land on Town Hill, earlier acquired by the town from William Williams of Maesygwernen) and the Swansea Technical College (the mathematics, physics and engineering building of 1909 is shown here) which were originally intended to form the nucleus of the new university college recognized, the scheme was untidy and uncertain and allowed no scope for long-term development: its one redeeming feature was that it was close to the railway station! Other proposals had, it is true, been canvassed, such as a site on Town Hill not far from the training college that had been earmarked for municipal housing developments; but they had all been dismissed as being currently impracticable. It was, therefore, with a university college comprising the existing training and technical colleges and ultimately to be concentrated on Mount Pleasant in view, that, in November 1918, the Corporation petitioned for a new charter.

The college promoters – the Technical College Sub-committee – had been spurred to think positively about an arts faculty by the appointment in the summer of 1918 of the special advisory committee recommended by the commission. After a lengthy exchange of views between the Privy Council Office and the Board of Education and with the approval of Sir William McCormick, the chairman of the Advisory Committee on University Grants, it had been agreed, on the Privy Council's suggestion, that the task of advising on the admission of the technical college as a constituent college of the university should be made a matter for a committee appointed by the university. Nevertheless, the view in London was quite positive that the composition of the committee was far too important a matter to be left to the university alone, and both the Privy Council Office and the Board of Education had a major say in the selection of the members. Indeed, it was made abundantly clear that the Lord President 'would wish to approve the constitution of the special committee' to ensure not only that the most appropriate academics would be appointed but also that the traditional susceptibilities of Swansea in respect of the university court would be unprovoked.

Eventually, after a number of suggestions and counter-suggestions had been considered, rejected or approved it was agreed that a small committee 'mainly unconnected with the University of Wales' should be appointed: T. Hudson Beare of Edinburgh, and previously Professor of Engineering at Heriot-Watt College where he had 'gained experience likely to be very useful in considering the case of Swansea'; Harold Carpenter, Professor of Metallurgy at the Royal School of Mines and previously a professor at Manchester; George Gibson, Professor of Mathematics at Glasgow, previously a professor at the Royal Technical College, Glasgow, and someone who possessed an 'extensive first-hand acquaintance with the teaching of mathematics in relation to the work of Applied Science Departments at University institutions'; E.H. Griffiths, retiring Principal of Cardiff, and a physicist like his predecessor, John Viriamu Jones; and W.J. Pope, Professor of Chemistry at Cambridge. Only Griffiths and Pope had been among the list of first choices submitted by the University.

The composition of the committee had been finally agreed when the Board of Education suddenly realized that the problem of the provision of an arts faculty raised by the commission had not been covered in its membership. Diplomatically, enquiry was made as to 'whether the absence of any representative of the Faculty of Arts from the names suggested for the Committee means that arrangements will be made otherwise to satisfy the [University] Court on this point'. Three names were forthwith suggested and of these Sir Gregory Foster, Provost of University College, London, and Percy Matheson, Regius Professor of Greek at Oxford, were chosen.

In the event, two distinct reports were submitted to the university court, one by the science members and the other, separately, by Foster and Matheson. The scientists were unconvinced that the existing level of work at the technical college was sufficient to justify its admission as a constituent college of the university but they were greatly impressed by the serious view that the promoters took of 'the magnitude of the problem which confronts them, and by their determination to deal with it in a comprehensive and liberal spirit'. Generally, they appeared sanguine about the direction of the developments proposed but they considered that the scheme would involve a considerable increase in staff, although the services of the existing technical college teachers should be 'substantially and sympathetically recognised'. The general impression made upon the arts visitors was that Swansea was 'well fitted to become a centre of such influence as may be exercised by a constituent College of the University of Wales and that the present moment is peculiarly opportune for a forward step in this direction:

> A 'growth of a new spirit' . . . promises strong and increasing support for an expansion of the Technical College, which will make it more efficient as a scientific centre for the metal industries of the district, and also, by bringing its technical studies into relation with more general education will give it a wider outlook and an influence which would be beyond the reach of a College confined to purely technical education.

What did emerge clearly from the arts advisers' report, however, was the revolutionary concept of arts studies for those days that the Swansea promoters were putting forward. Their approach was not to set up a full faculty of arts in the accepted sense, but rather 'to provide the Arts teaching in Mathematics and Natural Science which form the foundation of technical studies, and also to build up around the Training College a staff of teachers in education, modern languages and economic and historic [sic] studies which would serve to give a complete four-year course to Training College students, and at the same time supplement the scientific and technical interests of the College by bringing its students into relation with those who are going through a course of more general study in the "humanities"'. The emphasis was still very much on the higher scientific and technological needs of Swansea and to a remarkable degree views had changed little since the 1880s. Locally, the humanities were still seen merely as a cultural handmaiden to the real work of technological training, to 'enlarge and quicken the higher education of this rapidly growing community, and give to its technical and commercial studies a background of wider range and interest, which will bring them into relation with general education and culture'.

It was a scheme, though, which appealed to the Welsh Department of the Board of Education, advised by its chief inspector, Sir Owen M. Edwards, who was still concerned whether Swansea could 'evolve a Science and Technology University College which will at the same time have a University atmosphere by having a subsidiary Arts side or, what I would prefer, humanising science and technology'.

While the Mount Pleasant site was not wholly unsatisfactory, in practical terms the committee felt that it was hardly sufficient for the long-term development of the college over a period of, say, thirty years, and was lacking in facilities for recreation or athletics. The building plans for science and applied science needed thorough revision to achieve a better use of space and should not be embarked on without the advice of the appropriate heads of department. 'In any case it is advisable that the Principal should be appointed before the plans are sealed.' The arts members agreed and drew attention to the need for library, common room and refectory accommodation. Generally, the proposal to incorporate the training college was approved but the science advisers stressed that the lecture rooms and laboratories at Town Hill should not be used for science and technology, these subjects being centrally catered for at Mount Pleasant. Adequate provision had to be made for classics, history and modern languages and for general biology. The linkage of the Swansea School of Art with the university college scheme was also thought sensible 'so as to co-ordinate as far as possible all the activities of the town in the sphere of Higher Education'.

The committee stressed the undesirability of evening teaching work which would militate against original research, and the necessity of co-ordination with Cardiff for engineering. There was a need, too, to increase the staff both in numbers and quality and to ensure adequate levels of salary especially on the arts side. In general, however, apart from the question of the building plans and with its misgivings about the adequacy of the Mount Pleasant site, the committee viewed the Swansea scheme favourably.

Having justified its own position by a formulaic expression of concern that the scheme should give due weight to the study of Welsh language, literature and history, the university court, in April 1919, endorsed the reports with a strong recommendation to the Privy Council that Swansea should be granted a charter as a constituent college. The Privy Council acted promptly, actuated not only for Swansea's sake, but also because of the urgency of setting up the proposed faculty of Technology – impossible without Swansea's participation as a constituent college – to establish some order 'in the chaos of technical and evening work in South Wales'. By June it had been able to comment in detail on the Corporation's draft charter and statutes, stressing that its final approval would 'depend on a pledge being given by the Promoters to follow, as far as may be, the advice of the Special Committee'.

Events moved rapidly and before July was out the Privy Council had approved the admission of the technical college to constituent membership of the university. The university and the other colleges were all supportive, even Cardiff, which had most to lose by the creation of the new college. Percy Watkins, though, with an eye to the past, questioned whether the community served by the new college 'will not underestimate the responsibilities that it brings in its train' (*The Times Educational Supplement*, 4 April 1918).

Already, however, a development had taken place which, while not altogether unforeseen, was unexpected in its immediacy and was to have profound implications for the new college. In the summer of 1919 the 250 acre Singleton estate, the Swansea home of the Vivian family for more than a century, came on to the market. Little used by the Vivians since the death of the first Lord Swansea in 1894, Singleton Abbey had hardly ever been visited by his son, Ambrose, the second baron, who preferred to live in Breconshire. Singleton Abbey itself, the house built by John Henry Vivian and extended by his son for the visit to Swansea of the Prince and Princess of Wales in 1881, was in a dilapidated state and the grounds were sadly run down. It was, however, a prime site, extending from the Mumbles road to the expanding suburb of Sketty in the north and only a short distance from the western edge of the town itself. The Corporation saw the potential of the estate immediately, for it would provide not only further recreational space for the town, but it could be used for municipal housing developments hitherto scheduled, as part of the town's slum-clearance scheme, for the less suitable Town Hill.

To the college promoters it was an opportunity not to be missed. As soon as the Corporation entered into negotiations for the purchase of the estate the Technical College Sub-committee suggested that, if Singleton was acquired by the town, the new college should be built there. The recommendation received short shrift, however. Singleton was a veritable honey-pot and the Corporation was besieged by contending interests so that within the council chamber there was a powerful lobby opposed to any such move in favour of the new college. In June the Corporation asked its officers to examine the suitability of the estate for a variety of purposes, including building, playing fields, allotments and a cemetery: the principle of erecting a new college at Singleton was not to be decided upon until further and fuller investigations had been carried out – a polite dismissal of the promoters' ideas.

The opponents of siting a college at Singleton – like Alderman Tom Merrells (1868–1922), 'Honest Tom', the dockers' leader – were reflecting a vocal body of popular opinion in Swansea which convinced itself that the university college would have an adequate site at Mount Pleasant and was now proceeding to filch from the townspeople land which was rightfully theirs. It was now that the persuasive powers and authority of Gwynne became of paramount importance. Little is known of the political horse-trading that took place in the Guildhall but, eventually, by September 1919 Gwynne was able to obtain reasonably solid support for a site for the college at Singleton and it was agreed that part of the estate should be reserved for the college, judges' lodgings and 'other corporate purposes'. Already by 16 July 1919 agreement had been reached – although contracts had not yet been signed between Lord Swansea and the Corporation – on the purchase of the estate for £90,000. Two days earlier, the *Cambria Daily Leader* had explained that of the 254 acres to be conveyed to the town 'a considerable portion' would no doubt be used for housing schemes, but it was also proposed that 'about 25 acres shall be set apart for the new Technical College, but this had yet to be definitely decided. Some sections of public opinion favour the idea that the mansion shall be the nucleus of the new college buildings while others express the view that the Abbey should be utilised as a Museum.'

It was to be some considerable time before a permanent site for the college was to be decided, and, when it was, the decision was due more to the pragmatic situation that had developed by then, than from any considered policy. Even as late as December 1920, when the college had already completed its first term, the Corporation was still reluctant to settle on a definitive area at Singleton arguing, rather lamely, that this could not be done until it knew the exact requirements of the college.

The promoters had decided to open the new college in October 1920 and they had other more immediate matters to concern them than even the worrying problem of a permanent site. Their most pressing task was the appointment of a principal. The commission had stressed that much of the prosperity of the college would depend upon a wise choice: someone who would help to win for the college its due weight in the counsels of the university, and would also keep constantly before his own mind and that of the people of Swansea the duty of giving the college such a range of studies as would save it from the narrowing effects of a too utilitarian standard. From the outset it was obvious that the existing principal, sterling as had been his work for the university college movement, was not the man to steer the new venture. Varley, highly qualified and experienced as he was, did not have either the background or breadth of vision. His

The distribution of the twenty-eight United Kingdom universities and university colleges in 1920, on the eve of the foundation of the University College of Swansea. They catered for some 40,000 full-time students. In 1921 Leicester was founded as a university college and Hull in 1927, but they were not admitted to the UGC grant list until 1945.

world, in no pejorative sense, was that of the technical college and he himself recognized this. Before he could be publicly passed over, Varley, wisely, decided to leave and to free the sub-committee from any claims it might think he had upon it. No doubt at one time he had expected the appointment for which in a sense he had worked so hard, but he had been overtaken by events. It was no longer the Swansea Technical College that was being elevated to university status but a completely new institution that was being created. Swallowing whatever bitterness he may have had, Varley left Swansea to take up the principalship of the Brighton Technical College in September 1919.

In the meantime T.J. Rees was appointed acting principal of the technical college as an administrative stop-gap. But speed was of the essence. There was grave concern that the permanent appointment of the principal of the new college should not be delayed until after the apparatus of court and council had been set up. The views of the Privy Council Office were sought and the persuasive powers of Sir Alfred Mond were enlisted to gain the agreement of Lord Curzon, the Lord President, to the 'extreme desirability . . . that the appointment should be made by the existing Committee. All the information that has reached him [Mond] from the best informed quarters show [*sic*] that the members of that Committee are anxious to make a first-rate appointment and to be guided solely by the opinion of the best men, such as Mr. Fisher, the President of the Royal Society, Lord Haldane etc. It can be trusted absolutely to take the necessary trouble and to make an honest appointment, whereas a Provisional Court of Governors would be a very large body, and an unknown quantity, and might easily fall into error.'

Everyone was aware of the dangers of seeking candidates of the right calibre through private soundings of leading educationalists rather than through public advertisement although this had become current university practice. Very much in their mind was the spectre of the failure of Cardiff to appoint a new principal the year before. There, the college council, following established precedent, had decided not to advertise the post on the retirement of Principal Griffiths but to sound out the 'great and the good' in the educational world for eligible candidates. Although confidential, in the manner of these things in Wales, it was not long before the names of the final shortlist of four candidates[1] were out and leaked to the keeper of the nation's conscience, the *Western Mail*. Despite pleas to avoid 'the petty intrigues of cliques and cabals, whether denominational or political' a bitter campaign was mounted against the favoured candidate, Thomas Jones of the Cabinet Office. Disguised, humbuggingly enough, as a demand for a wider field through advertising – for, it was hinted, compared to Principal Griffiths the chosen candidates were 'as moonlight unto sunlight or as water unto rich wine' – a public grievance was engineered, finding expression in press and parliament, that at the eleventh hour led to the postponement of the appointment (*Western Mail*, 4 February 1919).

Throughout the summer and the autumn of 1919 the Swansea sub-committee carried out its informal soundings. H.A.L. Fisher, the reforming president of the Board of Education, freely gave his advice to Gilbertson and T.J. Rees when they called on him and Haldane was equally helpful. The latter, responding to Gilbertson's expressed wish for an 'organiser' for the college and drawing on his experience as war minister, suggested that if it was an organizer Gilbertson wanted he could not do better than General von Donop, the commandant of Woolwich Arsenal. The message that came through clearly and consistently, however, from Haldane, Fisher, Hadow and the others approached was that to be able to enter effectively upon an equal footing with older, established institutions required the leadership and direction of someone imbued with the university ethos. The new college was emphatically *not* to be seen as a 'glorified technical school doing work that would be lop-sided and that would be incompatible in its restriction of spirit with the University idea' (*South Wales Daily Post*, 16 November 1920).

In the event six candidates were eventually shortlisted. Unhappily, the record is silent on who they were. According to Sir Lewis Jones who was especially close to Gilbertson at this time – he had become the first full-time secretary of the South Wales Siemens Steel Association in 1917 and had known Gilbertson even before this through his wartime service in the Ministry of Munitions – the sub-committee originally favoured the candidature of Dr Charles Edwards who was, at the time, Professor of Metallurgy and Dean of the Faculty of Science at Manchester. Edwards apparently expressed little interest in academic administration, however, and while he was enthusiastic about the creation of a department of metallurgy at Swansea he was not prepared to come to the college as its principal. The approach and Edwards's reaction were well known even to the earliest students of the college.

Haldane, in more serious mood with Gilbertson, suggested the name of Dr Thomas Franklin Sibly. As Professor of Geology and Dean of Science at Cardiff, Sibly had greatly impressed Haldane when he had given evidence before the royal commission, both on behalf of the college senate and with the Business Committee. No academic in the university had 'displayed higher qualities of university statesmanship or carried more influence with his colleagues and with . . . the Commission than . . . Dr Sibly'. Following his disappointment over the principalship of Cardiff, he had since moved on to Armstrong College, Newcastle upon Tyne, as Professor of Geology. Sibly, at thirty-six, was a teacher of quality whose intellectual distinction was established and who had acquired a considerable reputation as an academic administrator and far-sighted university statesman. He had held a chair for seven years. Born in Bristol and educated

Thomas Franklin Sibly (1884–1948), principal
(1920–6) and vice-chancellor of the University
of Wales (1925–6).

at the university college there, he had taken first-class honours in experimental physics
in the London B.Sc. degree in 1903 and in 1908 he had been awarded the London D.Sc.
in geology. In the latter year he had been appointed to a lectureship at King's College,
London, and in 1913 had taken up the chair of geology at Cardiff, which he had held for
five years before going to Newcastle. Despite the war, his influence on his subject had
been considerable. He had spent a great deal of time on field research on the Lower
Carboniferous strata and had pioneered the understanding of the Carboniferous
Limestone of south Wales. During the war, too, he had served in the Geological Survey
and had been concerned with the investigation of mineral resources, both in south Wales
and the Forest of Dean, so that he had a more than passing acquaintance with local
extractive industries. Sibly, too, had been the main architect of the south Wales scheme
for the co-ordination of higher technological education in Wales.

In January 1920 Sibly was unanimously appointed principal at a salary of £1,500 a
year – incidentally, more than double the salary paid to Varley the year before. Swansea
was fortunate in securing him as its first principal. A man of kindness, patience and
sparkling clarity of thought and expression, he brought to his office not only a
knowledge of the workings of a Welsh university college but also, from Newcastle,
experience of a technological university institution. He had a keen mind and a flair for
seeing far ahead without missing the minutiae of the present. Above all, he possessed an
abounding faith in his college and a persuasive advocacy on its behalf. He was,
moreover, still young and the council could feel confident that it was committing the
charge of the college to a man of energy who was in sympathy with its pattern of
development. To Gilbertson, Sibly had 'the right instincts and will do his best to
develop the institution in the way [the governors] wish it to be developed'. Perhaps
Gilbertson's very choice of words were an augury of difficulties that were soon to arise
but it was to be due to Sibly more than any one that the new college was to establish its
position so quickly both in the local community and in the University of Wales.

Although time was desperately short, all seemed set fair for the embryo college and even before his arrival in Swansea in the late spring of 1920 Sibly had turned his mind to forming the nucleus of a staff and planning for the opening of the college in October. In June 1920 Edwin Drew (1885–1963) was appointed the college's first registrar at a salary of £550 a year. Sibly had known Drew at Cardiff where, since 1914, he had been chief clerk and finance clerk – effectively deputy to the registrar – and this critical appointment was the first measure of Sibly's judgement. Drew took up his duties on 1 August 1920 and was to serve the college for thirty-two years. If his relations with his own staff were sometimes strained and often autocratic, it cannot be doubted that he was a skilled administrator with a profound knowledge of the varied ramifications of university business, and an able officer of the college who contributed much to its smooth running in its formative years. While he lacked a certain imagination and his approach to college business was of the 'old school', his rapport with his senior academic colleagues was good, and his integrity and devotion to his duties inspired confidence in him both as registrar and as secretary of the council and the senate and their multifarious committees.

If the college was fortunate in its first principal and registrar it was no less successful in attracting teachers of distinction to head its original departments. 'It is hardly to be expected', Foster and Matheson had declared, 'that the new University College will be able to attract men and women of established reputations.' What would be required would be distinguished academic records coupled with youth and enthusiasm and this is what the college achieved. Initially, it was decided to set up five chairs, one each in metallurgy, chemistry, physics, mathematics and engineering, and two independent lectureships, in history and geology. Metallurgy, naturally, was regarded 'as the characteristic speciality of the College'. The chair of metallurgy was, therefore, unquestionably accepted as the most important post after the principalship and carried the handsome salary of £1,250 a year – £450 more than the other professorships.

To the industrialists involved in college affairs there was only one possible candidate. Dr Charles Edwards 'was pre-eminently the man for our Chair' and it was only owing to the insistence of Professor Harold Carpenter, one of the external assessors and Edwards's former chief at both the National Physical Laboratory and Manchester, that other names were considered by invitation. Edwards was in due course appointed. Reporting the appointment, the college council explained that it was the natural duty and ambition of the college 'to build up a Department of Metallurgy which will be of the first rank alike in teaching and in research, and to establish a close relationship between University education and Metallurgical practice. Great importance therefore attaches to this appointment and the College is fortunate in having secured the services of Professor Edwards.'

Born in Canada but brought back to Britain by his parents at a very early age, Edwards, at thirty-eight, had already achieved a major reputation as a distinguished metallurgist. His influence in Swansea was to be vital in establishing the college's academic status and in forging intimate links between its metallurgical research and the metal industries of south Wales which expected so much of the college. His great success was all the more remarkable when one realizes that he had himself begun his working life as an apprentice in the foundries of the Lancashire and Yorkshire Railway at sixteen years of age and had received no formal undergraduate education at either university or

Charles Alfred Edwards (1882–1960), principal (1927–47) and vice-chancellor of the University of Wales (1931–3 and 1939–41), *left*, and Evan Jenkin Evans (1882–1944), *right*

technical college. Awarded an Iron and Steel Institute Carnegie Research Scholarship in 1907 while a lecturer and demonstrator at Manchester, he had been awarded an M.Sc. – his first degree – for his published work in 1910. After some four years as a research metallurgist in industry, he had succeeded Carpenter as Professor of Metallurgy in Manchester in 1914 at the age of thirty-two.

The other four professors who were appointed by the council were also in their late thirties. Dr Evan Jenkin Evans, an expert in spectroscopic work, who was appointed to the chair of physics, had been a contemporary of Edwards at Manchester where he had been senior lecturer in physics and assistant director of the physical laboratories. Dr Joseph Edward Coates, the new Professor of Chemistry, was a year younger than Evans and Edwards and had been lecturer in physical chemistry at Birmingham. Coates had studied at Bangor with Orton, at University College, London, with Ramsay and, what made a lasting impression on him both with regard to research and cultural interest, at Karlsruhe with Haber. During the Great War he had served as a senior technical officer with the rank of lieutenant-commander, RNVR, at the Royal Naval Experimental Station in London and had been awarded an OBE for his contributions to the development of the smoke-screen.

The Professor of Mathematics was Lt. Colonel Archibald Read Richardson who, shortly before, had been appointed Professor of Aeronautical Science at the Royal Air

Joseph Edward Coates (1883–1973), *left*, and Archibald Read Richardson (1881–1954), *right*

Force Cadet College at Cranwell and who came to Swansea as an expert in hydro-mechanics. Richardson and Evans, personal friends of long standing, cemented the close associations that have always existed between the departments of physics and mathematics. Before the Great War, Richardson had been Assistant Professor of Mathematics at Imperial College, but he combined with his scholarship the qualities of a man of action, having served with great bravery in both the Boer War and the Great War, in which he had been severely wounded.[2] Academically, his was, perhaps, the most distinguished of all the new appointments and, occasionally, as one might expect, he lived on a different plane from his colleagues. At one end of term meeting of examiners Jenkin Evans turned to Richardson and expostulated, 'Richardson, there is something wrong here. One of my men has got 70 in Physics and nothing in Mathematics'. 'Well, Evans,' Richardson replied, 'I will say this; he was the best of those that got 0.'

To engineering the college appointed Professor Frederic Bacon (1880–1943), who had been a professor at Cardiff since 1913 and, at thirty-nine, was the oldest of the new professors. Educated at Trinity College, Cambridge, Bacon had had a varied career in industry before becoming a lecturer in applied mechanics and electrical design at the Royal Naval College at Greenwich and subsequently a lecturer in the photo-microstructure of metals at University College, London. During the war, in the RNVR, he had been very much involved in the experimental development of anti-mine and anti-submarine devices.

Unfortunately, lack of accommodation forced the college to postpone the introduction of arts courses for a year but it decided to proceed immediately with the appointment of a head of the department of history. To this post – an independent lectureship – the council appointed E. Ernest Hughes. A graduate of Aberystwyth and Jesus College, Oxford, Hughes, after a short spell as a teacher, had joined the history department at Cardiff. A born teacher and inimitable raconteur, Hughes was already well known throughout Wales as a popular lecturer closely associated with educational and social work; to R.T. Jenkins he seemed to have done more 'to popularise Wales than any other man since Sir O.M. Edwards'. His blindness – Hughes was deprived of the sight of an eye as a child – limited his capacity for original work but in no way diminished his devotion to the Workers' Educational Association or extra-mural work generally. During the first session, before the faculty of arts was established and while he had no formal teaching duties at the college, he threw himself into the creation of an extra-mural organization which was to have a profound influence over a large area of south-west Wales.

In sharp contrast to the position of the first principals of the other Welsh colleges, and indeed to that of Dr Rattray, who was shortly to be appointed the first principal of the University College of Leicester, Sibly had no formal teaching duties or departmental responsibilities, although he took a particular interest in the activities of the department of geology and especially students' fieldwork. As independent lecturer, and head of the department of geology, the college appointed Dr Arthur Trueman, then a twenty-six-year-old assistant lecturer in Sibly's old department at Cardiff. Trueman had previously studied under Swinnerton at Nottingham and by the time he came to Swansea he already held a London D.Sc. awarded to him for his work on Liassic rocks and fossils.

This, then, was the devoted little band of 'high quality, determined purpose and

Ernest Hughes (1878–1953), *left*, and Arthur Trueman (1894–1956), *right*

Dumbarton House, the original administrative centre for the college. In 1921 it became a hostel for women students and, subsequently, for men students until it was sold in 1925

self-dedication' which was to be the heart of the new college. But even before the new heads of departments could take up their duties, there was still a great deal to be done, and a lot of planning to be carried out. Although the original idea of establishing the new university college at Mount Pleasant had been overtaken by the Corporation's agreement to offer part of the Singleton estate to the college, no positive decision had yet been taken on the exact site to be made available. It was clear, however, that if students were to be admitted to the college in October 1920 temporary accommodation additional to that already existing at Mount Pleasant would have to be found quickly. While arrangements were made with the town council to allow science classes to be held at Mount Pleasant, no accommodation could be found in the technical college for administrative offices, and, as the arts visitors had foreseen, there was little in the way of facilities for students. Gilbertson and a fellow industrialist and philanthropist, Roger Beck, immediately rose to the occasion and through their generosity the college obtained the use of Dumbarton House in Brynymor Crescent as an administration centre and a meeting place for students.

While all the problems of finance, accommodation and staffing were exercising Gilbertson and Sibly, the public mind was looking forward expectantly to what was to be the great event in the Swansea calendar for 1920, for in July King George V and Queen Mary ended a prolonged national tour by visiting the town. Monday, 19 July was

The foundation stone ceremony, 19 July 1920. The ceremony, north of the 'archery lawn', was notional only because the permanent college site had not been agreed by the Corporation. For a number of years the stone itself remained 'safely lost' in a Corporation yard

the climax of their visit, and after touring Vivian's Copper Works and Baldwin's Tinplate Works and opening the new Queen's Dock, the king, as chancellor of the university, came to Singleton Park to lay the foundation stone of the new college. On a gloriously fine day in the picturesque parkland setting of the archery lawn the aspirations of over forty years were at last formally realized. Appropriately enough, among those presented to the king with the college officers was Richard Martin, 'the father of the University movement in Swansea', brought up to the platform amid cries of 'good old Dick Martin', and later to be knighted for his public services. Amid all the euphoria Gilbertson expressed the hope, in almost Haldanesque terms, that the college would become 'the home of high ideals and lofty purpose and of unfailing efforts for the advancement of learning, the improvement of industry, and the betterment of civilisation'. But the high-flown words could not disguise the fact that the site of the ceremony was merely a 'notional' one. Even the king could not be told where the eventual home of the foundation stone would be. As it happened, after the ceremony the stone was removed for 'safe-keeping' to a Corporation yard and for many years remained firmly 'lost'. It was eventually found, only after some difficulty, just in time to be incorporated into the 'new' library of 1937.

By September a further eight members of the teaching staff and three administrators – including Charles Hearne who, as chief clerk in the registry, was to serve the college devotedly until a breakdown in health forced his retirement after the Second World War – had been appointed, and at the same time the last of the original chairs was filled by the appointment of Bacon though he was not able to take up his duties fully at Swansea until the Lent term of 1921.

Detailed discussions took place throughout the summer with the Technical College Sub-committee about the use of the teaching buildings at the technical college, and syllabuses of studies were drawn up. Unhappily again, no records seem to exist about the admissions policy which was adopted. No doubt the college was glad to get what it could. Three types of full-time student were accepted: students wishing to read for degrees of the University of Wales in pure and applied science, those students of the technical college who wished to transfer to the university college to continue reading for the final B.Sc. examination of the University of London in 1921, and students wishing to take college diplomas in metallurgy and engineering. The difficulties and limited nature of the accommodation available to the college in its first session precluded the admission of arts students, and indeed restricted the number of places available to science students. It was thought that about ninety students would be a manageable number and it was naturally anticipated that a fairly high proportion of these students would be transferring from the technical college. In due course, eighty-nine full-time students were accepted, and on Tuesday 5 October 1920, the college's first session began. Of the eighty-nine, eight were women and fifty-five had been students at the technical college, while forty-seven were ex-servicemen in receipt of government grants,

The cover of the first issue of *The Undergrad*, the original college magazine

whose boisterous maturity of outlook did much to set the tone of the college in its earliest years. While Gilbertson could try to assure himself and, more to the point, the Swansea public, that the students he met 'had shown themselves to be nature's gentlemen', that public's susceptibilities were sorely tried on rag-days when the students gave vent to their animal spirits. But, however much Swansea was unused to the spectacle, the antics of these days were small beer to what was to come in later years. November 1920 was to see a procession marching 'from the college through the streets in the centre of the town bearing balloons, some fantastically clad, and preceded by a more or less expert squad of drummers, the while bugles, cornets and toy trumpets, reinforced by "squeakers", blared out a symphony more easily heard than described'. Despite the darkening days of depression there were fun times.

It has to be admitted that most of these students would never have set the Tawe alight with their academic brilliance. Most had their eyes set on careers in teaching or in the middling ranges of industry. From the start, though, there were some stars. Evan James Williams had transferred from the technical college. The son of a stonemason from Llanybydder, he had won a scholarship to the college after a hectic pillion ride on his brother's motor-cycle to Swansea to sit the examination, having missed the last train. In

Two early students of distinction and later Fellows of the Royal Society: Evan James Williams (1903–45), *left*, with a 'first' in physics in 1923, and Donald Holroyde Hey (1904–87), *right*, with a 'first' in chemistry in 1926. The informality of the early days of the college is brought home by the fact that Hey fortuitously took his scholarship examination on the suggestion of a porter during a chance visit to the college. Not having a pen on him, Hey had to borrow the principal's

1923 he got his expected 'first' in physics. He went on to work with W.L. Bragg at Manchester, with Rutherford at Cambridge and with Niels Bohr at Copenhagen and eventually settled at Aberystwyth, 'a decided "find"' for the college, as Professor of Physics. Elected a Fellow of the Royal Society at thirty-six he became internationally recognized as 'one of the most brilliant physicists of his generation'. Tragically, he died of cancer in 1945 at the age of forty-two but not until he had made 'contributions of decisive importance to the winning of the [U-boat] campaign'. In 1924 T. Neville George became the first student to achieve a 'first' in geology and embarked on a career of distinction of which more will be said later.

Conditions in the college for the few staff already appointed and for their students during the first session were far from being fun: not only was the accommodation at Mount Pleasant austere and the equipment there woefully inadequate, but for most of the staff there were further practical and psychological disadvantages of having to work in laboratories which were not regarded as their own and were largely intended for evening students of the technical college. Professor Coates recalled the dreadful shock he and his colleagues, used to established university laboratories, experienced when they first saw the facilities available at the technical college. In chemistry and metallurgy, especially, the shortcomings were serious even at the outset with a small number of students. Accommodation for undergraduate students was stretched to the utmost while

The problem of toing and froing between Singleton and Mount Pleasant and missing the tram from Bryn Road is highlighted in this student cartoon in *The Undergrad* (1922). The lecturer is Professor Coates

research was seriously hampered. The conditions in Brynsifi which housed geology were no better; the atmosphere at Mount Pleasant was also not a happy one. A number of the staff there had nursed the expectation of being appointed to the new university college. Their attitude, not surprisingly, varied from an unwelcoming toleration to one of open hostility towards the new university college personnel. That the first session was to be so successful says much for the resilience of the staff in coping so well with these difficult teaching conditions, isolated as they were from their principal and central administration in another part of the town. Obviously in such a situation little serious research could be undertaken, either by staff or by students, but the little that was achieved was by no means unimportant. Four full-time postgraduates had enrolled for the first session: three in metallurgy and one in geology. By the end of the session the college could boast its first M.Sc., gained by one of the eight full-time women students, Agnes MacDonald, for research under Trueman's direction on the evolution of Liassic gastropods.

One term at Mount Pleasant was enough for the staff to make it clear to Sibly that they could not carry on indefinitely under such conditions. The principal, well versed in such problems from his early days in Cardiff, took action swiftly and convinced Gilbertson, who had become the college's first president, and the college council that an approach should be made forthwith to the Corporation to elicit its future intentions towards the college, especially in the short term. The Corporation had already, in May 1920, agreed in principle to the college's temporary use of Singleton Abbey for arts subjects and general college purposes, but little had yet been done to put this decision into effect, despite pressure from the UGC, largely, it would seem, because of the cost of rehabilitating the house which in a period of rapidly rising prices was falling into an increasingly sad state of repair. At the same time, the allocation of a specific permanent site for the college at Singleton had not yet been determined because the overall use of the estate had not so far been decided.

Sibly was anxious to begin arts degree courses in the new session and there was consequently a considerable degree of urgency if the abbey was to be made good in time. Thus, in December 1920 a deputation from the college council met the Corporation's parliamentary and estates committees to impress upon them the college's vital need to have the promised use of Singleton Abbey as soon as possible. The previous month Sibly, in his inaugural lecture to mark the first session of the college, had dilated publicly upon the munificence of the Corporation. It remained to be seen, now that the college had slipped out of the control of the Corporation, whether the town council would be as ready to support it as it had professed in the heady days of the campaign for a university college for Swansea and whether Sibly's eloquence would strike sympathetic chords of conscience. Sibly proceeded to explain to the Corporation committees the urgent need for Singleton Abbey if the new college was to launch its projected arts departments effectively at the beginning of the 1921–2 academic session. He pointed out, too, the dire straits of the science departments temporarily housed at Mount Pleasant and emphasized that the facilities there were already so stretched that within another two years conditions would have become virtually impossible, especially in the key department of metallurgy. It would be to the advantage of the college if all its departments could be concentrated together as soon as possible, the science departments being accommodated in temporary buildings until their permanent quarters could be built. He, therefore, asked for the use of a small piece of land to the west of the abbey where the temporary buildings could be erected.

With David Matthews as chairman of the joint committee meeting, the college deputation was at least assured of an understanding hearing and the outcome was by no means unproductive although, as was expected, no patently permanent solutions to the college's difficulties emerged. As a result of the meeting the Corporation agreed to grant the college the tenancy of Singleton Abbey and some adjoining land at a nominal annual rental until the permanent college buildings were erected on another site at Singleton yet to be specified. At the same time the Corporation approved the expenditure of £10,000 towards the cost of necessary repairs and alterations to the abbey, any necessary balance being found by the college.

Within a few months, however, the college was faced with an added problem. The escalation of prices in a crippling inflationary period after the war had driven the cost of the temporary science buildings that the college wanted to build far beyond its expectations. The estimated cost of £45,000 naturally forced the college to the conclusion that such expenditure would necessitate a life-expectancy for the buildings far longer than the period for which the Corporation was prepared to let the temporary site at Singleton. As a consequence, further discussions were held between the college and the Corporation in March 1921. The Corporation made it quite clear that, while it wished to support the college in every way it could, a hurried decision on the future of Singleton was impracticable. Furthermore, it was not prepared to allow its future freedom of movement over Singleton to be pre-empted by 'the erection of buildings involving the outlay of so large a sum of money and the use of the abbey in the way proposed. This could not be agreed to as a permanent understanding.' To people like Tom Merrells it was the thin end of a wedge. To get its buildings the college had to agree that it would not lay claim to the abbey or to the small piece of land and that it would face the risk of scrapping the temporary buildings, but only on the understanding that some portion of Singleton would eventually be made over to the college.

At least the principle of having its own undivided home, if only on a temporary basis, had been established. It was to take much longer to settle the question of a permanent site. In fact it was not to be until August 1923 that the problem was finally determined. In the wake of an immense amount of political infighting among the Corporation and after the exertion of considerable pressure by the college council, it was at last agreed that the Corporation should honour its obligations to the college. The originally earmarked site at Mount Pleasant – the technical college, Brynsifi and the grammar school – together with the planned extensions, had been valued at £90,000. The Corporation now decided to discharge its undertakings to the extent of this sum by making over to the college Singleton Abbey and nineteen acres of surrounding land to the south and west of the mansion with a further fifteen acres on the western side of Sketty Lane for use as playing fields.

The total property in question was valued at £40,000. But the previous year the Corporation had made the college a forty-year loan of £50,000 to enable it to construct the temporary science buildings and this loan the Corporation decided to write off as a subscription to the college funds. The college now had a permanent home and the sad story of its site, which had been fraught with so much difficulty and unpleasantness, had been resolved. In the light of the unfortunate events that had dogged the young college

Right, Ivor Evans, first president of the Students' Representative Council. The first four student presidents were ex-servicemen, an element which had a marked effect on the early years of the college and the organization of student activities. *Below*, the *South Wales Daily Post's* impression of the first college rag day, 18 November 1920

SWANSEA STUDENTS RAMPANT.

Dear old Sandfields Lady: " Dear me, now I s'pose that mus' be one o' them there universal granulated rags agen. '

so far one cannot but appreciate the foresight of David Davies in 1918: things could have been much worse. Even so, there were conditions attached to the gift: the land on the southern side of Singleton Abbey, for example, was reserved to the occasional use of the Corporation for public events such as fêtes and agricultural shows when sufficient accommodation could not be found on its own adjoining land and, until the major development of the college began in the 1960s, this area was often the picturesque and exciting scene of sheep-dog trials. Nevertheless, as Sibly had pointed out earlier, the college had enjoyed a unique advantage in its close connection with the Corporation that had promoted its foundation. It occupied the 'finest site in the country and the Abbey . . . with the park made an inspiring habitation'.

Whatever opposition there might be to the surrender of Singleton Abbey and the prime parkland fronting it on the shore of Swansea Bay the Corporation had discharged its obligations to the college comparatively cheaply. For, as Owen Edwards was to point out: 'It is, of course, far less costly for the Corporation to dispose of their obligation to the University by the means now suggested than to hand over the Grammar School and the Technical College which would involve building another Grammar School and Technical College.' 'If they can retain both for £50,000', the Board of Education added, 'they don't seem to lose, especially from the educational point of view.'

Soon after the decision had finally been taken by the Corporation in March 1921 that the college could have the temporary use of Singleton Abbey, work began on the repairs and structural alterations necessary to the house, with its thirteen staircases but only one bathroom, to get it ready for the new session. By the summer its transformation had been completed. It was a difficult enough operation to provide sufficient light and air in the building and to put it into such a condition that no one would get lost in it, but thanks to the skill of Ernest Morgan, the borough architect, who had been commissioned to undertake the work, accommodation was provided for all the proposed departments in the faculty of arts, for a library and for administrative offices. Provision was also made for the departments of geology and biology and for common rooms for both staff and students. The dining hall – one of the more notable features of the old house – was converted into an assembly and lecture room, while the former orangery was reconstructed into a refectory which could double as a large lecture hall.

Work began, too, on the temporary science buildings or 'pavilions' as they were called. This, also, was undertaken for the college by Ernest Morgan, who worked to a simple rectangular design, getting the scientific staff of the college to fit their laboratory and workshop space into it. During the course of the college's second session, 1921–2, the accommodation for metallurgy and physics was completed, equipped and brought into operation; Jenkin Evans's design of the physics laboratories being based on his experience of Rutherford's laboratories at Manchester where he had been in charge during the Great War. Chemistry followed early in 1923 and in July of that year the first set of buildings was opened by Sir Alfred Mond.

Because of the ever-present financial problems engineering could not be brought from Mount Pleasant to Singleton until 1925. Its building was designed by a young local architect in private practice, Oliver Portsmouth, who was responsible, too, for a further light construction building for the library, the arts departments and the department of education, freeing accommodation in the abbey for other departments. By 1925, therefore, the whole college had at last been concentrated on the one site at Singleton.

Early days at Singleton, with Miss Busby (1894–1984), the librarian, in the library and Leonard Wright, assistant lecturer in physics (later lecturer and senior lecturer), in the honours physics laboratory

The acute difficulties and frustrations that both students and staff had to face at Mount Pleasant and the constant toing and froing between sites had become things of the past. The science laboratories, that of metallurgy in particular, were considered to be among the most up-to-date buildings of their kind, while a former student later recalled the way Lord Eustace Percy, then President of the Board of Education, justified the temporary science buildings when he officially opened the second range in October 1925. Were they not 'better for scientific teaching than permanent Greek-temple architecture; a lab. was a building that should be knocked about and altered and even a science professor would hesitate to knock down bits of a Greek temple'. Percy was, perhaps, more prophetic than he realized, for the temporary 'pavilions', hardly calculated to win any award for aesthetic charm and given a life of ten years or so, went through three or four distinct changes of use and, eminently practical, lasted for over half a century.

As we saw earlier, the problem of limited accommodation obliged the college to postpone the introduction of internal arts courses for the first session. From the outset, however, it had been concerned to establish a firm grass-roots link with the locality. Ernest Hughes was very much the driving force in this task and took upon himself the mantle of the college's unofficial public relations officer. With a view to bringing classes to the people and, at the same time, stimulating interest in the college itself, a Joint Tutorial Classes Committee representing the college and the WEA was quickly set up to launch tutorial classes. The public response to these classes exceeded the college's most optimistic expectations. During the first session 388 students registered for tutorial classes and by far the bulk of the burden of organization fell on the shoulders of Ernest Hughes. Hughes was also primarily responsible for initiating the series of public lectures which began in the first session and which were held at the YMCA in Swansea. Already by May 1921 it had been calculated that Hughes had himself delivered over one hundred public lectures in south and mid Wales and it was obvious that the college was justifying the role that the arts visitors had envisaged for its teachers, becoming 'by means of public lectures and personal character . . . leaders in the educational work of the town and district'. In all this there was, no doubt, an underlying anxiety to counter the militant influence of the Central Labour College movement and the growth of 'syndicalism' in industrial south Wales: what the 1917 Commission of Inquiry into Industrial Unrest in the area had explicitly seen as the need to impress upon the workers 'the duties and privileges of citizenship and right living' and 'a mutually clearer understanding of the methods and conditions of employment'. But to Hughes it was missionary work in itself.

During the course of the first session the college consolidated its plans for strengthening the teaching staff. Besides assistants in the science departments, the first group of senior appointments was made in the arts to enable internal classes in that faculty to begin in October 1921. Authority was obtained from the University of Wales for departments of classics, English language and literature, Welsh language and literature, modern languages, and education to be introduced and, in science, biology; thus permitting not only the foundation of the new faculty but also the introduction of a training department for teachers and of a complete preliminary science course for medical students.

The college did meet with one rebuff, however. It had been hoped that a department of philosophy could be set up as one of the essential constituents of the new faculty but the university had refused to approve this proposal on the somewhat specious grounds that no mention of the subject had been made by the original promoters of the college in their petition for a charter. The sympathetic support of Haldane was enlisted when he delivered his inaugural address. 'In a true University and in a true University College', he argued characteristically, 'you must have a Chair of Philosophy. It is the widest of all subjects.' The university council was not impressed. Financial considerations carried more weight, the proposal was deferred and was not finally sanctioned until 1925.

Lack of resources, too, stifled any notion of a department of economics. It was a development that had captured the imagination of the arts visitors in 1919 for they had envisaged that the work of the department could be 'specially directed to the economic and social problems that arise in a community like that of Swansea'. The college thought on a much wider canvas, however. Although it was 'fully alive to the importance of this branch of University work in an industrial and commercial community', it considered that 'Economics should be established only on a broad basis, compatible with a new University Faculty of Economics and Commerce.' While such a departure was beyond its immediate resources the college hoped that no opportunity of securing the necessary endowment would be neglected. Sadly, such funds were not forthcoming and a department of economics was not introduced until 1937.

The secondary nature of the arts faculty was reflected in some of the new appointments to the second series of departmental headships in 1921, for while some of the new members were as distinguished as their scientific predecessors, others lacked any considerable degree of experience, although in the event their contribution both to their subjects and to the development of the college was to prove to be as great. D. Emrys Evans (1891–1966), assistant lecturer in classics at Bangor, was appointed to the chair of classics and the gentlemanly W.D. Thomas (1889–1954), Junior Professor of English in the University of Saskatchewan, to the chair of English language and literature. To the chair of Welsh language and literature the college appointed Henry Lewis, assistant lecturer in Welsh at Cardiff. At the time, one of the youngest professors ever appointed in the university, he was someone with a distinctly limited university experience. Lewis had served with distinction in the Welsh Guards and the Royal Welsh Fusiliers in France during the Great War and had been severely wounded on two occasions. F.A. Cavenagh (1884–1946), lecturer in education in the University of Manchester, was appointed to the key post of Professor of Education.

The other three headships of department were taken up by women. The new head of the department of modern languages and Professor of French Language and Literature was Dr Mary Williams, Reader in Romance Philology in the University of London. Dr Williams had already achieved a dual reputation for herself as an expert in romance philology and also as being the first woman aeroplane passenger to fly the English Channel, only a year after Bleriot's historic crossing. She now achieved her hat trick in being the first woman to be appointed to a university chair in the United Kingdom. But the appointment was not unopposed; indeed it was opposed quite vehemently by George Arbour Stephens, now a member of the college council and chairman of the Swansea education committee, on the simple grounds that a woman could not possibly hold such an important appointment. Their mutual interest in Arthurian romance should have softened Stephens's anti-feminism. Eventually it must have done, for four years

Henry Lewis (1889–1968), *left*, and Mary Williams (1882–1977), *right*. It could never be said that the relationship between these two distinguished scholars was over cordial

later Dr Williams and he were married. The second woman appointed to the staff was Dr Florence Mockeridge, who had been lecturer in botany in the University of London and was appointed head of the department of biology and lecturer in botany at Swansea. The appointment of librarian was made the same year and Miss Olive Busby, assistant librarian at Bedford College, London, was appointed to the post. But despite these and other female appointments the presence of women on the staff was barely tolerated by their male colleagues. Drew, for instance, would always give vent to his disapproval by referring to Dr Mockeridge as 'Miss' Mockeridge. Women were not admitted to membership of the senior common room until after the Second World War, and when Charles Edwards discovered this he never went there again.

The novelty of the college was now beginning to wear thin and less attention was being paid to these appointments, although the distinguished war career of Henry Lewis did not pass without remark. His appointment also gave rise to one of those artificially generated flurries of disatisfaction that result in public expressions of unease. The campaign against him was public, bitter and personal and arose from the resentment of some of the bypassed candidates, in particular Dr John Jenkins ('Gwili') who was at the centre of the vortex. In the nature of these things the episode was soon widened into a question of principle revolving around the authority of the college council. Lewis had been the sole candidate seen by the council and the college was forced into the public explanation that while it was the council that was empowered to make appointments to chairs, following the pattern set by the Haldane Commission it was advised by expert committees. These committees, commented the *Western Mail* (22 June 1921), were 'not meant to supplant, but rather to supplement the work of the College Council . . .

A student view of (*clockwise from left*) Professor Mary Williams, Professor Ernest Hughes, Professor Emrys Evans and Miss Nesta Jones (history) – shortly to become Mrs Evans – and Professor W.D. Thomas, in *Dawn* (1925)

which . . . has in this way the benefit of the advice of a body of experts upon the academic qualifications of candidates'. The council's powers, concluded the newspaper, calculatingly stirring the pot, could only be encroached upon 'by an action resolved upon by itself, viz., to ask the joint standing committee of selection to virtually make the choice by asking that only one name be recommended'.

Herein lay the nub of the issue, for the presentation of only one candidate by the committee to the council, as in this instance, was conjured up as an infringement of the council's power of selection, however cogent the academic arguments of the committee might be. The result of the controversy was to establish a practice of bringing forward at least two, and sometimes three, 'chairworthy' candidates before the council, one of the two normally being more strongly recommended than the other. It was a practice that was fraught with dissatisfaction that occasionally erupted into argument between the principal, as chairman of the special committee, and the council. Not until the 1960s, and then only with the utmost reluctance on the part of some of its most senior members, was the council persuaded that single candidates should, as a matter of course, be brought forward. But by then it had generally become recognized that the former practice had become outmoded and that the selection procedure was primarily an academic matter. As far as Henry Lewis was concerned, it can only be said that he more than justified his appointment both on grounds of scholarship and dedicated service to the college. In due time he was to become one of its most powerful personalities.

In Swansea, also, there was some unease about the college's early appointments. In 1918, the science visitors had stressed that the services of the existing technical college staff should be 'substantially and sympathetically recognised'. Local perception was that this was not happening and an appointment that had caused particular stir was that of Professor Bacon who was, with Hughes, Trueman and Drew and, later of course, Lewis, seen to be yet another of Sibly's imports from Cardiff. Varley, some felt, had been shabbily treated. Now, once more, a leading member of the technical college staff had been passed over for a senior appointment, on this occasion Gilbert Jones, Varley's successor at the technical college, and head of its engineering department since its inception in 1896. Moreover, it could scarcely be ignored that of some seventeen teaching appointments made in science and applied science in the first year of the college only six were of technical college staff and of these only two (Henry Coe of metallurgy and Reginald Isaacs of engineering) were appointed to the grade of senior lecturer.

A happier subject of spirited discussion in the earliest days of the college was the question of the provision of a coat of arms. The college, helped by Grant Murray, Director of the Swansea College of Art, and the indefatigable local antiquary, W.H. Jones, Director of the Royal Institution of South Wales, suggested to the College of Heralds that a suitable design might be a thirteenth-century shield bearing representations of learning and industry, preferably the metallurgical industry as being characteristic of the Swansea district, with the old seal of the borough as a crest. By Christmas Eve 1920 Ambrose Lee, York Herald, had put forward his interpretation of the college's basic idea: a shield containing the head of Minerva, suggesting learning and wisdom; the hammer of Vulcan, the arts and industry of metal working; and, below these classical allusions, a scroll, the record of both. These somewhat *outré* proposals were, not surprisingly, not taken up and instead a rather more conventional design was adopted. This depicted within the shield a dragon, for Wales; the usual book, for higher learning; and a hammer, pickaxe and anchor, for the metallurgical and extractive industries of the area and the commercial activities of the port of Swansea. The problem of what should be written in the book was neatly overcome by putting in nothing that was legible.

A question which could not be dealt with quite so dextrously was that of a suitable motto for the arms. Welsh was the obvious language: *Meddwl diwyll, diwall berchen*[3] was one suggestion and it was only after much heart-searching that *Gweddw crefft heb ei dawn* was chosen from the collection of proverbs in the *Myvyrian Archaiology*. The adoption of the motto by the court in April 1921 gave rise to a lively debate both on questions of orthography and meaning. Archdeacon Robert Williams of Carmarthen – responsible for the 'Introduction' to the first *Everyman* edition of the *Mabinogion* – explained in the *Cambria Daily Leader* (18 March 1921) that 'what the Council wished the motto to convey was that technical skill without culture is *gweddw*, i.e., widowed or bereft'. He concluded happily that 'whether *dawn* ever meant culture is more than a little doubtful but there can be no doubt that the suggested motto is euphonious and apt'.[4]

The majority of the earliest students came to the college from the immediate Swansea area and lived at home. It was only natural that this should be so in the first years, but the promoters had regarded the college as a national institution and saw it, at the very least, as serving a wide area of south-west Wales. Indeed, this territorial designation had been included in the first drafts of the college charter. From its inception, therefore, the college authorities had laid great stress on the need to provide residential accommodation, especially for women students. When the college's administrative offices moved to Singleton Abbey in July 1921, Dumbarton House, which had been placed at the disposal of the college by Gilbertson and Roger Beck free of rent, was bought and converted into a hostel for fifteen women students taking teachers' training courses. Attempts had been made to acquire other houses for conversion into hostels for both men and women but these had failed because of the high prices suitable property was commanding at the time. Men students not living at home thus had to resort to lodgings. However, as a result of an appeal through local churches an adequate supply of lodgings was found surprisingly quickly, especially in the nearby Brynmill area, thereby beginning the close association of the landladies of that part of the town with the college which lasted until the major expansion of student residences in the 1960s and the current changes in student accommodation habits.

As the 1922–3 session approached it became clear that the number of applications from women students for admission to the college was such that the accommodation in Dumbarton House would be insufficient. The yet unsettled question of the incorporation of the Swansea Training College with the hostel facilities that it could have provided made the problem still more critical. Fortunately, the council was able to come to an arrangement with the local education authority to take over a training college hostel in Gwydr Gardens, Uplands, on a temporary basis to accommodate twenty-three women students from the university college. Dumbarton House became a men's hostel but the succeeding three years' operation resulted only in a continuing deficit because the fee-income of the thirteen residents could never match outgoings. Demand for hostel accommodation by men students had never risen to expectations either and so it was decided to abandon the hostel in June 1925 and sell off the house.

SPEED THE PARTING GUEST.

Miss Mary Wilkinson (d. 1989), the third warden of Beck Hall, small in stature but determined in discipline, deals with unwelcome visitors

The story of residential accommodation for women was a far happier one. The hostel in Gwydr Gardens proved a success under the able supervision of the college's first women's warden, Mrs Elsie Mathias. Then, shortly before his death in July 1923, Roger Beck, who had repeatedly affirmed his interest in the college by numerous benefactions, gave six of the houses and surrounding land in Gwydr Gardens for hostel purposes. One of these houses was that already in use by the college and gradually as the tenancies of the other houses lapsed and they came fully into the possession of the college they were adapted to form Beck Hall, as the hostel was named in 1925 in memory of its benefactor. By 1926–7 a block of four of the houses had been taken over and connected up as one unit with the warden and thirty-two women students in residence. In these years, however, the number of students fluctuated considerably, largely because of the general economic situation. In 1927–8, for instance, there were only twenty-three students living in Beck Hall, apparently due, as the council reported, 'to depression in trade, an unusually small number of women students having been admitted to the College'.

But if parents and students were finding it desperately hard going in these difficult post-war years, neither did the college have a superabundance of funds. True, it had the foundation of grant-aid from the UGC and the umbrella of the university. It did not have the struggles that Aberystwyth or the early university colleges in England – and, indeed, the contemporary Leicester – had to face because of the absence of government support. There was, too, the ever-present generosity of local industrialists, even if this was more limited now in a period of acute recession than the expectations aroused by the euphoria of the recent boom years would have led one to believe. David Davies's ultimate hope of £150,000 or even £100,000 was never realized but a respectable £69,605 5s. 3d. was handed over to the college as the final capital figure of the endowment fund in 1920. And the local industrial and commercial leaders continued to demonstrate their support by donations and by annual subscriptions, which for over a decade exceeded £8,000 each year. Their gifts of equipment and materials for laboratories and workshops were also many and varied – from a lathe for chemistry to 1,200 yards of three-core armoured cable for engineering – and were more than valuable at a time when such items were often beyond the means of the college. It was not only local firms that were generous in this way, for many gifts in kind came in from national concerns outside the Swansea area to help equip the new engineering laboratories in particular. The academic departments were not alone in benefiting and one especially important accession to the library in its first year of operation was a collection of some three thousand volumes belonging to Professor Harold Littledale[5] bought through the generosity of David Glasbrook, son of that John Glasbrook who, half a century earlier, had opposed the establishment of a public library in Swansea.

The greatest degree of financial support came naturally in respect of the college's building fund. The gross cost of the new light-construction engineering and library buildings and the consequential reorganization of the abbey in 1924 was estimated to be £34,260 including 'a bare minimum of £5,000 for the purchase of nucleus equipment for the Department of Engineering'. The college, however, had available only some £22,450 – mostly in the form of donations – and to embark on all that was necessary it had to increase its overdraft facilities with the Midland Bank to the considerable sum of £30,000, secured by college investments, and to launch a special appeal for £12,000.

The magnitude of such a figure is perhaps made clearer when one realizes that a substantial house of the period could be bought for less than £500. That the necessary funding was attained in a comparatively short time underlines the continuing support of local industry. Of the donations received, some £7,000 was subscribed by members of the Cleeves coalowning family alone, while substantial amounts came from the Coal Owners' University Trust Fund.

In spite of such support, it remained the case that the college was poor. Resources had to be carefully husbanded and it is all the more remarkable, since development was so inhibited, that so much good work was achieved in those early days. The college had been created at what, in economic terms, was arguably the most difficult time in British history. In 1919 the sum voted by parliament for the universities had risen, for the first time, to £1,000,000, of which broadly two-thirds were allocated to general recurrent expenditure and one-third to non-recurrent expenditure on capital projects and the purchase of equipment. By 1921 the universities' vote had been increased to £1,500,000, but in the following year, during the period of austerity that saw the wielding of the 'Geddes Axe', the vote was cut to £1,200,000. Later, the UGC was to comment that this twenty per cent reduction in grant-aid 'came at a most awkward time, when the springs of increased local support were also beginning to dry up'. Although Swansea in the 1920s escaped the worst rigours of the Depression that devastated south Wales because of the greater variety of its industrial base, the continuing buoyancy of the tinplate industry and its export trade in anthracite and oil, the college, nevertheless, still felt the bitter wind that was blowing elsewhere.

To meet exceptional expenditure at the inception of the college a special non-recurrent grant of £5,000 was made direct through the UGC while, to cover the costs of salaries, administration and general maintenance during the college's first year, an equivalent recurrent grant was made. Due emphasis was laid on the fact that the recurrent grant was not to be seen as additional to the recurrent matching grant to be made to the university on a pound for pound basis. The college, therefore, in common with the other constituent colleges and institutions of the university, was dependent upon the university council for its share of the public funds which the university received from the Treasury and the county councils. In the earliest years *ad hoc* grants were made by the university council to enable the college to contain its working deficit and it was not until 1922 that a policy scheme was worked out for the allocation of grants to the constituents of the university. By this time, however, the 'Geddes Axe' had fallen, leading to a reduction in the Treasury grant. As today, the early 1920s were years of financial anxiety in the universities. For 1922–3 and 1923–4 the college was receiving some £16,000 for recurrent expenditure from the university but it was far from satisfied over the distribution of part of the funds available. It was not to be for another thirteen years, until 1936, that the disagreement was resolved to Swansea's satisfaction, but in the meantime, in 1925, the Treasury grant had been restored to its previous figure so that by 1925–6 the college allocation had exceeded £19,000 (together with a further £7,500 arising from the equivalence grant on private benefactions) which became stabilized at about £21,000 (+£7,500) the following year. Progressively during the 1930s the allocation was to rise, until by the last session before the Second World War it had reached £37,848, although since 1936 the equivalence grant had ceased.

To problems of finance were added academic problems of major dimensions.

The Mighty Atom

COLLEGE PERSONALITIES. *No.1.*

THE NEWCOMER – PROF. HEATH – WHO, DURING
A SHORT WHILE, HAS TAUGHT US A LOT WE
DIDN'T KNOW ABOUT PHILOSOPHY. IS APT, ON
OCCASION, TO FORGET HIS PHILOSOPHIC VIEW
OF LIFE, ESPECIALLY WHEN DEALING WITH THE
LATE COMERS TO LECTURES.

Archie Edward Heath (1887–1961), a
student's impression in *Dawn* (1926)

Reference has already been made to the refusal of the university to sanction the
establishment of a chair of philosophy at the college. In part this was said to be on
grounds of financial stringency and in part because the promoters had made no mention
of the subject in their petition for a charter of incorporation. Eventually, the university
conceded the college's case and the new professorship was established from October
1925, Archie Heath, senior lecturer in education at the University of Liverpool, being
appointed to the post. Heath had never taught philosophy before coming to Swansea. A
Cambridge natural scientist, he had studied the subject under Bertrand Russell and had
developed a special interest in the philosophy of science. But his sweep was wide and
embraced contemporary movements in art and literature. To Heath, in particular, was
due the breaking of barriers in the early college between science and the arts; and he was
much in demand as an extra-mural lecturer. Revered as he was by his students, he was
disliked by many of his colleagues. A bouncy little man – he was the smallest man in
college – he was prickly, prejudiced and downright to the point of rudeness. In his later
years he sported a goatee beard and cultivated it with all the vanity Poirot displayed over
his moustache. But he was haunted by tragedy and his burden was heavy for him.

Even more important to the immediate development of the college was the question
of the incorporation of the Swansea Training College, which had been included in the
petition. It had been hoped that the training college could be transferred to the
university college on 1 April 1922 on the basis of a ninety-nine-year lease and at a
nominal rent. Before the end of 1921 the broad conditions of transfer had been agreed
between the university college and the local education authority, subject only to the

approval of the Board of Education and the Treasury. An overriding condition was that the training college could be used only for the training of teachers, with the hope that it would provide for training under the four years' scheme, the facility for two-year students being gradually phased out. Although in the year before his death Sir Owen Edwards had been sceptical about the proposal, in April 1921 it was provisionally approved by the Board. The college, confident now that there would be no impediment to the merger, proceeded to the appointment of Cavenagh as Professor of Education and administrative head of the training department which would include the Swansea Training College when that had been taken over. The whole scheme, however, had to be deferred by the abrupt refusal of Treasury approval on the grounds that the merger 'would increase the liability of the Exchequer in respect of grants'.

There began a very trying period for Sibly, who was concerned not only with the natural growth of the college but also with the immediately practical problem of hostel accommodation for women students. Eventually, after lengthy discussions, in May 1923 both the Board of Education and the Treasury agreed to the merger of the training college on the basis that the departments did 'not think it desirable that the University College should be under any obligation to incur expenditure in providing training for two-year students'. This meant that the residual cost of training two-year students from the Swansea area, on which the merger hung, became a matter between the university college and the local education authority. Obviously, from the point of view of the education authority the main advantage of the merger would have been the shifting of the responsibility of the fifty per cent cost of the training of such students to the university college. Unhappily, no agreement between the two bodies could be reached: the college required a permanent grant from the education authority to meet the residual cost of the students, while the authority felt itself unable to guarantee such a grant. As the matter was put by the college, 'the question of the transfer was postponed *sine die*'. It was never to be revived and died a natural death.

Such major setbacks did not serve to ruffle unduly the close-knit society which was establishing itself at Singleton. A staff club was quickly established and the periodic social gatherings of council, staff and students on the 'archery lawn' if weather permitted proved to be ever popular. Facilities for the normal social life of students were meagre and called forth a degree of staff participation that would be unwelcome today but which in these early days served to cement relationships between the various component parts of the college. Evening functions, including the Saturday evening 'dancing classes' which eventually developed into the later institution of Saturday night 'hops', were held in the 'Refectory' — the old orangery — which was the only room of sufficient size in the college and which therefore had to serve its turn for both social events and more formal college occasions, including public lectures. Spartan as the facilities were, there was always the possible excitement of stumbling into a sleeping cow as one negotiated the unlit and unfenced grounds after a function. Little was available, either, for student union facilities but as the houses in Gwydr Gardens were taken over, some rooms were put at the disposal of the Students Representative Council there and equipped with second-hand furniture by the students themselves.

Time was already beginning to take its toll, however. Sir Richard Martin, the last link with the original college movement of the 1880s, died in September 1922, and

Two early benefactors: the steel and tinplate magnates, Roger Beck (1841–1923), *left*, and Henry
Folland (1877–1926), *right*, president of the college, 1925–6

Roger Beck, most generous and self-effacing of benefactors, less than a year later. In
1924 Henry Coe, senior lecturer in metallurgy and formerly head of the metallurgical
department at the Swansea Technical College, died suddenly. A candidate for the chair
of metallurgy in 1920, Coe was again a link with the movement for a university college
and someone who had played a major role in the formative development of the new
college. A grave setback to the college's aspirations was the retirement of Gilbertson
from the presidency in 1925 because of a serious heart condition brought about by his
strenuous industrial activities during the Great War. His wise leadership and natural
conciliatory flair had done much to ensure both the smooth development of the college
in its earliest years and also the positive support of his industrial colleagues. He was
followed as president by a fellow tinplate manufacturer, a thrusting self-made man,
Henry Folland, who contrapuntally possessed all the assertion that Gilbertson did not.
In many respects Folland was the very man the college needed to lead its next stage of
development. Tragically, he died suddenly in Egypt before the year was out.

But, by then, the college had suffered an even greater loss in the resignation of the
principal. Thanks to Sibly's guidance and inspiration, the college was rapidly beginning
to establish itself as a centre of teaching and research in the Welsh university system. He
himself had won the confidence of the local industrial leaders, who were such a powerful
influence in the counsels of the college, and, through his active proselytization, he had
begun to create an awareness locally of the true nature of a university. When it suited the

work in hand, he could adopt a character of formidable dignity, but, personally, he was a kindly and a generous character, never remote and always ready to help or advise colleagues and students. Thanks to Sibly the intimate *esprit* of the early college was rapidly established. Now, perhaps, Sibly saw his formative skills being extended to a broader canvas. In 1926, therefore, he left Swansea to become the Principal Officer – shortly to be restyled 'Principal' – of the University of London, an exacting post at a troubled period of transition for the university. Though the move was a natural promotion for someone of Sibly's capacity, it was not to prove a happy one. He could never adjust to the impersonal corporate institutionalism of London and it was with relief that, after three years, he could retreat from the complexities of South Kensington to Reading, the youngest, smallest and probably least financially secure British university. Sibly was to spend seventeen happy years at Reading until failing health forced his retirement. But this was not before he had laid firm foundations for the university and, as chairman of the Committee of Vice-chancellors and Principals from 1938 to 1943, had enhanced the reputation of 'redbrick' with the government and created a receptive atmosphere for post-war developments.

But, in 1926, there was still much to accomplish at Swansea and there was more than a hint of deteriorating relations between a vigorous principal and some members of the college council in what had already been achieved. On occasion there were bound to be conflicts of ideas, but there were some council members – and perhaps this was a problem that lay in the very genesis of the college – who, in their dealings with the

Back row: J. Saunders Lewis, E.S. Keeping, T.K. Rees, R.G. Isaacs, J.C. Arrowsmith, L.B. Pfeil, J.S. Caswell, H. Hill, P. Dienes, P.S. Thomas, Alan Stuart, Idwal Jones, Thomas Taig, G.M.A. Grube, J.A.V. Butler, L. Wright, R. Wilson. Middle row: L.E. Hinkel, A.L. Norbury, A.A. Fordham, W. Morris-Jones, Miss Ethel Martin, Miss G. Jones, Miss I.M. Westcott, Miss Phyllis Jones, Miss Nesta Jones, Miss O.M. Busby, Prof. C.A. Edwards, The Principal, Edwin Drew, Miss D. Bliss, Miss D.M. Williams, Miss I.A.F. Hilton, Miss E.M. Pool, Miss Evelyn Matthews, Mlle. Y. Marec, A.E. Trueman, A. Hanson, E.E. Ayling. Front row: Prof. F. Bacon, Prof. A.E. Heath, Prof. E.J. Evans, E.E. Hughes, Prof. J.E. Coates, Dr. F.A. Mockeridge, Prof. D. Emrys Evans, Prof. W.D. Thomas, Prof. A.R. Richardson, Prof. Henry Lewis, Prof. F.A. Cavenagh. Of the forty-four academic staff included in this 1926 group (Prof. Mary Williams and Dr Paul Diverres are absent), five (Prof. Edwards, Prof. Richardson, Dr Butler, Dr Pfeil and Dr Trueman) later became Fellows of the Royal Society college staff, saw more than a hint of a master/man relationship. No doubt it was a reflection of the paternalism that existed in the industries of the Swansea Valley, but even by the 1960s it was something that had not been wholly eradicated and was to bring forth difficulties once more. It was all too symptomatic of the dangers David Davies had seen in a narrowly based governing body and with hindsight its seeds could be seen in the words with which even Gilbertson, that most forward looking and conciliatory of men, had welcomed Sibly as someone who would do his best to develop the college in the way the governors wished it to be developed.

Sibly's departure from the principalship was more than some convenient but artificial time break in a sequence of events. It was a real watershed which marked the end of the beginnings of the college.

LOOK OUT, HERE COMES MR. DREW!

This student cartoon of the pre-war college captures the all-pervading presence of the registrar, Edwin Drew

Notes

1. The shortlisted candidates were: Thomas Jones, S.J. Chapman, Professor of Political Economy at Manchester; T.F. Sibly, Professor of Geology at the college; and Ernest Barker of New College, Oxford – all eminently suitable for the post and all to have distinguished futures.

2. It is said that Richardson was recommended for a Victoria Cross for his bravery during the German Somme offensive in March 1918. In 1922 he married Dr Margaret Harris, assistant lecturer in modern languages at the college.

3. Loosely translated as, 'The possessor of a cultured mind is a man without fault'.

4. The *Western Mail* ran a competition for the best translation of *Gweddw Crefft heb ei Dawn*. The adjudicator, Professor W.J. Gruffydd, divided the prize between the best of the proverbial, and the best of the literal renderings submitted: 'A lack of parts makes widow'd Arts' ('Brynchan') and 'Art hath no mate if without wit' (Revd J. Harries Williams).

5. 1853–1930; Professor of English at Cardiff, 1899–1921. The acquisition of the Littledale collection was of major consequence to the college's embryo library.

CHAPTER FOUR

'A MOOD OF ACUTE ANXIETY'

S ibly was followed as principal on 1 May 1927 by Charles Edwards, who had held
the office of vice-principal since the foundation of the college and had been
appointed acting principal for the interregnum. Again, as in 1920, it seems that
Edwards was reluctant to accept the principalship and was induced to do so only on the
understanding that he would still be able to maintain substantial contact with the
department to which all his energies had been directed since his first coming to Swansea.
His continued involvement with metallurgy entailed supervision of the honours
students and direction of the research activities of the department. However, although
he was able to devote himself to a considerable amount of productive scientific work,
mostly in collaboration with postgraduate students, and did some lecturing in physical
metallurgy, his responsibilities as principal naturally reduced the time he could give to
the overall charge of metallurgy. The burden of day-to-day administration was,
therefore, entrusted to an assistant professor who in effect ran the department: Leonard
Taverner, from 1927 until his appointment to a chair at Witwatersrand University in
1940, and subsequently Robert Higgins (d. 1983). The latter was a Scotsman, lacking totally
in his chief's delicacy of expression, who devoted his all to the department until Edwards's
retirement in 1947 and the appointment of Hugh O'Neill (1899–1986) as professor.

At last, the industrialists on the college council had brought about what they had
wanted in 1920. Nevertheless, despite Edwards's acknowledged contributions to
metallurgical research for which he was elected an FRS in 1930, and the vital
encouragement he gave to generations of research students, it has to be recognized that
both the development of his department and the broad direction of college affairs
suffered from his dual responsibilities. Policy decisions that should have been taken by
the principal himself often slipped imperceptibly into the hands of the registrar. The
reputation of the college which, on the basis of the work being carried out with strained
facilities in so many departments, should have been high soon came to receive less than
the recognition it merited in the councils of the university. 'There goes Edwards',
waspishly remarked the principal of another constituent college after a particularly
important university meeting, 'back to Swansea to report to Drew and be told what he
should have done.'

This said, Edwards was, in many ways, the right man for the times. Outside the
college he fostered the vital links with industry, both local and national, which were so
much a part of the life-support of the college. His intimate understanding, built up over
many years, of both the industrial and the university worlds made him an effective
bridge between college council and senate, even if his background nurtured a deference
to the former which Sibly would never have contemplated. Within Singleton, too,
Edwards, very much supported by his wife, helped to create the friendly, fraternal –

almost too cosy – atmosphere that was such an appealing characteristic of the college until the great leap forward of the 1960s.

If there was little enough dynamism in the direction of the college in the years before the Second World War, nationally they were the years of 'the ordeal' and, for much of the period, of general economic stagnation. If Edwards was cautious in his leadership it must be recognized that these were times when caution was a prerequisite in university planning. In some respects, the universities fared better than did other sectors of British society. Although the sums dispensed as recurrent grants by a UGC still feeling its way may now seem derisory – across the board they were no more than a third of what was to be committed to the development of Swansea alone in the early sixties – they relieved the universities of the gravest of their anxieties.

By 1929–30 the exchequer grant to the college stood at £21,933. In the following year it was dramatically increased by over £10,000 to £32,835. But the increase allowed the college to do little more than tread water, since the bulk of what was additionally available was swallowed up by a much-needed increase in the salaries of independent lecturers and of the non-professorial staff generally, for the library staff, and for the purchase of books and equipment for the library.

Financially, the first few years of the college had been troubled. As Sibly had been at pains to point out, and as he was to discover again at Reading a decade later, they had been a time when it was essential to cultivate a sense of proportion and to economize wherever possible. At the end of the first operative financial year (30 June 1921) there was a deficit of just over £3,276. In part this was due to a delay in the receipt of full grants from the university; but obviously the initial expenditure in establishing the college, and furnishing and equipping it, was heavy. Although the council could congratulate itself that the deficit had not been higher, it made great play with the fact that this had been achieved only through the exercise of 'the most stringent economy consistent with efficiency'. For the next two years, in a deepening economic crisis, the accumulated deficit crept up to £4,343 and then to £4,694, with the university urging every possible economy and the college continuing to look closely at every tittle of expenditure. By June 1924, as a result of an enforced housekeeping that would have done credit to the unregenerate Scrooge, the deficit had been converted into a surplus which was maintained annually until the immediate post-war period, though on a number of occasions – in 1929–30 for instance – this was only achieved by a hair's breadth. Even today, in the far-from-easy world of the 1990s, it is perhaps difficult to appreciate to how fine a financial tolerance the college was obliged to work. But Swansea was not alone. As the UGC discovered at the time of its 1924 visitation, most universities were 'in a position of grave difficulty . . . Economy had already been carried to its utmost limits by the university authorities, and further savings in expenditure could only have been obtained at serious risk to the academic structure of the institutions in their charge. The general mood of the universities was consequently one of acute anxiety' (UGC *Report 1928–29*, p. 3).

After the euphoria of the days of promotion and foundation, and as the subscriptions began to be cut or be allowed to run out, the income at Swansea from endowment and donation settled down to about £6,000 per annum for most of the 1930s. It was maintained at a somewhat lower level for the war years, but afterwards the incidence of high taxation and the austerity economy, coupled with the visibly greater support being received from the state, reduced it to an almost insignificant proportion of the college's income. Not for Swansea the kind of private generosity that even in the bleakest days of the 1930s some of the English civic universities were able to attract from their localities or from the London livery companies.

The First World War and the Depression of the 1920s and '30s cast a severe blight on the staples of local industry, including many of those firms that had been most involved in the foundation of the college. By the late thirties the long decline of the copper industry ended with the closure of the last of the copperworks. Many of the zinc and spelter works also disappeared during the inter-war period, though the refining of nickel continued at Clydach. Because of overseas competition and its resistance to technological change the tinplate industry experienced many closures and a drastic reduction in capacity which led to a large fall in employment. As early as 1929 Swansea had lost its dominant position as the world's major producer and exporter of tinplate. The Siemens steelworks, tied as they were to the tinplate industry to which they supplied the bulk of their output, suffered from the latter's increasing dependence on the import of cheap tinplate bars, but there were still thirteen steelworks producing bars for tinplate manufacture in the early thirties. The introduction of protective tariffs under the Import Duties Act of 1932 provided the steelworks with a much-needed fillip and, as the nation's rearmament got under way in the immediate pre-war years, the industry began to recover. The anthracite-coal industry of the district actually expanded in the thirties with a consequent benefit to the port, so that Swansea never experienced the sufferings of the steam-coal valleys or the stagnancy of the port of Cardiff that was so totally dependent on them. There was, too, another glimmer of hope for the future. The early twenties had seen the coming to Swansea of the Anglo-Persian Oil Company (later BP), which built the first major oil refinery in Britain at Llandarcy. But before the war the plant was small and its real impact was not felt until the 1950s.

While Swansea in general never endured the distress of the mining valleys to the north and east, and never allowed its social fabric and cultural vitality to crumble, there was individual hardship, and in business and industry a continual retrenchment that directly affected beneficiaries like the college. Any tempering of generosity to the college that there might have been was thus due rather to the influence of external economic forces than to any lessening regard for the institution; local industry simply could not afford to support the college financially to the extent that was done elsewhere. Nevertheless, it would be wrong to suggest that local industrialists and business firms did not continue what support they could in both cash and kind. In 1924, for example, the South Wales Siemens Steel Association, always staunch in its support, doubled its original annual grant of £2,500 to the college's general funds. At the same time, help was still forthcoming in the form of subscriptions and gifts to departments; and when it came to answering specific appeals for capital building projects, local industry was certainly not behindhand even for non-technical developments. Most valuable, in a period before universal student grant-aid, was the funding of entrance scholarships. At the outset the borough council endowed eight annual scholarships, four of £50 per annum, one of which T. Neville George won in the first year, and four of £25 per annum. To these were added in 1921 five more awards, each of £50 per annum, this time financed by industrialists and a bank: the King George V Scholarship (by Gilbertson); the Queen Mary Scholarship (by Sir John Wright); the Princess Mary Scholarship (by W.T. Farr);

University College

The Great College Photograph 1928, taken by the London Panoramic Photograph Company. At least one student cheated the sweep of the camera and succeeded in appearing at the extreme left of the back row and the extreme right of the first row standing

the Chamber of Commerce 1921 Scholarship (endowed anonymously); and the Lloyds' Bank Scholarship.

For its recurrent needs the college was almost entirely dependent upon the public financial provision made through the university; but as a result of the effective husbanding of its resources – and here one cannot undervalue the care that Edwin Drew took over every trifle of expenditure – by 1932 the long-standing deficit on the building fund had been extinguished and, despite the critical reductions in grant-aid, the college had achieved a surplus of £635 on its income and expenditure account. Even so, before the year was out the university council was again pressing home the need for economies and was putting an embargo on additional commitments. The critically narrow financial margin within which the college had to operate throughout the inter-war period gave little room for any development and was in any case constructed on a low base line. In fact, it was not until the next substantial review of the Exchequer grant in 1936 that any major new development could be embarked upon out of recurrent income. The augmentation of Swansea's government grant-aid by over £4,000 between 1935–6 (£34,397) and 1937–8 (£38,708), despite decreasing fee-income in these years because of declining student numbers, allowed the college at last to offer some increase in the maximum salaries of professors and independent lecturers in 1936 and to convert the independent lectureship in botany held by Dr Mockeridge into a professorship.

This last proposal, though welcomed by many, especially on personal grounds, gave rise to lively public controversy because it was perceived to be in competition with the creation of a department of economics. Over its first decade the department of biology had grown rapidly to reach a pre-war peak of 179 registrations for its various courses in 1933–4. The bulk of the departmental teaching was in the first year and also in general

ansea. 1928.

biology for teachers in training. The number of students taking honours in botany was never more than a handful, but if most teaching was conducted at a low level, this handful consistently achieved good results. It was a story to be echoed across the board in the college as, indeed, were the continuous and prolonged complaints about teaching conditions and accommodation in this department. However, deficient as were the facilities for undergraduate teaching, those for research were parlous in the extreme, so much so that students were positively discouraged from pursuing research. Library provision at this level, too, was woefully inadequate. Nevertheless, in the midst of such alarming discouragement much was achieved in a department critically based in a coastal environment so richly diverse in flora and fauna.

Dr Mockeridge's own studies mainly centred on plant growth substances and later, through a succession of research students, she carried out important work on the water relations of the *bryophyta*. By 1922 two assistant lectureships had been established and with the appointment of T. Kenneth Rees (d. 1975) (botany) in 1924 and Percy Little (1894–1966) (zoology) in 1927 the academic base of the department was secured. It says much for the resilience of the staff in those days – and by no means only in biology – that worries about lack of money, cramped accommodation and scant facilities, not to mention their teaching loads, did not submerge them completely. Rees's enthusiasm was unabated and it was due in large measure to him that what was euphemistically called a 'marine biological station' was established, jointly with the university college at Cardiff, in a cottage at Port Eynon. Today, this centre would be regarded as unwarrantably primitive but for a few years it proved to be of real value for marine and ecological work. When, eventually, the cottage was sold, the work was transferred to a rented room in Mumbles Lighthouse, 'a situation at least as favourable for the work in hand', it was said, and 'far more accessible than the cottage'. Rees's own research interests were in freshwater and marine algology, based on his investigations of Lough Ine and along the south Wales coast. Little's work was focused on trematode parasites and the effects of oil pollution on fish. In addition to their research work and their university teaching and fieldwork, Rees and Little committed themselves heavily to extra-mural studies and adult education. Through their popular lectures they became very well-known in the community and made a considerable impact for the department locally.

This local awareness of the department and its work was to be reflected in the public debate that developed over the desirability of establishing a chair of botany rather than a chair of economics. These were days when the college as a whole was much closer to its community than it was ever to be after the expansion of the 1960s. What today might pass unnoticed even in the college itself was in those days likely to be given a thorough and universal public airing. To the *South Wales Evening Post* (20 May 1935) the need for a chair of botany was self-evident: 'visiting educationists can scarcely believe that there is no professorship in Biology [*sic*] at the College since there is no more important science from the point of view of the community's life and livelihood'.

Economics, on the other hand, was a subject that the college had been anxious to develop since the earliest days. It had been very much alive to the view of the arts visitors (see p. 99) that the work of such a department could be especially relevant to local economic and social problems. It was an attitude that found favour with the local correspondent of the *Sunday Times* (26 May 1935). To him there was 'no gainsaying that the most fundamental problems of society are economic and political in character, particularly at the moment, and that, as Swansea is the heart of a highly industrial area, it is strange that a Chair of Economics and Political Science has not been established at Swansea long ago'. Music, too, threw down its perennial challenge in the press, to be

Florence Mockeridge (d. 1958)

dismissed out of hand by the supporters of economics. 'If we are to make light of the seriousness of our economic and political problems, it is not unlikely that we shall be having music of a kind which has not as yet been experienced throughout the whole history of mankind.' In the event, Dr Mockeridge was appointed Professor of Botany in October 1936 and a department of economics was also sanctioned from the beginning of the 1937–8 session.

Steps were taken during 1937 to appoint a professor of economics and K.S. Isles (1902–77), then a thirty-five-year-old lecturer in political economy at Edinburgh, was appointed to the post. He immediately embarked on a study of the problems of technological unemployment in the tinplate industry, financed by the National Institute of Economic and Social Research; it was intended for publication as part of an economic and industrial survey that members of the college staff agreed to carry out for the Corporation. What would undoubtedly have proved to be an invaluable study does not seem to have been finished before Isles left Swansea for his native antipodes and the chair of economics in Adelaide in the summer of 1939.[1] A parallel investigation, which his colleague in the department, A.E.C. Hare, the assistant lecturer, had begun on his appointment in 1938 was completed and appeared as the fifth monograph in the seminal series of pamphlets on the economic and industrial setting of the Swansea district that was published by the University of Wales Press on behalf of the college at the beginning of the Second World War. There were six of these notable monographs, inspired by Councillor A.E. ('Alfie') Harries and sponsored by the Corporation. Published at 6*d*. each, they deserved to be more widely known than the disruption of war permitted. The first was by T. Neville George on *The Geology, Physical Features, and Natural Resources of the Swansea District* (1939). Then followed Glyn Roberts's *The Municipal Development of the Borough of Swansea to 1900* (1940); P.S. Thomas's *Industrial Relations . . . in Swansea . . . from about 1800 to Recent Times* (1940); D. Trevor Williams's *The Economic Development of Swansea and of the Swansea District* (1940); A.E.C. Hare's *The Anthracite Coal Industry of the Swansea District* (1940); and Wynne Ll. Lloyd's *Trade and Transport* (1940).

The foundation Professor of Classics, D. Emrys Evans, left Swansea in 1927 to take up the principalship of Bangor following Sir Harry Reichel's reign of Methuselah-like proportions. Evans's two immediate successors – S.K. Johnson (subsequently Professor of Classics at Newcastle) and R.B. Onians (subsequently Professor of Latin at Bedford College, London) – remained at Singleton for only comparatively short periods. In 1936 the post was advertised for the third time in nine years. One of the twenty-four candidates was a young Cambridge don, J. Enoch Powell. Years later he was to say, 'Never, I think, having been guilty of underestimating my claims, I didn't consider myself suitable for being a Lecturer or a Reader. So I thought I'd better get a chair. I put in for professorships and quite a number of them went jolly well until they discovered that I was only twenty-three, and then there was a marked coolness' (quoted in Cosgrave, *The Lives of Enoch Powell* (London, 1989), p. 54). The coolness in Swansea was such that Powell was not even shortlisted and he went off to Australia. Thirty years later, however, his name was one canvassed for the principalship.

The successful candidate, Benjamin Farrington (1891–1974), was to remain at Swansea for the next two decades and in that time made a considerable impact both in the college and outside it. He came to Swansea from a lectureship at Bristol, which he had held briefly after spending fifteen years in Cape Town, latterly as Professor of Latin.

One of those many Irishmen who have brought great enrichment to classical studies in the twentieth century, Farrington, like other Irish classicists abroad, had embraced Marxism and the Communist Party, influenced, it is said, by his experiences in South Africa and by the views of his first wife. His Marxism, however, found its expression less in politics than in the history of ideas and in the association of science with the practicalities of life. A writer of elegance and clarity, he became widely known for his frequently reprinted Pelican, *Greek Science*, a book regarded in its time as the best and most readable introduction to its subject. Highly esteemed for his intellectual gifts, it was said by a close colleague that Farrington held on to his Marxist views only out of respect for the memory of his first wife: 'how could he, otherwise?' it was pointedly asked. However this may be, his natural Irish charm and capacity for long-lasting friendship, and his quiet, if sometimes biting, wit not only made him an agreeable colleague but a highly regarded and much loved one.

The recent lack of continuity in staffing had not been confined to the professoriate, and the increasing pressure of student numbers in the faculty of arts, imposing a heavier teaching load at the expense of research, necessitated an additional permanent post in the classics department. Engineering was also given an additional assistant lectureship (in electrical engineering). Here again the teaching load was critical and the department had been asking for an extra post since the mid-twenties. The compartmentalization of the subject allowed little or no flexibility of teaching across its three branches and the serious illness of R.G. Isaacs in 1936 brought matters to a head. No University of Wales honours courses had yet been introduced in engineering and extra help was required to institute them. Hitherto, the most able engineering students had sat for external London honours degrees but the adoption of new London regulations closed that option. The disruption of the war, however, delayed the introduction of final-year honours courses in all three branches of engineering for another ten years until 1947.

The development of the college in these years up to the Second World War was slow and unspectacular. By the last full session before the war the number of full-time students stood at 485 (discounting the handful of students who took pre-medical courses). This total, however, did not represent any steady increase over the years and was some 250 less than a peak in 1933–4. Furthermore, the overall total conceals the imbalance that had developed between the numbers of arts, pure science and applied science students at Swansea. The following table sets out the situation in respect of full-time student numbers (again discounting pre-medicals) at five-year intervals from the opening of the college in 1920 until 1938–9.

		Arts		Pure Science		Applied Science		
		Men	Women	Men	Women	Men	Women	Total
1920–1	Postgraduates	–	–	–	1	3	–	4
	Undergraduates	–	–	21	7	57	–	85
								89
1925–6	Postgraduates	3	2	10	3	6	–	24
	Undergraduates	106	129	73	11	39	–	358
								382

		Arts		Pure Science		Applied Science		
		Men	Women	Men	Women	Men	Women	Total
1930–1	Postgraduates	5	5	22	1	–	–	33
	Undergraduates	162	117	86	32	55	–	452
								485
1935–6	Postgraduates	7	3	29	3	3	–	45
	Undergraduates	292	103	137	32	63	–	627
								672
1938–9	Postgraduates	8	2	16	–	2	–	28
	Undergraduates	216	66	77	14	81	–	454
								482

What calls for special note is the comparatively small number of applied science students in what had been an avowedly technological university college at its inception and particularly the miniscule number of research students. In two of the sample sessions, 1930–1 and 1938–9, there were no research students at all in metallurgy. The stark fact was that, as the college expanded, its numbers increased primarily on the arts side which, already from 1923–4, its third session, had annually enrolled more students than science and applied science put together. And within the arts faculty until the session 1927–8, women students outnumbered the men. This stress on the arts was a phenomenon by no means peculiar to Swansea; it applied across the board to British university colleges.

The reason for this concentration of students is not hard to find. It lay in the attraction of a teaching profession with an established superannuation scheme which offered security and some measure of status in the harsh economic world of the 1920s and 1930s. Entry to what was seen as a 'soft' profession was, moreover, facilitated by the Board of Education under the 'pledge' system, whereby students were obliged to accept teaching appointments for a period of years in return for financial assistance during their college careers. It was a commitment that not a few of these RSTs, as they were called – Recognized Students in Training – found irksome and which some came to regret bitterly, but for the majority it offered the attraction of a possible sanctuary from the bleak realities of unemployment and the dole queue. At this time the university colleges generally 'owed the very existence of their arts faculties and in many cases their pure science faculties to the presence of a large body of intending teachers whose attendance at degree courses was almost guaranteed by the State' (Armytage, *Civic Universities*, p. 256). It was, though, a situation that contained the seeds of future difficulties, especially as the number of students anxious to obtain teaching posts not only outstripped the employment potential in the dark days of the 1930s but also found increasing difficulty in gaining entry to training departments being systematically reduced by a Board of Education alarmed by the spectre of overmanning in the teaching profession. In the event, because of the scarcity of jobs, the 'pay-back' requirement was not invoked against some lucky RSTs who eventually broke their contracts and abandoned their chosen career.

In terms of staff numbers at the college, the group of thirty-one who had been present for the session 1921–2, when the first full arts courses had been introduced, had grown steadily year by year to sixty-five. There were no sudden and dramatic increases. In fact, the level of staffing was totally inadequate and the teaching load on individuals was immense. The lack of money, however, meant that there could be little alleviation and there was a natural reluctance on the part of the college to enter into long-term contractual commitments over such funds as did become available. At this time, therefore, and until well after the end of the war, the college tended to depend on temporary appointments. It was a state of affairs which, taken together with the normal movement of staff and unforeseen illnesses, was not calculated to create stability or inspire confidence. It says much for the commitment and resilience of the staff of those days that they coped so well in both teaching and research.

For student numbers did not demonstrate the same measured progress as those of staff. They had increased steadily until 1930–1 (485) and then leapt up by almost a hundred students each year, reaching a high point of 751 in the session 1933–4. For two consecutive sessions (1931–2: 567; 1932–3: 668) the growth in numbers showed an increase of more than sixteen per cent, compared with a highest figure of eight per cent for the immediately preceding years. The high intakes of the early thirties – the figures for 1933–4 were not to be exceeded until the influx of ex-servicemen after the Second World War – are not difficult to explain. They were a result of the Depression and the associated dearth of employment possibilities which encouraged school leavers, frequently cushioned by the tempting 'pledge', to think of entry to university when they might previously have sought a job immediately after leaving school.

This increase in student numbers, which was a phenomenon by no means confined to Swansea despite the peculiarly harsh economic conditions in south Wales, coupled with the widespread stagnation of job opportunities, brought a serious rise in the unemployment of university graduates. It was a new but immensely worrying situation that generated a vocal heart-searching on problems of national planning for universities, their curricula and the kind and numbers of university graduates the country needed. Principal Edwards became a well-known figure on the south Wales scene promoting 'The place of the University in Industry and Commerce' and advocating a fifteen-year plan for prosperity. More immediacy and realism were brought to the unemployment crisis by universities through better considered careers advice. In the case of Wales, the university made available to each of its constituent colleges a grant to help meet the cost of providing such advice. It was only £50 a year, which now seems a pitiable amount. Nonetheless, it allowed Swansea to create a part-time careers advisory post to which, in July 1934, it made the heaven-sent appointment of P.S. Thomas, since 1924 the college's first full-time – and remarkably lively – tutor in extra-mural studies.

During the dark years of the mid-thirties, Thomas did sterling work in advising on possible careers and encouraging students to think of avenues that might not otherwise have occurred to them. The vast majority looked to little other than the teaching profession and most of Thomas's time and energy was devoted to trying to wean students away from such a career. It was far from easy. As a survey carried out by the president of the Students' Representative Council, D. Andrew Davies, in 1937, showed, sixty-five per cent of arts students and forty-five per cent of science students wished to become teachers, while sixty-five per cent of arts students and fifty-five per cent of science students had not explored the possibility of any other career. The greatest difficulty Thomas had to face was a marked 'reluctance on the part of students and their parents to show initiative, create opportunities and possibly take some risk'. To *The Times Educational Supplement* (21 November 1936) such reluctance was only natural:

> A university training in South as in North Wales is still an avenue of escape, of freedom from the grim conditions which the parents have had to face. It is not surprising that when the latter risk their savings on the higher education of their children they should not be inclined to venture upon further uncertainties in the hope of quick returns.

By seeing Thomas at the start of their undergraduate careers, the college hoped that students might be persuaded to make a better choice of degree subject, and that to some extent the all too-pervading and unsettling feeling of insecurity about the future would be eased. As the thirties drew to their close and the industrial position of the country began to improve, science graduates, especially chemists and metallurgists, were facing far less difficulty in getting jobs than those in the arts. The problem of coaxing the latter away from the limited, but still prevalent, ambition of entering the teaching profession persisted, and, though Swansea had a greater proportion of grant-earning places to applicants in its training department than the other Welsh colleges, the dilemma of placing graduates who failed to enter the profession remained acute up to the outbreak of war. A good deal of time was spent in attempting to convince students of the alternative attraction of a career in the civil service and a special course in English was introduced to familiarize them with civil service examination requirements. It was to prove an uphill task.

If the economic stagnation of the period and the financial sacrifices that the great majority of parents made for their children are reflected in the career pattern or expectancy of students at a college like Swansea, the same problems are brought out by an analysis of the residential location of students at the college in the quarter-century between 1920 and 1945. Although the figures for the war years are distorted by the effect of the national emergency on the size and character of the student population, those for the two decades up to the war reveal that, as student numbers increased, an increasing proportion lived at home, reaching a peak of 85 per cent in 1937–8.

The figures show that throughout this period the primary influence of the college was felt in Swansea itself and the area immediately surrounding it and that the rise in student numbers in the pre-war years resulted from a marked increase in the intake of students coming from those areas of Swansea, Glamorgan and Carmarthenshire which were within daily travelling distance of the college. In 1935, for instance, of the 685 students at the college, only thirty-eight women were 'living in'; of the rest, seventy-seven men and seven women were in lodgings. The great majority, therefore, lived at home and commuted to college each day, returning home in the evening to study, more often than not amid the distractions of the family living-room and in a milieu weighed down with the anxiety of unemployment and financial sacrifice. It was an extension of school and 'homework', however, that served to provide another organic anchor for the college in its community and to help make it a real part of the locality, where its goings-on and the foibles of its personalities could be retailed with an almost familial relish. It was a phenomenon repeated up and down the country where redbrick

'The Young People – Learning to be Metallurgists and Engineers. Swansea University has a fine tradition of science. The young man comes from Morriston, travels in to his lectures by 'bus.' From *Picture Post*, 1 January 1944

universities or university colleges were the *local* universities in a way they have forever ceased to be. In part this 'localization' of students reflected a genuine reluctance to move out of the home environment by students who had little experience of living away from home before and whose social habits and expectations were restricted and parochial to a degree that can hardly be grasped today in an age of almost frenetic mobility. In Wales, moreover, there was a cultural hesitancy to move outside the principality and, perhaps, an even greater disinclination on the part of English students to venture into the Celtic fringe. In practical terms, too, it was a phenomenon that related directly to the greater expense involved in attending a more distant university, for many of the students would not have been able to afford the expense of attending any university institution that necessitated residence away from home. This was something constantly borne in upon Sir Lewis Jones, himself the proud product of an aspiring working-class family from Brynamman whose sacrifices had allowed him to make his way to the university college at Reading. He frequently made the point at meetings of the court that the majority of the college's students came from lower middle-class and working-class homes.

This social complexion of the student body, and the overriding worry about what lay in the outside world after graduation, tended to create an underlying seriousness of attitude and attention to study – if not brilliance of achievement – that was relieved only by the excitement of Rag Week, Saturday night socials, society dances at the Baltic

Lounge, or visits to such meccas of conviviality as the old Kardomah Café in Castle Street. Coffee rather than beer was the order of the day; wine, however cheap, was virtually unheard of. Much of the rumbustiousness that seemed to have stamped itself on the first post-war generation of the college was dissipated by the gloom of depression and slump. This is not to say that the predominance of the earnest, hard-up student meant that there was a total absence of fun-loving colleagues or that no 'swells' were to be found about the college; ersatz 'Brideshead' types with sportscars and armfuls of tennis-rackets were to be found loudly monopolizing the streets and pavements of the Uplands, but they were far from being characteristic of the majority. College societies flourished, especially those connected with departments and those which gave an outlet to political feelings. It was only natural that the Socialist Society should be active, and there was always Tom Jenkins. Tom was the college's totally self-educated boilerman who fancied himself as a political philosopher and who would gather groups of students around him in the boilerhouse to discuss socialism and the ills of the world. Given the highly-charged political atmosphere of the time, it seems surprising how tolerant the students were. It was to be three decades before the college would witness the distressing scenes that greeted Dr Christian Barnard when he visited the college. In 1936 a German debating team came to Swansea, having been warned elsewhere that they would be far from welcome. They lost the debate – 'That communism is a menace to Europe' – but the behaviour of the audience was exemplary and afterwards the visitors were treated with a visit to the cinema. Such sedate behaviour was not mirrored in the comments of

'Forgotten Masterpieces' from *Dawn* (1927). *Clockwise from left*: the awesome colossus of Watkyn Thomas (1906–77), capped fourteen times for Wales between 1927 and 1933. Captain of Wales three times, he led the first Welsh XV to defeat England at Twickenham (1933); W.H. Beynon, president of the Students' Representative Council (1926–7); and Tom Jenkins, the college's 'alternative' political philosopher

John Jenkins, a Swansea solicitor, who saw the college as a hotbed of socialism and used the annual meeting of the court that year to allege that in certain departments honours degrees were being awarded on grounds of political favouritism rather than merit. He suggested that socialist students had been visited in their lodgings and given details of examination papers, while non-socialist students had been given misleading information. That there were no grounds for Jenkins's accusations and insinuations, which had arisen out of an unsubstantiated grievance of three years before, became patent and he left the court meeting with a well-deserved drubbing.

The uncertainties, austerity, and lack of dynamism in the general direction of the college during the inter-war years did not mean that good work was not carried out by the departments. Despite laboratory and teaching conditions that might be considered impossible today, firm foundations were established for the college. In chemistry, for example, although Coates and his staff were very much concerned in the earlier years with planning the laboratories and establishing teaching courses, publications dealing with researches undertaken in the department began to appear as early as 1923. With the growth in the number of postgraduate students, from three in 1922–3 to twelve eleven years later, research activity increased markedly in a number of physical and organic studies. By 1933 overall student numbers had reached a total of 125 and for the second year running Coates was complaining that 'the department was working at the limit of its capacity as regards both accommodation and staffing'. These numbers marked the pre-war peak for the department, however, and, as we have seen, were conditioned by economic forces at work beyond the college. Thereafter, numbers steadily declined until the influx of students after the war; but a consistent quality of teaching and research was maintained until national service regulations during the Second World War limited the numbers of honours students and brought about a cessation of postgraduate work.

Much the same picture may be painted of other departments. In geology, Arthur Trueman was promoted to a professorship in 1930. Over the decade he had spent in Swansea, Trueman, an inspired teacher, built the foundations of a flourishing department and research school. It was once said of him that he could always make his students achieve things that they never thought possible. Despite demands on his time that would have overwhelmed many a lesser mortal, Trueman was able, also, to make some outstanding research contributions in a variety of geological fields, particularly the palaeontology of the Liassic rocks of south Wales and south-west England, and, what was to be the primary research interest for the rest of his life, the stratigraphy of the coal measures of the area. All the while his burden of teaching – for civil engineers and metallurgists as well as degree students in geology – was exeptionally heavy, especially in the early years, when he had the help of only one assistant lecturer, Alan Stuart (1894–1983), and one technician, Trevor Marchant, the sheet-anchor of the department for fifty-three years. Nevertheless, virtually single-handedly, Trueman could still respond with enthusiasm to a request from local teachers for instruction in geography and his Saturday morning classes, leading to a certificate in the subject, became something of a local institution. It was a growing development. Despite the aggravation of accommodation problems, by 1932 a Final (Pass) Degree level course in geography had matured, Dr D. Trevor Williams, an historical geographer and Reader in Geography at Exeter, was appointed lecturer in geography; and the title of the department was changed to 'Geology and Geography'. In the following year, when

Thomas Neville George (1904–80)

Trueman took up the Chaning Wills chair of geology at Bristol, he left behind him a well-found department at Swansea.[2]

Trueman was succeeded by Dr T. Neville George, a former pupil and at the time a twenty-nine-year-old officer with the Geological Survey. One of the college's original band of eighty-nine students, George had won a Swansea senior scholarship from the grammar school at the exceptionally early age of sixteen. His original intention had been to read chemistry but he was enticed away from that subject by Trueman. While he was still an undergraduate, 'TN' as he was known from his student days published two research papers and he was the first student to gain a 'first' in geology at Swansea in 1923. With his own research lying chiefly in studies of the Carboniferous Limestone, palaeontology, and evolutionary developments, George consolidated the department and, at the same time, contributed actively to many aspects of adult education locally until his own departure to the chair of geology at Glasgow in the steps of Trueman in 1947. Possessing a puckish sense of humour, George enjoyed debate and liked nothing better than relaxing at the piano. His manner could be brisk, however, and he could occasionally be rather domineering; in Glasgow he played to the full the role of the archetypal Scots professor. Nevertheless, his students loved him. His distinction as a scholar – he was elected to the Royal Society in 1963 – his effectiveness as a teacher and his continuing interest in the college at Swansea were to mark him out as a possible contender for the principalship on the resignation of John Fulton in 1959.

In 1940 Archie Richardson was forced to resign from the headship of the department of mathematics owing to increasing ill health, the legacy of his severe First World War wounds. He retired to Cape Town, continuing there his algebraic researches for which he was elected an FRS in 1946, until shortly before his death in 1954. Throughout their exile, and for both of them it was very much an exile, the Richardsons never forgot their host of friends in Swansea, especially those with children. And during the war there was a never-ending stream of food parcels from South Africa for those whom they thought might be in need. During his tenure of the professorship Richardson had built up an honours school of algebra which was both outstanding and unique in Britain. However, the total number of honours students over the entire period of his professoriate was only thirty-two, and while Richardson laid great stress on postgraduate studies it was unfortunate that few research students came to Swansea to take advantage of his pre-eminence as an algebraist, only eight M.Sc. degrees and one Ph.D. degree being awarded up to the war. On personal grounds it was right that Richardson, a progressively sick man, should have stayed in Swansea so long, the more effectively to pursue his research; for the college, however, it was a tragedy that its lack of reputation in these days never allowed him to build up the research school that he deserved. He was followed as professor in 1941 by Dr Rowland Wilson (1895–1980), who had first joined the department as a temporary assistant lecturer twenty years before. Although honours courses in mathematics were suspended for the duration of the war, Wilson soon found his teaching being spread in a variety of directions not contemplated before.

In physics, Jenkin Evans maintained his major interest in the field of spectroscopy and instigated work in magneto-optics and in measurements on the extreme ultra-violet. An excellent lecturer, with a powerful voice in keeping with his massive build, he laid great stress on the training of students in the methods of research and a high proportion of his old pupils went on to fill positions of responsibility, among them at least five Fellows of the Royal Society (six, if one counts J.H. Beynon, who went on to become a chemist): Evan Williams, whom we have already mentioned, W.C. Price, later Wheatstone Professor of Physics at King's College, London, E.G. Bowen (1911–91), Ieuan Maddock (1917–88), and Granville Beynon, a successor from 1958 in Williams's chair at Aberystwyth, all to become scholars of international reputation. As was fitting in a metallurgical centre, Evans encouraged a great deal of work on the physical properties of alloys.

The departments of the faculty of arts, even more handicapped than those of science by the small numbers of postgraduate students and the scarcity of bibliographical and other resources for research, nevertheless succeeded in producing some excellent work. In the department of Welsh, for example, Henry Lewis published a succession of notable linguistic and philological studies. His literary colleague, Saunders Lewis, appointed to the departmental assistant lectureship in 1922 and later to become the greatest Welsh-language playwright and a first-class poet, wrote some striking works of literary history and criticism. Stephen Williams, who was to succeed Henry Lewis as professor in 1954, joined the department in 1927. Also an essayist and literary critic, Williams won for himself an enviable reputation as a teacher. While his work on medieval Welsh texts will stand the test of time, it will always be for his radio lessons on the Welsh language that he will be most widely remembered. They exemplified his true *métier*, and the immense popularity they brought him was a public acknowledgement of his sincerity and his personal concern for his students. It was through such solicitude and genuine

Physics staff and postgraduate and honours students, 27 April 1935. Seated are, *left to right*, Maurice Davidson, Leonard Wright, Professor Evans and Frank Llewellyn Jones. Frank Homeyard, the departmental technician, is at the extreme right of the first row standing. Granville Beynon is second from the left in the second row standing and Melville Hopkins, later senior lecturer in the department, is behind Beynon to the left

interest in their future – a characteristic of many university departments in these pre-expansionist days – that the emergence of many younger scholars was encouraged. Students of the calibre of T.J. Morgan (1907–86), Melville Richards (1910–73) and Simon Evans, for instance, all three professors of Welsh in later years, and Hugh Bevan, whose withdrawn manner, not relieved by his later, harrowing, wartime experiences in the north Atlantic, belied his accomplishment as a literary critic and lecturer of exceptional brilliance.

In the department of history, Ernest Hughes's blindness in no way diminished his dedication to the cause of education in the widest of spheres. His physical disabilities curtailed any urge he might have had for serious scholarship, but his infectious enthusiasm for popularizing the history of Wales extra-murally and his dedication to his students remained unabated until the end of his life. Limited as he might have been as an academic himself, Hughes was unerringly wise in the appointment of his departmental colleagues and he gathered about him a small group of distinguished staff: Glyn Roberts (1904–62), for instance, later to become registrar and then Professor of Welsh History at Bangor for all too short a time; and W.N. Medlicott (1900–88). With so small a staff, required to cover all the courses in English, Welsh and European history, there was little time for specialization, but Medlicott was already beginning to write books that were to establish him as one of Britain's leading historians of international relations – *The Congress of Berlin and After* is one example – and he achieved the notable feat of developing a 'school' of diplomatic historians among his postgraduate students. After the Second World War, Medlicott occupied the chair of history at Exeter and then, in 1953, became Stevenson Professor of International Relations in the University of London. In fact, it is remarkable how in these years before the Second World War, the arts faculty recruited a number of able young men to the lecturing staff, some of whom were to occupy distinguished chairs in the post-war period but who, because of the interruption of war-service, never made quite the same impact on Swansea that they might otherwise have done. Among those who spent some of their formative teaching years in this Swansea 'nursery' but who left during or soon after the war were Edward Thompson of classics, Angus McIntosh and Thomas 'Cobber' Taig of English, Karl Britton and W.B. Gallie of philosophy, Medlicott and Roberts of history, Hare of economics, and Richards of Welsh.

The financial constraints under which the college was forced to operate during the inter-war years allowed little in the way of physical development at Singleton. Not until 1932 was the deficit on the original building programme extinguished and by that year, with student numbers approaching their pre-war peak, the pressure on accommodation was such that urgent stop-gap efforts had to be made to meet even partial needs. Additional laboratory accommodation was provided for the two natural science departments in the abbey but this was at the expense of the rapidly expanding arts faculty and, while a palliative, was no long-term solution.

Such a makeshift arrangement must not be interpreted as suggesting any lack of planning. It was an expediency forced on the college through lack of money. Plenty of thought had been given to *planning* and, as student numbers increased, there was little prevision that the expansion might be short-lived. Already in 1930 the college had appointed, as development architects, a local firm, C.S. Thomas and Herbert Jones, to advise on a permanent building scheme on the land immediately in front of the temporary pavilions. The most desperate requirement was additional accommodation for the library. Within the year, the college had received an outline development plan including a perspective sketch and plans of a 'library block'. But there was no money and no action could be taken. Nevertheless, a new permanent library remained the college's priority. The original library facilities had been envisaged as providing for a college with a student population stabilized at some 350 or 400 at the end of twelve years. Now there were prospects of a student body of 750. Already conditions were becoming intolerable; cramped and unsuitable areas had to be shelved, and the growth of the student population led to such extreme overcrowding that even additional accommodation found in the abbey was proving insufficient.

The university had agreed that an allocation of £1,000 which it had been making annually towards the reduction of the capital deficit should be continued for the time being as the nucleus of a college building fund, but it was obvious that most of the £40,000 estimated as the cost of a new library building would have to be found outside public grant-aid. In the teeth of stiff opposition – there was a strong body of opinion opposed to the development as singularly ill-timed in a period of recession – an appeal for funds was launched but it met with a variable reception. The Corporation, when approached for a contribution, made it abundantly clear that a previous donation of £2,000 in respect of the playing fields in 1926 had been made on the distinct understanding that it would be its last contribution to the college, and the new request caused the town council to raise the whole question of its representation on the college council. But if financial support was not forthcoming from the Corporation and if relations with that body, cordial as they might appear on the surface, were becoming increasingly strained, the college pressed ahead with its appeal on the basis of private invitations. By June 1934 the amount in hand, or promised to the fund, stood at £18,675, the largest single donation (£1,000) coming through the good offices of the college's president, Sir George Barstow, from the Anglo-Persian Oil Company Limited. Substantial sums came, too, from many of those local industrialists who had always been open-handed in their support of the college – and not-inconsiderable amounts, bearing in mind the level of salaries at the time, were contributed by members of the college staff.

Although the appeal yielded very much less than was needed, and far less than had been hoped for, the college decided to press on with the library project on the basis of a cost-limit of £34,000. A limited competition was held to appoint an architect, W.G. Newton, Professor of Architecture at the Royal College of Art, being nominated as assessor by the president of the RIBA. As competitors, the latter also nominated six architects practising in Wales and six from outside the principality.

The commission was awarded to Verner Owen Rees (1886–1966), a London architect of Welsh extraction, in December 1934. Rees had already been successful in a number of architectural competitions and was to go on to be outstandingly so. He had – in partnership – designed the London School of Hygiene and Tropical Medicine in Bloomsbury and the War Memorial at Soissons. Four years earlier, he had come third to Percy Thomas – on this occasion an unsuccessful competitor – in the competition for the design of a new guildhall in Swansea. As required in the conditions of the competition, Rees's scheme was designed to form part of a future college centre with buildings for the faculty of arts and an assembly hall linked by a series of grand terraces.

By September 1937 the building, which in its scaffolded and unfinished state had, according to ever-ready local complaint, been far too long a 'blot upon a gracious scene', was available to readers and was officially opened by the Duke of Kent on 19 October. As the librarian pointed out at the end of the new library's first session, 'To anyone acquainted with the Arts building, and the noise which surged continually around the old Library, it is unnecessary to stress the advantages enjoyed by readers in the new building; but one point should be noted – the marked improvement in quietness and dignity of demeanour which has been the students' response to the new conditions'. For over a quarter of a century, with student numbers increasing from 550 to over 2,000 and with pressures on reading accommodation latterly becoming even more critical than they had been before its construction, Verner Rees's simple neo-classical creation, this 'very notable building', as the local newspaper described it, performed sterling service for the college. But libraries are not simply bricks and mortar, nor even just the books that they contain. One must not forget the dedicated direction of the library service by Miss Olive Busby, for almost forty years (1921–59) the college's indefatigably energetic, dedicated – and to students and even some staff at first meeting – fearsomely formidable librarian.

The unsympathetic response of the Corporation to the plea from the college for some degree of financial support for the new library scheme stemmed from an unfortunate

THE ARCHITECTS' JOURNAL for January 13, 1938

UNIVERSITY COLLEGE LIBRARY, SWANSEA

D E S I G N E D   B Y   V E R N E R   O .   R E E S

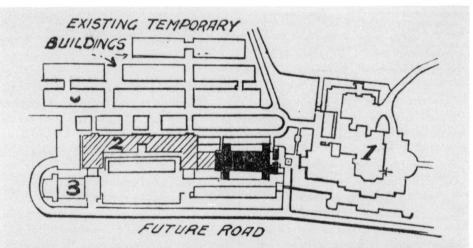

EXISTING TEMPORARY BUILDINGS

FUTURE ROAD

KEY PLAN, showing the Library in relation to the Abbey, and the future Arts Department and Great Hall as the scheme progresses to the west ultimately screening the whole of the temporary buildings, shown in rear of the new blocks. Block in black is the library; No. 1, Singleton Abbey ; 2, future arts department; and 3, future great hall.

Verner Rees's proposals for a new library, arts building and great hall, 1935

misunderstanding that had arisen even before Sibly had left Swansea. When the Corporation originally made over to the college part of the Singleton estate in 1923, some fifteen acres of land on the western side of Sketty Lane was given for use as playing fields. Because of the college's other capital commitments on the construction of the 'semi-permanent' buildings at Singleton – as the 'temporary' science pavilions increasingly came to be called with the passage of time – it had not been possible to develop the recreational area at the time of the gift. Indeed, in 1923 the college had been under the firm impression that the actual laying out of the playing fields would be the Corporation's responsibility.

Nothing having been done by 1926 and the sporting needs of the student population, by now over 450 in strength, being inadequately catered for by the temporary facilities provided by the Corporation in Singleton Park, the college approached the Corporation to confirm its intentions. It was dismayed to learn that there was no question of the Corporation handing over the playing-fields site 'level and sewn with grass ready for playing on'. The most the Corporation was prepared to do was to remove trees and undergrowth from the 'swampy and unreclaimed' land and raise the surface to a suitable level. This, it was emphasized, was all that the Corporation had ever intended; the provision of pitches was entirely a matter for the college to meet out of its own resources. Among some members of the college council, at least, there was a strong feeling that the college had been misled. The Corporation eventually recognized that the resolution governing its original gift of land was ambiguous and open to differing interpretations. It, therefore, agreed to make the college an *ex gratia* payment of £2,000 towards the total cost of some £4,000 for laying out the playing fields – adding the pointed codicil that it was to be distinctly understood 'that no further request for financial assistance is to be made by the university college in respect of this or any of the matters included in the settlement made in July 1923'.

Relations between the corporate manifestations of 'town' and 'gown', which had once seemed so cordial and productive, had now reached their lowest point and it was to be many years and the coming of a new principal before there was any true meeting of minds again. There were many on the town council who thought that more than enough had been done for a college that lay firmly outside its control and direction. That there lingered in civic circles resentment at the college's independence and that, in its own turn, the college council exhibited a marked insensitivity to the town council's viewpoint cannot be doubted. But these were failings sharpened increasingly by the potent factor of politics. For while the Corporation was distinguished for its considerable, if paternalistic, civic pride, there was a widening division between what was an increasingly Labour-dominated town council after 1933 and what was seen as the 'employer controlled' college council – 'that council of industrialists', forty per cent of whose members were intimately connected with commerce and industry. The bitter social assumptions and conflicts of the time, unconnected though they were with the development of the college, came to dominate the relationship of the two bodies in spite of many individual attempts, especially those of 'Tee Jay' Rees, to bridge the gulf.

Before the thirties were over it had become a gulf that gave rise to a considerable degree of bitterness. In the meantime the college continued with its arrangements for developing the playing fields. A grant of £4,000 from the UGC in 1928 towards the cost of a sports pavilion encouraged the college to look rather more imaginatively at the development of recreational facilities. In 1930 the construction of the pavilion was put in hand to the design of a local architect, Glendinning Moxham (1865–1946), famous for Swansea's covered market, the town's pride and joy until the blitz of 1941, the Glynn Vivian Art Gallery, and the Bristol Channel Yacht Club. At the same time, a rugby pitch was laid out under the supervision of Arthur Fordham (1888–1978), the college's lecturer in civil engineering. By the early summer of 1932, when the sports pavilion was opened, two football pitches had been laid out, and in addition a temporary cricket pitch and three temporary tennis courts had been prepared, with the provision of four permanent tennis courts sanctioned as the next development.

Much of the incentive for developing these sports facilities – and, indeed, four-fifths of the capital needed for the sports pavilion – came directly from the UGC which, on its visitation to the college in 1929, was dismayed by the lack of recreational resources available for students. When the committee next came to Swansea five years later, in April 1934, the picture had dramatically changed. By now there were three grass and four hard tennis courts, together with a hockey pitch and a netball pitch as well as the other games pitches that had been laid earlier. No doubt it was due, at least in part, to the superiority of these facilities for training that the college rugby team achieved renown by reaching the finals of the Universities Athletic Union Championships on five successive occasions in the 1930s and a clutch of brilliant players was produced. In 1935, when Swansea devastated New Zealand, the whole of the town side's three-quarter line came from the college, past and present, with Willie Davies at outside-half. These were days when there were names to conjure with: Claude Davey, Idwal Rees, the 6 ft 3 in, 15 stone Watcyn Thomas, and the immortal Haydn Tanner, all capped for Wales on innumerable occasions and all captains of the Welsh team.

The thirties were marked over much of Europe by an enthusiasm for outdoor recreation and, with the German emphasis on sport and physical fitness very much in mind, in 1936 the government set up a National Advisory Council for Physical Fitness with a budget of £2,000,000 to try to meet the deficiencies in capital provision for physical training throughout the country. It was in keeping with the general mood for physical culture that, in the same year, the UGC provided another special capital grant of £3,500 towards the cost of building and equipping the sorely needed facility of a gymnasium at Sketty Lane. This was completed, once more to Moxham's designs, by 1938 when Vernon Jones was appointed the college's first full-time 'instructor of physical training and swimming' in view of 'the urgent need for improving the physical education of the students'. In 1938, too, the college, again through the good offices of the UGC, received a grant of £7,500 from the National Fitness Council towards the cost of a swimming bath and two squash courts adjacent to the pavilion. This project, though, was beset with problems. With water seeping down from the allotments further up Sketty Lane drainage was difficult and until Fordham solved the predicament the swimming bath remained nothing more than a large hole. Not until the summer of 1940 was the bath completed and before long it had to be closed down for the duration of the war; it was not to be reopened until 1947. The playing fields, over which there had been so much contention and on which so much care was expended, were requisitioned by the military for an army encampment, while the pavilion and gymnasium became home for the officers and men of 239 AA battery of the Royal Artillery, manning the emplacements by the Mumbles Road.

The establishment of the National Fitness Council and the development of sporting and recreational facilities at Sketty Lane had encouraged, in some minds, the possibility of siting at the college a National Physical Training College of a kind that the government proposed setting up in England. Not only was it felt that this would cater for the 'new need of the times' but it would help in the drive against unemployment by diverting students from training as teachers to training as physical-fitness instructors. In

One attempt to alleviate the canker of long-term unemployment was the Summer Camp, which gave the unemployed the possibility of a seaside or country holiday. The first Llangennith holiday camp for the unemployed was organized by Swansea students during 5–19 July 1935 at a cost of about £110, with equipment borrowed from students at Cardiff. It gave 120 men a week's holiday and was a great success. The student at the extreme right of the group is D. Andrew Davies, student president in 1936–7

this the Corporation was at one with the college, but nothing came of the scheme. The English college went to Loughborough but nothing came to Wales.

The lack of hostel accommodation for male students exercised the college more than the problem of sports facilities. If the judgement of *The Times Educational Supplement* (21 November 1936) was accepted, it was a need common to all the Welsh colleges. Swansea might, in principle, echo the paper's plea that 'few of the real advantages of a university training can be obtained if students have to travel to and fro by train to college and meet their tutors only in fleeting visits to the classroom or laboratory', but past experience suggested that such accommodation was not popular and the current economic situation was not likely to make it more so. In any case, it was a luxury that the college had no means of affording without some handsome benefaction – which was far from likely. Nevertheless, even if the college could not yet provide hostel accommodation for men, it could try to furnish more adequate social and amenity facilities at Singleton itself. Mention has already been made of how the students' union made use of spare rooms in Beck Hall and equipped them with oddments of second-hand furniture bought cheaply from local dealers. Social functions were held in the refectory or in the town, and Principal Edwards, in particular, recognized how necessary it was for the students to have a centre of their own which could be a focal point for their activities and help to increase the *esprit de corps* of the college. The students themselves had first raised the cry for a union building in the early 1920s, but little constructive effort was made by them to achieve their purpose until 1934, when a special levy was made upon the amalgamation fee to provide an annual contribution to a building fund. Even with this income, allocations from the union's own general funds and a special subscription list, it was calculated in 1936 that sufficient capital would not have been accumulated by the students themselves for at least twenty years. It was not unnatural, therefore, that the students should look longingly at the original library building when it was vacated in 1937 and suggest that it would provide adequate union accommodation until permanent purpose-built quarters were eventually made available. With all the other pressures on accommodation at Singleton it was not something on which the college was likely to see eye to eye with the students, and in due course the old library building was turned over to teaching purposes.

At last, in 1939, the college council decided to proceed with the construction of the first stage of a union building at Singleton to the south of the 'lion' entrance gates, having secured a grant of £6,000 for the project from the UGC. Verner Rees, who had earlier so successfully disarmed possible criticism by his sympathetic treatment of the new library adjacent to the abbey, was appointed architect. His proposal was for a complex costing about £26,000, the first stage of which would include common rooms for students and staff, a students' union council room and offices, games facilities, and residential quarters for a steward. Owing to the war, however, the whole project had to be postponed. It was never revived.

The cost of the first stage of the abortive union building was estimated at about £13,000. This meant that, allowing for the grant from the UGC, some £7,000 remained to be found. What encouraged the college to initiate the project was the arrangement which had come into force in 1938 by which Swansea was enabled to receive a quarter-share of the constituent colleges' allocation of the Welsh Church Act funds, the release of which had been secured by Act of Parliament two years earlier. The university, with the co-operation of the colleges, had agreed that the government stock accruing to them from the redemption of Church tithes following the disestablishment of the Anglican Church in Wales, should be distributed as a capital sum. This was to be devoted primarily to objects bearing directly on student welfare, such as hostels for men students, financial aid to poor students, capital payments, where necessary, to existing hostels for women, and, in general, the provision of student amenities.

The excess of cost of the first stage of the union building over the UGC's capital allocation would, therefore, have been met from the college's share of the proceeds of the Tithe Redemption Stock which, when it was finally distributed to the college in 1948, amounted to nearly £114,000. In addition to the capital sums available from the

Verner Rees's perspective drawing of the abortive students' union building at Singleton, 1939

redemption of the Church tithes, there was also revenue accruing from the capitular estates transferred to the university under the Welsh Church Acts which in the 1940s and 1950s brought to the college a not inconsiderable sum of about £1,500. Again, this money had to be used primarily for the welfare of students and has been a useful support for developments such as the college's health service, which was instituted in 1962 with the appointment of the college's first medical officer.

If the college council, in the problem years of the 1920s and 1930s, was exercised about the need to provide adequate social and amenity facilities to enable students to enjoy the benefit of a university education to the full, there were many members of staff, themselves in much closer personal, everyday contact with individual students, who had this concern borne in upon them even more deeply. To some, face to face with the uncertainties and perplexities of a comparatively unsophisticated student body, it seemed that the council was not doing enough and was dragging its feet in the whole area of student welfare. The development of the playing fields, important as it was, touched only one aspect of the problem. The seemingly intractable issues of providing an adequate tutorial system, sustaining students intellectually and socially, securing sufficient facilities for both social and leisure activities, of the underlying lack of money, seemed to some to militate against the well-being of the students and their academic progress. The harsh problem of graduate employment merely served to etch more deeply the difficulties, the doubts and the tensions that sprang from them.

It was not long before the inborn stresses and strains began to tell, in spite of, or, perhaps because of, the close society that existed at Singleton. In 1936, Kenneth Rees, the lecturer in biology, frustrated by what he considered to be the continued lethargy of the college council, submitted to the university court a memorandum proposing the establishment of a permanent court committee to inquire into the academic, social and physical needs of the students of the university. He felt that the absence of a tutorial system and the lack of hostel facilities for men students meant that many of the less tangible but none the less important features of university life were lost. His approach, however, honest as it was, was weakened by overstatement; and his suggestion, in what was essentially a public document, that the lack of such facilities severely limited the development of a large proportion of students, inhibited their cultivation of 'social graces' and, thus, told against their employment prospects was, in the minds of many, both unfortunate and mischievous.

Rees had intended his document to be of general application throughout the university but it was immediately interpreted as a personal indictment of the situation in Swansea. The corporate pride of the college council was severely hurt. While it recognized that some of his arguments rang true it was dismayed that Rees had aired his concerns in public and he was rounded upon for not having presented his paper to the college's own governing bodies first. Rees had, of course, acted injudiciously and no doubt the college authorities, imbued with the almost proprietorial feelings that characterized the councils of most provincial universities and colleges at that time, were harsh in their condemnation of him for having apparently brought the college's name into disrepute. But perhaps, in the event, his action did accelerate the programme for improving student sporting facilities, even if, because of continuing financial difficulties, little could be done about tutorial provision or residential accommodation.

Although it was no 'storm in a tea-cup', the domestic affair of Kenneth Rees in 1936 paled into insignificance in comparison with a *cause célèbre* which brought the college considerable public notoriety at much the same time. In September, three leading members of Plaid Genedlaethol Cymru, Saunders Lewis, its current president, the Revd Lewis Valentine, a Baptist minister from Llandudno, and D.J. Williams, a schoolmaster-author from Fishguard, attempted to set fire to a Royal Air Force bombing school at Pen-y-Berth, near Pen-rhos in the Llŷn peninsula. Local protest at the proposal to build the installation had been vocal and a great deal of play had been made of the physical and cultural harm that it was alleged would result to a traditional farming community in this heartland of Wales. The three thus saw their action as a grand politico-cultural gesture, devoid, in their terms, of criminality and, setting out to draw greater public attention to their cause and to attract increased sympathy for it, they promptly gave themselves up to the local police. The failure of a jury at the Caernarfon winter assizes in October to agree on a verdict led the government to play into their hands when it decided to have the case against Lewis, Valentine and Williams reheard at the Old Bailey. It was an overreaction in what was already a highly charged situation and caused immense uproar in Wales from men and women of all parties.

Saunders Lewis, already a celebrated writer who, ironically, had had a distinguished career in the First World War, had been a member of staff of the Welsh department at Swansea since 1922. The small community of the college – in 1936–7 there were 629 students and fifty-nine teaching staff – was as riven over the episode as the rest of Welsh society. The college council took the only step that, in those days, it saw as properly open to it, since Saunders Lewis had been charged with a criminal offence, and in

Saunders Lewis (1893–1985)

October it suspended him from his lectureship. This in itself, though unexceptional, was precipitate and, in the emotional maelstrom of the episode, immediately provoked a storm of protest, with petitions on Lewis's behalf being organized among staff, students and outside organizations. In November, following the college's refusal to reinstate Lewis, the students were called upon to strike for two days. On a ballot, however, the proposal was overwhelmingly defeated by 427 votes to 110. As the *Western Mail* (26 November 1936) put it with evident glee, the vote had 'served the useful purpose of making known the feelings of the College as a whole'. This was a premature assessment.

In January Lewis, Valentine and Williams were, not surprisingly, found guilty at the Old Bailey after refusing to give evidence in English, and were sent to prison for nine months. A month after the trial, the college council, at the end of a two-hour meeting mainly given over to the question of Saunders Lewis's future, decided that as from 19 January, the date of the verdict at the Old Bailey, his appointment with the college was terminated. The college's legal advice had been 'that Mr. Saunders Lewis, by his own act and as the result of his conviction for that act, ceased to be in the employment of the University College on January 19, since he has rendered it impossible for him to carry out his duties'. In other words, by his action and his subsequent imprisonment Lewis was in breach of his contract and, in effect, had removed himself from his post. To Lewis's supporters the argument was a specious one. To them he was no criminal, for his act had been a symbolic one. He had been *dismissed* by a council composed of 'ignoramuses and traitors . . . the most contemptible lot of ruffians you could possibly imagine' (J. Walter Jones quoted in the *Western Mail*, 24 May 1937).

Legally, the council had no doubt acted perfectly properly. Technically, Lewis *had* removed himself from his teaching post. There could be no argument about this. But the council had acted with considerable insensitivity and in striving to keep itself aloof from politics – and there is no question that this was what Sir George Barstow, the president of the college, was attempting to do – it found itself pulled into a political arena, bitterly divided over the Nationalist cause and the recent sequence of events. The council, however, now went further, and declaring Lewis's post vacant, let it be known that it had decided to fill it forthwith. Its intention was to avoid further calls for his reinstatement when he came out of prison. But, as was only to be expected, this action only served to bring upon itself an even greater outburst of emotion and sympathy on Lewis's behalf. Especially was this to be expected when the council's action was contrasted with that of D.J. Williams's local education authority in Anglicized Pembrokeshire which allowed the schoolmaster-author to return to his teaching post. Petitions in Lewis's support poured in to the council, while the atmosphere surrounding the affair was not calmed by one, normally most docile, colleague who roused a public meeting by raging that 'his blood boiled when he thought of the rotten and putrid thing that had been perpetrated in Swansea' (Stephen J. Williams quoted in the *Western Mail*, 17 February 1937). But not all Lewis's colleagues took his part, and some distinguished academics in his own field remained hostile, among them his head of department, Henry Lewis, with his own stark memories of the Somme and Passchendaele. To some, Lewis had patently brought the name of the college and the stature of Welsh scholarship into disrepute. Others, though he had never intruded his politics into his teaching, saw his political activities as an abuse of his academic position. None of this criticism was relieved by his reputation for a somewhat cavalier attitude towards his academic responsibilities in a college where many of his colleagues worked so unremittingly hard.

Outside the gates of the college, feelings were as mixed as within. There were some like Percy Morris, a Labour alderman and local politician of great power and influence in the 1930s and '40s, who, concerned about the element of double punishment involved, could not understand the college council's attitude and questioned how Lewis's 'efficiency as a lecturer has been impaired by what has happened'. He persuaded the Corporation to ask the college to postpone its notice to Lewis, defer the new appointment, and in the meanwhile 'endeavour to gauge public feeling by convening a special meeting of the Court of Governors, representing all sections of the community associated with the University'.

To some degree Morris, a moderate – he was an official of the Railway Clerks' Union – and a Congregationalist lay preacher, was motivated by an altruistic desire to see full justice done to Saunders Lewis. There was no love lost between the Labour Party and Plaid Genedlaethol Cymru, however, and Morris's skilful deployment of the Corporation by an almost three-to-one majority – supported by all his Labour colleagues – was, not altogether unjustifiably, seen by the officers of the college as a disingenuous political move to discomfit the college council. Certainly this was the view of Lewis Jones, the college's senior vice-president and Liberal-National MP for Swansea West since 1931. Lewis Jones, a considerable figure in local politics, whose seat Percy Morris had contested in 1935 and was to win in the landslide Labour victory of 1945, had been closely involved in the negotiations with the Corporation over the playing fields affair a decade earlier and, rightly or wrongly, as a representative of industry himself, he saw political antipathy to this influential element of the college council guiding the Corporation's attitude.

It was not altogether surprising that when the college council met in March it should be unmoved by petitions, or by what it regarded as the improper interference of the Corporation. Lewis's supporters, by the virulence of their campaign, had put the possibility of any compromise completely out of the question. He was not reinstated and Melville Richards, research assistant lecturer in the department of Welsh, was appointed to fill his vacancy. Impolitically, this was done without public advertisement, an action neither calculated to calm the storm nor to ease the future and, ultimately, tragic career of Richards. The sound and fury continued on their course, but an unseemly public meeting at Swansea and an attempt to have the affair reopened at the university court failed in their objective.

Although scars remained and recriminations reverberated for many years, the college seems to have returned to the even tenor of its everyday life very quickly and, even if it was never forgotten, the affair soon became an unhappy event of the past at Singleton. Perhaps if Gilbertson had still been president of the college the whole matter might have been handled differently, for much of the esteem in which he was held by both management and labour in industry was due to his extraordinary powers as a conciliator. Bearing in mind the powerful divisions in Welsh society that the burnings at Pen-y-Berth created, however, even Gilbertson's talents would have been sorely stretched. As it was, he had died on 8 October 1929 from diphtheria contracted during a motoring holiday in Romania. His death at the age of fifty-six, and at the prime of life, was an incalculable loss to the college.

What struck most observers about Gilbertson – those close to him, like Lewis Jones, and others like Professor Coates, less close but with a clear perception of what Gilbertson had set himself to achieve for the college – was his combination of high human ideals and far-sighted business acumen. From 1918 to 1925 he was chairman of the South Wales Siemens Steel Association and thus a central figure in the steel and tinplate industry. It was owing to his influence and the esteem in which he was held that the college received the support that it did from local industry. Gilbertson was, of course, fortunate in his time in that the rise of foreign industrial competition and the apparent inadequacies of British technological expertise had at last implanted a local recognition of the need for greater provision of higher scientific education. Nevertheless, it remains true that it was due to his influence and reputation that the interest and support of his fellow industrialists were captured, where earlier pioneers like John Jones Jenkins and Richard Martin had failed. It was thus only natural that when Clyne Castle was acquired as a hall of residence in 1955 it should be renamed Neuadd Gilbertson after the man who, more than any other, had been instrumental in the founding of the college.

Gilbertson was succeeded as president by Sir George Barstow. A former senior civil servant in the Treasury, where he had risen to be Controller of Supply Services, Barstow had at one time been the Treasury official responsible for that department's relations with the UGC. He, therefore, brought to the presidency of the college a profound knowledge of the operation of university finances at the highest level and an understanding of the 'civil servant's mind'. He brought, too, a degree of business flair for, since his retirement from the civil service, he had made a second career in finance and industry. His prime interest was the Prudential Assurance Company, of which he

Sir George Barstow (1874–1966), president of
the college 1930–55

was to become chairman in 1941; but he was also involved in a wide range of other national concerns, such as the Midland Bank and the Anglo-Persian Oil Company (of which he was a government director from 1927 to 1946), and, more locally, the firms of Vivian and Sons and W. Gilbertson and Company. He was well rooted in the business world of London and the industrial and commercial life of south Wales. He was able to continue to draw on the support of Swansea's industrial and mercantile community, therefore, and was likely to carry on Gilbertson's work.

Perhaps as a former civil servant, he did not possess the flexibility of approach to problems that had characterized his predecessor but he had an acute sense of judgement and a deep interest in higher education – he was deputy chairman of the court of the University of London. One cannot emphasize too much the extent to which the early years of Barstow's presidency were a period of disheartening difficulty in terms of finance; but the cautious policy that both he and Edwards pursued at least allowed the college to consolidate its position and reputation, however much a more adventurous policy might have been desired by others. It was not until the later and more buoyant years of the decade that a more positive degree of physical and academic development became possible. But even as the college seemed less chronically crippled by financial shortage, and the chance of significant growth seemed more than a chimera, the looming clouds of war grew darker and any future at all became more problematic.

The nature of the political menace in Europe had been brought home to the college staff in an immediate and personal way in 1934. The persecution and displacement of academics from German universities following the rise of Nazism was alleviated in a small way by the welcome – if not always warm – which those who were able to leave Germany received in Britain. As early as 1933 a fund, administered through the Academic Assistance Council, had been opened to place academic refugees in British universities and through its aid a large percentage of the 170 or so displaced scholars who came to Britain found temporary shelter to continue their research and teaching. The staff at Swansea were consistently handsome in their support of the scheme and through their efforts Professor Otto Piper, an eminent Protestant theologian and the successor to Karl Barth's chair at Münster, was able to come to the department of philosophy for a brief sojourn of two years from 1934 to 1936 as a guest of the senate, before he moved on to Bangor and thence to the United States where he ended his days as a professor at Princeton.

The outbreak of the Second World War in September 1939 had less immediate effect than one might think. For some time, preparations had been in hand against air-raids by cleaning out the abbey cellars to serve as shelters and building a bunker and ARP station nearby. Universities were asked to provide their own ARP and were given a fifty per cent grant to meet the cost. Harold Jenkins, the College's senior finance clerk, became a senior Air Raid Warden and Incident Officer at HQ, Swansea with responsibility for the college and the surrounding area, and E.E. Ayling of chemistry was appointed the senior Gas Identification Officer for Swansea. A unit of the Local Defence Volunteers – later known as the Home Guard – was set up at the college; the unit was virtually an extension of the metallurgy department, with Professor Dannatt, exiled to Swansea from Imperial College, initially in command and Robert Higgins as his second-in-command until the latter eventually took over. An Air Training Squadron, too, was established under the professional control of Wing Commander W.C. Mitchell, but with Professor W.D. Thomas and Thomas Taig also very much in evidence. By 1942 it became a requirement that most men students of military age had to belong to one organization or the other but from their inception both activities were popular and attracted enthusiastic support from students, many of whom would be facing the realities of service life in all too short a time.

The Home Guard at Singleton, *c.* 1944

In the first session of the War a Joint Recruiting Board was set up with the Ministry of Labour to assess the suitability of students, not covered by reserved occupation schemes, for commissions in the forces or other forms of national service; and a number of students were interviewed by the ministry's Director of Personnel himself, C.P. Snow. Miss Mossman (d. 1971), the college's academic clerk, acted as secretary to the board in addition to her normal duties. In spite of this she still found time to enrol as a Red Cross Auxiliary.

For much of the 1939–40 session, the work of the college continued normally; and even the apparently interminable construction of the swimming bath and squash courts was allowed to be completed. Gradually, however, virtually all postgraduate work came to a halt and by October 1940 the twenty-four students present at the beginning of the previous session were reduced to a mere six. The pre-war problems of graduate employment disappeared almost overnight, most of the physical and applied science graduates being taken into scientific work of national importance. Indeed, the demand for scientific workers became so pressing that by 1943 a proportion of first-year honours students were also being required to undertake such work before completing their degree courses.

At the undergraduate level, two significant changes took place in the complexion of the student population. In the last session before the war, the total number of full-time undergraduate students was 460, but by 1944 this had dropped to 303. The internal make-up of these bare figures also altered considerably. While in 1938 there had been significantly more arts students than science students, by 1944 the balance was completely changed. In 1938, too, there were more than four men to every woman in the college, but by the last year of the war, this proportion dropped to less than two to one:

	Arts		Pure Science*		Applied Science		Total
	Men	Women	Men	Women	Men	Women	
1938–9	216	66	81	16	81	–	460
1939–40	189	62	79	19	94	–	443
1940–1	109	66	73	20	91	–	359
1941–2	81	59	94	22	97	–	353
1942–3	67	55	73	25	110	–	330
1943–4	53	59	68	28	89	–	297
1944–5	48	76	62	29	87	1	303

(* The figures for pure science include the handful of students who took first-year science courses before proceeding to medical studies.)

The second change that took place during the war related to the period of study. It was found possible, without any unacceptable lowering of standards, to permit students to complete a degree in a year less than the peacetime degree regulations required, provided they undertook nine months' service in the armed forces or on work of national importance.

Despite the curtailment of postgraduate work, the shortening of degree courses and the apparent reduction in student numbers, the college had to contend with serious staffing difficulties as members of the staff joined the forces or were seconded to government departments. Already by the end of the first year of the war, eight members of the teaching staff had been given leave of absence while on national service. The first to be released was Glyn Roberts, who was recruited at the outbreak of war into the new Ministry of Supply, where he rose rapidly through successive grades of the service to the highly responsible post of Deputy Head of the Anglo-American Raw Materials Board in Washington. Professor Dennison was drafted to the staff of the War Cabinet only a few months after his appointment to the chair of economics, and Kenneth Rees was seconded to the Board of Trade. In January 1940 Norman Hartshorne, with an MC from the Great War, was appointed a staff captain in the army chemical warfare section. After service abroad in East Africa and India, he eventually returned to the college as a lieutenant-colonel. Albert Devonald was another; a clerk in the registry, he volunteered for the Royal Artillery on the outbreak of war and ended it as a captain in the Ghurka Regiment, having been mentioned in dispatches. These were only the first to be engaged in some form of emergency service; by 1945 one-third of the total complement of the teaching staff – as well as members of the registry and ancillary departmental staff – had been absent from the college in some form of national service for the whole or a substantial part of the war. No member of staff lost his life but twenty-eight students or former students were killed and are commemorated on a memorial plaque in the library.

As Ernest Hughes pointed out in 1944, the depletion in student numbers hardly affected the acute staffing difficulties created by the war. Some relief was obtained as early as 1939 through the appointment of temporary assistant lecturers to replace those who were absent, and this method of reducing the teaching load of the remaining permanent staff was continued throughout the hostilities. Even in the darkest years of the war, up to 1943, teaching still went on as well as possible, and, although the chief contribution of individual members of staff and graduates to the war effort was made away from Swansea, some significant research work continued to be carried out at Singleton.

Accommodation was at a premium throughout the war. If there was a virtual cessation of postgraduate work and a contraction of the length of first degree courses and the numbers taking them, there was a flurry of activity in other areas. Immediately on the outbreak of war, there was an influx of visitors evacuated to Swansea from other institutions in areas regarded as more vulnerable to enemy air-attack. In September 1939 the chemistry laboratories and parts of the physics and metallurgy departments were largely taken over by the Department of Explosives Research of Woolwich Arsenal (later the Armaments Research Department) under the direction of Sir Robert Robertson, the former government chemist, with an initial staff of about seventy, which later rose to over 150. If the presence of this major government department strained the available accommodation, the situation was made all the more difficult by the need, from 1940 onwards, to provide hospitality for about 250 students from the metallurgy department of the Royal School of Mines at Imperial College and from the department of engineering at University College, London. These university departments remained at Singleton until 1943 and 1944 respectively, while the Armaments Research Department stayed on until 1946.

The reception of these exiles not only involved the provision of accommodation, creating special problems in chemistry, for example, but also entailed a sharing of

A wartime college hockey team and University of Wales Intercollegiate Champions in 1941–2. The variety of sports gear emphasizes war conditions, while two of the players are students of University College, London. The captain, Gilbert Bennett, *centre*, also captained the college tennis team and the university teams in both sports. Student president in 1943–4, he was a member of the education department and faculty, 1973–83

facilities which gave rise to unprecedented complications. None the less, the college and its guests settled down together cordially. A firm relationship was formed with the Armaments Research Department, and a happy consequence of its time in Swansea was that when it vacated the college in 1946 it left behind a number of temporary buildings which it had erected in the 'Grove' at Singleton. These were acquired by the college for £1,235 and were used to provide much needed additional accommodation for the faculty of arts, the departments of chemistry and biology, and for student purposes. In metallurgy there was a very happy fusion with the visitors, led initially by Sir Harold Carpenter of Imperial College, Charles Edwards's old chief and one of the science visitors of 1919, who was tragically drowned in Clyne Valley following a heart attack in September 1940. The college traditionally concentrated on ferrous metals, the School of Mines with its imperial commitments, on non-ferrous metals. Teaching could, therefore, be complemented and the London students entered fully into the life of the college, both socially and on the playing fields. Many of them stayed over in their lodgings, which had greatly increased because of the influx, during the vacations, causing some friendly jealousy because of the extra 'stripes' they got for Home Guard and Air Squadron duties and, not less so, because of their greater availability for the local girls.

Social life in the college thrived. Dances were popular and societies were well attended – especially the political clubs – but, because of the blackout and the danger of bombing, the latter were usually held during the lunch hour and the former after matches in the afternoon. The evenings and nights for many meant fire-watching. Beck Hall was understandably a popular venue for this but the gilt disappeared from the gingerbread if breakfast followed with Miss Wilkinson, the redoubtable warden, who might seek opinions of Pre-Raphaelite art or Eastern philosophy while the volunteer fire-watchers struggled with their tiny ration of over-crisp bacon. The college escaped unscathed from the Swansea blitzes and only one student was injured on college property – an engineer from University College, London – who was badly burned trying to defuse an incendiary bomb at Beck Hall.

Although, in most respects, there was a contraction of the normal work of the college during the war, there was enlargement in some areas. In 1942, in the light of the need for radar specialists, the government asked the college to participate in its Radio Bursary Scheme – the Hankey Scheme – and the normal courses of study in physics were expanded to meet the needs of the special syllabus. Organized by Leonard Wright, in conjunction with the department of engineering and with equipment loaned by the government, the courses were so successful that they were continued to the final (pass) degree stage as a course in electrical communications and in 1943 the number of entrants doubled.

Courses were also offered to servicemen in various branches of the armed forces as part of the work of the Regional Committee for Education in HM Forces, of which Edwin Drew was the secretary. A number of departments were involved in this work but most of the load of organizing the classes naturally fell on the education and extra-mural departments. In 1943 and 1944 special residential courses were organized at Beck Hall for Canadian servicemen on leave and, in the same years, two special courses for British army officers were held, designed to provide a background and training in conducting discussion groups. At the same time as it was helping to undertake this special work, the department of extra-mural studies, which tragically lost its dynamic senior tutor, P.S. Thomas, in 1941, was still very much involved in its normal activities. Although classes were obviously very much reduced in number, especially in the winters of 1941 and 1942, actual attendances at the classes remained surprisingly high in view of the problems of bombing and blackout. In 1941–2, the most difficult period of the war for Swansea, it was still possible to attract 458 students to the eleven tutorial classes and the fourteen sessional classes that were organized. The day schools held at the college during these years proved to be popular, too, and subjects such as 'German Nazism' and 'Science in Everyday Life' brought in large numbers of enthusiastic participants. As the tide of war began to turn in 1942–3 with the Allied victory in north Africa, the relief of Stalingrad and the capture of Guadalcanal, a new spirit of cautious confidence began to emerge in Britain and it is interesting to note, among the day-school topics for that year, the subject, 'Economic Reconstruction in Europe'.

Among the more popular books of the earlier part of the war were Sir Charles Oman's *Memories of Victorian Oxford* and G.B. Grundy's *Fifty-five Years at Oxford*, which doubtless offered a retreat from the discomfort and danger of the present into the apparently more tranquil and certain era of Cuthbert Bede. By 1943 signs of the new optimism were beginning to appear throughout the university world. In that year a 'university book' of a totally different character appeared when 'Bruce Truscot', alias Professor Allison Peers of Liverpool University, published his *Redbrick University*. This was, perhaps, the first detailed critique of provincial universities. Seeking to define their problems, it helped to bring them to the forefront of the public mind. In 1943, too, the Association of University Teachers embarked on a study of university developments and of the difficulties which it was considered would need to be faced once the war had ended. By 1944 the whole question of the post-war role of universities was a subject of considerable debate. Some of the problems confronting the universities had also become matters of concern to the government, which consequently set up specialist committees to advise on them. The McNair Report on the training of teachers and the Goodenough Report on medical schools appeared in 1944, while the Barlow Report on scientific manpower and the Clapham Report on social and economic research were published in 1946. The Education Act of 1944 was also particularly significant for the universities because it promised to increase greatly the number of students qualified for university entry.

The thread which ran through this debate on universities and their place in a reconstructed society after the war was the need for a radical expansion in the number of students and, in consequence, a greatly enlarged university system. There were, it is true, dissentient voices. In 1944 Sir Charles Grant Robertson (1869–1948), the historian and former vice-chancellor of Birmingham University, held forth that 'dredge or subsidize as you will, there is no large untapped reservoir of brains'.[3] But the majority view was otherwise. In the same year, Sir Ernest Simon (1879–1960, later Lord Simon of Wythenshawe) described university provision in Britain as 'parsimonious' compared with what was done in the USA and called for 'considerable expansion of university teaching and research and more positive planning in the field of university work'. The Barlow Report also envisaged almost a doubling of the country's scientists by 1955 and testified to the willingness of the universities to expand their numbers by 86 per cent; 'in some instances', the Report concluded, 'even this is an appreciable underestimate of what could be done'.

In Swansea, at the height of the war, thought was already being given to the post-war development of the college. In 1944 a five-year development plan was drawn up. Based on an immediate expansion of both undergraduate and postgraduate work as students returned from the war, it was an ambitious programme. Even in its immediate needs it called for an injection of capital of over half a million pounds at pre-war costs. Permanent laboratories for geology and biology, a students' union, two halls of residence – one for two hundred men and another for one hundred women – and additional accommodation for the faculty of arts and the college's administration were only the first priorities. Enhanced grants for additional staffing, library books and departmental equipment were called for and proposals were put forward for the establishment of new departments of Spanish, Portuguese and Russian. As later developments, an assembly hall and a further hall of residence for men were included with recurrent provision for more staff and equipment.

What was much more urgent than the new capital proposals, though, was the restoration of the existing college buildings. Maintenance, which had never been easy even at the best of times before the war, had been neglected almost completely for nearly six years and had been compounded by the demands made by the college's visitors. Extensive alterations to meet the needs of the Armaments Research Department, which were no longer appropriate to the normal academic requirements of the college, had to be undone. This restoration work was the first priority, and was vital if the college were to cope with the expected flood of new students. The final full peacetime session, 1938–9, had seen 482 full-time students enrolled. By 1944–5 the student complement had sunk to 303. Within four years this number more than trebled and, until the stabilization and then decline of numbers in the early 1950s, included a significant proportion of ex-servicemen.

	Total Number of Students	Number of Ex-servicemen
1945–6	475	82
1946–7	710	307
1947–8	872	436
1948–9	1,002	532
1949–50	1,078	527
1950–1	1,060	373

By 1946 it was possible to embark on some developments. But the post-war years of austerity, of fuel crises and of a Britain desperately trying to adjust to the problems of reconstruction allowed little scope for the practical implementation of the ambitious plans of only a year or two before. Actual development at Swansea was very limited but thanks to a UGC grant of £19,700, a start was made on a temporary building north of the physics department, to serve as a new refectory and thus free space in the abbey for common rooms and for teaching in geology and geography. In the physics department itself a whole series of additions and alterations was undertaken, on the basis of a capital grant from the UGC, this time of £13,500. These buildings and adaptations were essentially utilitarian in character and, like the original science pavilions, their only architectural merit was that they did not obstruct the view of Swansea Bay. They were a far cry from the philosophy of permanency underlying the library scheme a decade earlier or the programme of 1944.

There was, nonetheless, still some expectation that by 1948 a start might be made at Singleton on a range of permanent buildings for science and engineering, at least one hall of residence and conceivably a students' union. Percy Thomas, the eminent Welsh architect who had designed Swansea's new guildhall in the thirties, was commissioned to design the first two projects but, because of the financial constraints on the UGC, all that eventually materialized were some temporary additions to the engineering and chemistry departments. Indeed, with the exception of the library, it was not until 1957 that the first truly permanent buildings began to appear on a newly planned Singleton 'campus'. Yet amidst all the gloom of these years, there was at least one fillip to the college. This was a new complex, designed by Herbert Jones, for the arts faculty which, in terms of accommodation, had always suffered as something of a poor relation even compared with the generally austere conditions prevailing at Singleton. Though a temporary building, and not completed until 1949 at a cost of over £32,000, it contained the inestimable asset of a theatre. The 'new arts hall' had 'an exhilarating effect upon college life' and for several student generations was to be a nursery for budding actors and a cultural mecca for the college and the town.

The problem of student facilities was by now becoming critical, with the post-war expansion in student numbers and the ever-growing band of more mature ex-servicemen

Maes-yr-Haf

who saw a students' union building as essential for the well-being and organization of the student body. Despite the natural opposition of local residents, Maes-yr-Haf, a house on Sketty Road near Beck Hall was acquired by the college in 1946 at a cost of £8,000, for use as a students' centre. The cost was met by the UGC, but, once again Maes-yr-Haf was seen as only a temporary expedient, pending the construction of the planned permanent students' union at Singleton. This was not to come until the sixties and for sixteen years Maes-yr-Haf performed its function well, even if the student body failed repeatedly in its attempts to obtain a bar licence: a shortcoming that would be tolerated in no students' union today.

Much of the early planning of what had been envisaged as the post-war redevelopment of the college was inspired by Jenkin Evans, the foundation Professor of Physics. Unhappily, he died after a long illness in July 1944. Frederic Bacon, the foundation Professor of Engineering , died suddenly in 1943. By his death the college was robbed of one of the anchors of its formative years and a mechanical engineer of distinction who had devoted all his energies to building up his department at both Cardiff and Swansea. Another loss was the departure into retirement in 1944 of Professor Ernest Hughes. Retained for two extra years because of the war, Hughes had not only built up a history department of importance but had done even more to extend the interest of the college into the Swansea district and, through his lectures, to publicize its very existence.

The old order which had nurtured the growth of the college on the most slender of resources was changing. New blood was flowing into Singleton. In 1944 Bacon was succeeded by Dr R.N. Arnold who left after only three years to take up the regius chair of engineering at Edinburgh and be succeeded in turn at Swansea by L.J. Kastner. Evans was followed by Dr Frank Llewellyn Jones, who had joined the physics department as an assistant lecturer in 1932 and had spent much of the war at the Royal Aircraft Establishment at Farnborough, and Hughes by Dr D.B. Quinn. Moses Williams, who had succeeded Cavenagh as Professor of Education in 1934, left for the similar chair in Bangor in 1942 and his place was taken by Dr Fred Schonell. Early in 1947 T.N. George went to Glasgow, Dr Duncan Leitch succeeding him. Coates retired in September 1948 and was soon followed by L.E. Hinkel, lecturer in chemistry since the very beginning of the college, and latterly senior lecturer. Already in 1946 another link with the earliest days of the college was broken when Paul Diverres retired from the French department after twenty-three years at Swansea.

A number of staff did not return to the college from their war service or spent only a very short time at Swansea after 1945. Among them were Dennison who went to Cambridge in 1945 and was succeeded by E. Victor Morgan who had been promoted to a lectureship in economics only the year before, J.H. Jones (classics), Medlicott and Roberts (history), Taig and McIntosh (English), Richards (Welsh), D.T. Williams (geology and geography), Rees (biology), Hartshorne (chemistry), and Lang (education). A new generation that was to have a formative influence on the post-war development of the college and its academic stature began to emerge. Rush Rhees (philosophy) and Glanmor Williams (history) had come before the war's end, and Gwyn Griffiths (classics), James Bartley (English), and H.J. Godwin (mathematics) soon after. In 1946 new assistant lectureships were established in a whole range of subjects, English, history, Welsh, philosophy, economics, education, mathematics, physics, chemistry, botany, metallurgy and engineering, the first new posts since the establishment of Hare's assistant lectureship in economics in 1938. David Sims (English), Neville Masterman (history), Hugh Bevan (Welsh), R.O. Roberts (economics), L.R. Griffin (physics), R.H. Davies (chemistry), and R.R. Dale (education) were among those who now joined a teaching staff that by the beginning of the 1946–7 session had grown to eighty, nearly a third more than it had been just before the war. Quite a few of the new recruits were younger than many of their ex-service students and, as one wag put it, the wearing of gowns by lecturers was a necessary precaution to prevent classes seeing their teachers' knees shaking with fear.

For Charles Edwards April 1947 marked the completion of twenty years as principal and in the following September he retired. His had been a long and arduous stewardship, fraught with the constriction of inadequate grant-aid, the worries of the great economic depression and, finally, the problems of the war. The totality of the difficulties Edwards had to face gave little scope for any dynamic expansion of the college, but in husbanding its resources effectively he and his colleagues were at least able to maintain standards and ensure some development. The 1937 library was almost a personal triumph for Edwards and will remain his monument. His achievement, though, was less in his overall direction of the college, where his scope was limited by the dominance of the council and the administrative efficiency of his registrar, than in his direction of metallurgy at the college. He was already a metallurgist with a world-wide reputation when he came to Swansea in 1920, and his real importance lies in his creation of the metallurgy department, the fundamental research he carried out or directed and, especially, the links he forged with local and national industry. His influence was to be felt through the academic work of his colleagues and students many of whom went on to posts of distinction in their field. A gentle man, precious perhaps in some ways, he never lacked their respect and affection, and in his dealings with his younger colleagues he was always courteous and considerate.

The maturity of the ex-service element of the post-war student body is brought out in this photograph of the Students' Representative Council for 1947–8 with T.K.L. Nicholas as student president and Miss E. John as senior vice-president. Third from the right in the front row is the staff treasurer, a youthful Glanmor Williams, while at the extreme right of the row is H.L. Ebsworth, student president, 1948–9

Notes

1. Isles later returned to Britain to a chair at Belfast and subsequently was vice-chancellor of the University of Tasmania.

2. Three years later Trueman was to move to the chair of geology at Glasgow where he remained – he became an FRS in 1942 – until his appointment as deputy chairman of the UGC in 1946. He became chairman in 1949 and played a crucial role in the reconstruction of the universities after the war, sensitively balancing the universities' need for unprecedented government grant-aid with the government's own demand to provide guidance over its expenditure. Unhappily, ill health took its toll and Trueman had to retire prematurely in 1953, two years after having been created a KBE.

3. This was a view shared by Archie Richardson who wrote, also in 1944, 'I wonder what the future of the Universities will be. From what I gather they will be swamped with a mass of very poor material . . . somehow I feel that hard work and true scholarship will be at a discount, and social science, the science of the village pump, etc., will take its place.'

CHAPTER FIVE

'OPPORTUNITY AND CHALLENGE'

J ohn Fulton took up office as third principal of the college on 1 October 1947. His family background was thoroughly Scottish and academic. Brought up in Dundee, the youngest son of a principal of the university college there, Fulton took his first degree at St Andrews. Then, like many another high-flyer from Scotland before and since, he came south to Balliol where he took Greats in 1926. After a couple of years teaching logic and scientific method at the London School of Economics he returned to Balliol and a fellowship. Appointed originally as a philosopher, Fulton's interests soon began to turn more in the direction of politics and, in 1935, the college formally recognized the emphasis of his teaching by making him a fellow and tutor in that subject. Apart from four years of the war, Fulton was to remain at Oxford until his call to Swansea and it was for him a formative period. He came under the immensely powerful influence of his fellow Scot, the formidable A.D. Lindsay (1879–1952), Master of Balliol since 1924 and from 1945 ennobled as Lord Lindsay of Birker. He formed a lasting friendship, too, with a contemporary Balliol philosophy don, Charles Morris.[1] Lindsay was essentially an academic politician rather than a philosopher and it was his inspiration that led Fulton and Morris in the direction they took. By the 1950s and '60s Fulton, Morris and the latter's younger brother Philip,[2] the real architect of the Robbins

John Fulton (1902–86), principal (1947–59) and
vice-chancellor of the University of Wales
(1952–4 and 1958–9)

Report, had inherited Lindsay's mantle as the great proconsuls of higher education in Britain and the projectors of liberal Oxford thinking among the modern universities.

Fulton came to Swansea at the right time, because, although the college's foundations were firm, it was still very small, striving to cope with grossly inadequate resources with a flood of ex-service students – the Exchequer grant still only being just in excess of £90,000. What Swansea needed now was less the active scholar and more the policy maker and administrator-politician who could grasp the opportunities that new attitudes to higher education and its funding were creating: someone who was quite clear in his own mind as to his objectives, who had the conviction and persuasiveness to win others to his way of thinking, and who had the doggedness and determination to carry his plans through to practical completion. Fulton, in so many ways the antithesis of Principal Edwards, had just these qualities. While his own thought was by no means profound or original, he could assimilate ideas readily. He could be imaginative and innovatory, usually by borrowing and adapting other people's ideas, and, possessing remarkable powers of persuasion, could convince others of their validity. At times, in public performance, Fulton could cloud the gist of his own argument by the involutions of his eloquence but, generally, this only served to assure his audience of his judgement and his intellectual capacity.

In so many ways he bore comparison to that other Scottish philosopher-*manqué*, Haldane, and, like Haldane's, Fulton's influence over the college was seminal. When Fulton delivered his inaugural address as principal in February 1948 on the theme 'The University in a Free Society', it was a comparison that could not escape those who recalled Haldane's speech at the Central Hall twenty-seven years before. The speech was a *tour de force*; the audience 'had heard nothing like it in Swansea for logical, pure, even distilled, thinking'. Redolent of much that Fulton had imbibed from Lindsay, it was the new principal's manifesto to the college. Specialization, he declared, was a feature of modern society: it had to be; thus, the aim must be to liberalize it. This was the cultural base of much that was shortly to be encapsulated in the 'Keele experiment' and of what Fulton, in some small, informal, measure was to try to introduce to Swansea; unsuccessfully, as it turned out, owing to the hide-bound attitude of some of the more influential of his new colleagues.

Fulton was an energetic forty-five with a remarkable capacity for hard work. Although he had spent most of his academic career at Oxford, he had four years during the war as a civil servant, latterly as a principal assistant secretary in the Ministry of Fuel and Power, dealing with the vitally important problems of the coal industry. Here he had worked closely with the minister, Gwilym Lloyd-George, and with the Minister of Labour, Ernest Bevin. 'It was due largely to his work that we got through as well as we did,' said Lloyd-George a decade later. Assisting Fulton in the department as an economist and statistician was a young don from Jesus College, Oxford, named Harold Wilson. By the time he came to Swansea Fulton was thus no stranger to the 'corridors of power' and, in true Balliol tradition, he had cultivated a number of 'connections' that were to prove invaluable to his life's work.

In the field of university politics, he had already played a key part in the genesis of the new University College of North Staffordshire at Keele and, in the spring of 1947, at the instance of Lindsay, was recommended as its first principal. Since the beginning of the year, however, Swansea had been taking an interest in him and he was being pressed to make a decision on its offer. Attractive to Fulton as Keele was, with its unorthodox academic programme, its prospects at this juncture were problematic and, in Professor Gallie's words, he soon allowed himself to be 'whisked away to an important university post elsewhere'.

The atmosphere of reconstruction that had been gathering apace for the final two or three years of the war created new opportunities for the universities and presupposed an unprecedented central government commitment to their expansion. This was seen not only in terms of recurrent support but also of capital grants, which had been so rarely given before the war – though Swansea had been fortunate on a number of occasions – but which were now essential to meet the substantial building programme that would be required to meet pre-war deficiencies, war-time ravages and the projected 'national requirements', especially on the science side. The days when private benefaction could be expected to make much impact in financing university development were past, and, indeed, with spiralling inflation and high wartime levels of taxation continuing after 1945, there was little hope of much significant help from the private sector.

Of great significance was the Barlow Report of 1946 which urged the doubling of the output of science graduates within ten years and envisaged a strengthening of technological teaching and research 'to raise the currency of technological qualifications'. It suggested, too, that the need for more and better-trained scientists and technologists should not be met at the expense of the humanities and looked to some enlargement of the number of arts students provided there were sufficient employment to absorb them. Overall, it estimated that Britain would need 70,000 student places by 1950 and 90,000 by 1955, and it advanced a programme of 'positive discrimination' in favour of the modern universities. As part of this programme it recommended that full university status should be accorded to the remaining English university colleges (Exeter, Hull, Leicester, Nottingham, and Southampton) and that at least one new university should be created. The report was to be a beacon-light for the 1950s until it began to be overtaken by even more dramatic changes.

Already, early in 1945, the UGC, in a convincing memorandum to the Treasury outlining the tentative plans of universities for the succeeding decade, had brought home the absolute need for adequate central government funding if the universities were to achieve 'the expansion and improvement of facilities . . . which the public demanded'. Over the next twelve years successive governments of whatever political persuasion and in however bleak an economic climate responded and cemented the state's financial commitment to university development to the extent of some £232,000,000. Even to Stafford Cripps, Chancellor of the Exchequer in the dark days of 1948, the justification for a substantial increase in university grants in the midst of the rigours of austerity was clear: 'it is on the advances that we make in scientific knowledge and on the energy, initiative, directive capacity and courage of these young graduates that the economic future of the country will largely depend'.

Swansea shared in this state support. The recurrent grant which had been £46,474 in 1944–5 was increased to £69,277 for the following year and at the beginning of the first post-war quinquennium, in 1947–8, had reached £90,267. By the end of that quinquennium, in 1951–2, it topped £146,000. It then rose sharply again at the beginning of the new quinquennium 1952–7 to £182,072 to end the five-year period in 1956–7, after regular increases, at £253,182, or 79 per cent of the college's income.

Fulton's arrival at Swansea thus took place at a propitious moment. But there were still only two permanent buildings at Singleton – the abbey and the 'new' library of 1937. The new semi-permanent refectory was nearing completion and the arts building was at an advanced stage of planning. Most of the existing temporary buildings had more than exceeded their original life expectancy and, although some of them had been skilfully adapted and extended, they were ripe for redevelopment. The college site, though, was tiny. There could be little or no development south of the abbey and the library because of aesthetic considerations of vista and the practical difficulties of a high water-table in the 'meadow': whenever there was heavy rain a pond appeared there – and still does. Redevelopment of the land on which the temporary 'pavilions' stood to the north was a virtual impossibility. 'Decanting' the old laboratories and workshops and housing their inhabitants and equipment elsewhere during any building operations was impracticable and the associated disruption to teaching and research could not be contemplated. Yet Fulton knew that the college could not remain as it was: it had to swim with the national tide or sink into obscurity and eventual extinction. Nevertheless, unless the college could convince the UGC that it had room for expansion in land and buildings government largesse for university development would be lost or diverted to other institutions.

The tentative development plans of 1944 had been scotched by the immediate post-war austerity. Fulton's mind, though, was far in advance even of what had been seen as ambitious then. His ideas of expansion could only be effected by a sizeable movement west into land owned by the Corporation: otherwise it would have to be on a totally different site. For Fulton wanted more than a teaching centre at Singleton. He wanted an integrated site – the word 'campus' did not come into vogue in Britain until the early sixties – with academic buildings, halls of residence and amenities for staff and students all clustered together. So long as so many students were still the victims of a train or bus timetable they could not reach their full academic stature and the common life of the college would be ill-nourished and precarious. 'Making the most of a university is a whole-time job.' To Fulton, 'nothing else will do'. And this meant a site considerably bigger than the nineteen acres presently occupied by the college in the park.

An exhaustive search for an alternative to Singleton proved to be unavailing. Yet, while the college might cast a covetous eye on even just a shade more of the park, there seemed little likelihood that it would come its way. On past showing, the Corporation's reaction to any approach from the college was, like as not, to be unsympathetic if not downright hostile. Any change to an attitude that had become increasingly ingrained over twenty years would need a great deal of nursing – a task that would tax all the drive and dexterity even of someone who had successfully coped with the internecine intricacies of Whitehall. Fulton immediately set about rebuilding bridges with the Corporation and convincing both the university and the UGC that his ideas were viable. It was an exercise which brought out to the full Fulton's skill as an administrator, his mastery both of tactics and strategy, and his apparently intuitive sense of timing.

Already, within a few months of taking up his new post, he was considering what permanent building developments could take place when the new refectory, arts hall and certain other adaptations had been completed. Residential accommodation, especially for men, and highlighted since the influx of London students during the war and ex-servicemen after it, was a continuing problem. In his first public pronouncement he stressed the priority he gave to student residences. By November 1948 his campaign was taking shape and he was giving public vent to his vision of what he saw as a *complete* university community. 'If we seize our opportunities this College may well become unique,' he told the court.

> The civic universities were founded before residences were thought practicable for universities of their kind. Confined in the middle of great cities, they must now seek sites remote from the academic centre for student hostels and the like. We came late into the field. That is our opportunity. The sites are at our doors.

Fulton's first direct move was to enlist the support of the new chairman of the UGC, Sir Arthur Trueman, 'the fairy godmother of all our universities' as Fulton was to describe him. Trueman had a real and a personal understanding of the problems that were besetting Swansea and, when he inaugurated the college's 1949–50 session in the new arts hall, he was drawn to say that few institutions in the country were worse off for buildings. When he went on to suggest that the arts building was just a foretaste of a great expansion to come he was not jejunely tailoring his words to the occasion.

With a student population and staff complement more than double those originally envisaged in the 1920s, the college was bursting at its seams. Trueman, therefore, encouraged Fulton to embark on a permanent development plan for Singleton. The college forthwith re-engaged Percy Thomas. Thomas – by now 'Sir Percy' since he had been knighted in 1946 – was well versed in the needs of universities and he had

Sir Percy Thomas (1883–1969), *left*, and Alderman Percy Morris (1893–1967), *right*

undertaken similar plans for Bristol and Nottingham as well as for the university college at Aberystwyth. Nor was he a total stranger to Swansea or its principal, because for two years he had already been advising the college on the possibility of developing a hall of residence on a strip of land at Sketty Lane.

What now emerged from Thomas's thinking, inspired by Fulton's knowledge of the North American approach to university planning, was an elegant scheme which would, when completed, transform the non-residential, essentially 'nine-to-five', college, operating in makeshift, temporary quarters, into a mainly residential university precinct, housed in comparatively 'low-rise', brick-faced buildings, which would, commented the *Manchester Guardian*, 'challenge comparison with any in the country'. It must be a matter of regret that, as events were to unfold, this scheme could never be fulfilled. It would have continued the pattern set by Verner Rees's thirties 'modern-traditional' architecture and created a 'pleasaunce' in Singleton, conveying an impression of comparative spaciousness even within the bounds of a limited site. This is something that the later functional, impersonal, plate-glass 'international' style architecture can never recapture, despite its skilful conception and growing harmony with its setting.

Thomas's plan, submitted to the Corporation in June 1949, required virtually the whole of the south-western part of Singleton Park, an area of nearly thirty-two acres stretching from the abbey almost to Sketty Lane. What was envisaged was a scheme embracing five halls of residence each accommodating 120 students, a general amenities building incorporating a students' union, an assembly hall and four blocks of academic buildings built on an open-courtyard principle. The range of the college's current disciplines, including the social sciences which, thanks to Fulton's initiative, had been introduced from the beginning of the 1948–9 session, were catered for, with provision for expansion to a total student population of at least 1,000 to 1,200. Such an increase

Sir Percy Thomas's original development plan for Singleton, 1949. The virtual absence of cars in Thomas's perspective is worth remark. The mushrooming growth in the use of the car has been a prime factor in rendering the development plan and its successors impractical

would, it was thought, meet the college's share of the nationally agreed Barlow target of 90,000 by 1955. The cost of the total development was estimated at £4,000,000, but it was recognized that the overall project would be many years in the making. Still, if all went well, Fulton hoped that the first of the new buildings would be completed within three or four years and, true to his earlier pronouncements, he saw hostel accommodation as having priority.

Before putting the plan to the Corporation, Fulton secured Trueman's personal support; the scheme, it was felt, was practical, economical in its use of ground, and yet adequate for the foreseeable future. Within a few months Fulton had achieved considerably more. In November 1949 he could tell the court of governors that the programme could be 'contemplated in the assurance that, if a matter of 10 per cent can be raised locally, the rest will be forthcoming from the central purse. Is not this a moment of magnificent opportunity?' A moment of opportunity indeed, but to be able to grasp it an even greater challenge confronted Fulton. His development plan was in place, he had secured for it both academic and official approval, and he had a reasonable assurance of generous public funding. What he still did not have was the land and without it the whole house of cards would collapse. And there was still a strong body of opinion on the town council, reflecting – and in its own turn inspiring – a similar element among the townspeople at large, which was suspicious of the college and its ambitions. There remained more than a lingering feeling that the college had come to Swansea only at the expense of the town's surrendering a large part of one of its prime amenities and that in return the college had shown little or no interest in the town itself. A 'Common Docker', contributing a vexatious letter to the *South Wales Evening Post* (24 March 1950), expressed a not uncommon view:

> Of what material value is the College to us as overburdened ratepayers? Of course a number of local young people attend there, thus avoiding the expense of going further afield, and I have every reason to believe the degree to be of a high standard. But the bulk of the students are strangers, who obtain their particular qualification, and then off they go to posts elsewhere, even as the students of the Training College do.
>
> What part does the College take in the social or political life of our town? The staff and students never enter into the town's affairs and even in matters such as our yearly Mayor's parade they never grace it by appearing in the usual academic garb of a college to show that they appreciate the consideration which the town has always shown them . . .
>
> Do the college authorities ever remember what [*sic*] they have already had from us the finest site in South Wales, the very best part of Singleton, which they have littered up with temporary buildings, making a blot on a beautiful park. . . .

An inspired letter from someone who was probably neither common nor a docker. But it was symptomatic and the discussions and negotiations with the Corporation were far from easy. There were many who, in Sir Lewis Jones's words, were 'only too ready to say that the college was trying to filch yet more of the heritage of Singleton Park from the townsfolk'. Fulton's commitment to the college, however, and his fine appreciation of its place both in the national scene and in the local community, gradually impressed all but the most antipathetic town councillor.

One of his most telling points was to explain how much expenditure in Swansea the college was directly responsible for; an annual sum approaching £150,000. Indirectly, and taking account of the new arrangements for local authority grants, this figure would increase to something like £250,000. This was an impressive statistic. Fulton's ace, though, was to win the crucial support of Alderman Percy Morris, Lewis Jones's old political rival and the Labour councillor who had been such a thorn in the flesh of the college council at the time of the Saunders Lewis affair. Morris was now MP for Swansea West. More to the point, as leader of the town council and chairman of the parliamentary committee, he was the most powerful and influential local politician. To W.C. Rogers, 'His was a control that was complete'.

Yet, even with Morris's backing the effort of persuading the Corporation to let the college have more land proved to be an uphill task that was to take eighteen months of argument and counter-argument. The prime difficulty was not so much the spirit as the extent of the college's request. Thirty-odd acres – less than a sixth of what was available at Nottingham, Exeter or Reading and a mere twelfth of the Penglais site at Aberystwyth – was seen as far more than the 'nibbling at Singleton' that had been so vehemently criticized by the like of Tom Merrells thirty years earlier. Even some of the most sympathetic of the councillors saw in Sir Percy Thomas's plan a 'sprawl' of buildings that were not 'strictly utilitarian'; the college should 'do with far less ground and build north-west and upwards'. North-west, because one very real concern was the loss of the 'show ring' – roughly where Fulton House and the chemistry building are now – which would prevent popular attractions like the major agricultural shows and sheepdog trials being mounted at Singleton, though their popularity was such that the site was in any case becoming too small.

Eventually, in December 1950, the Corporation not only agreed to grant the college an additional 26.75 acres of parkland on its western boundary but to make it over as a free gift. It was not quite the acreage that Fulton had asked for, but the Corporation had to have in mind land for a new general hospital and, with some compromise on boundaries, it gave him enough although in the consequent revision of Sir Percy Thomas's plan one of the halls of residence had to be sacrificed. Fulton's exertions of the previous two years to repair the breach with the Corporation, and the positive encouragement he had had from Trueman, met with a degree of success that even the principal had not expected. The way was now open to expand and develop a university institution of a breadth of interest and quality not truly contemplated before.

Any expansion of student numbers was bound to be dependent on an increasing number of entrants from outside the college's immediate area. And, in any case, now that maintenance grants, from both central government and local education authorities, were becoming more readily available and financially more valuable, there was a growing trend for undergraduates to study away from home. In fact, although still maintaining its local affinities, the college was already drawing students from the wider regional areas of south and mid-Wales. This was a tendency that was to increase in the fifties and, even before the great expansion of the college, students were beginning to come from an even wider constituency.

Coupled with this there was a steady decline in the percentage of students living at home and therefore within easy commuting distance of the college. In 1938–9, the last full session before the war, eighty-two per cent of students lived at home. This figure does not quite equate with that for local students *stricto sensu*. That would have been slightly higher because there were always a few local students who chose to live in lodgings or, if women, in Beck Hall; but it is near enough. By 1948–9 the percentage of

A French Society performance of *Knock, ou le Triomphe de la Médicine* in the new arts hall in February 1953, produced by Guy Millot, the departmental *lecteur*, who also starred in the leading role

home-living students had declined to sixty-four per cent, although one should recognize that the figures of this period may be distorted by the influx of ex-servicemen after the war. However, the percentage of home-living students continued to decline in the 1950s even when the disappearance of the ex-service element caused a fall-off in the student intake so that one might have expected the percentage to rise. In fact, between the years 1950–1 and 1956–7 the percentage went down steadily each year from fifty-six per cent to thirty per cent. By 1960–1, when the expansion of the college had begun in earnest and yet before the Singleton Halls had opened to inflate the numbers of non-local students, the percentage had become a mere twenty per cent. Already by this time, therefore, in terms of the geographical spread of students, Swansea had matured into a college of national standing. It was, too, beginning to attract students from far wider social groups than ever before.

Thus, the most pressing of all the manifold problems of expansion was still the question of the adequate housing of students. Since 1920 some hostel accommodation had been provided for women, and by 1930 a gradually expanding Beck Hall – known as Neuadd Beck since 1969 – accommodated some forty students, although numbers were later to fluctuate considerably in tune with the varying economic climate of the times. There had been no hostel for men students since 1925, when Dumbarton House was disposed of because it was not proving a viable economic proposition. Although in these pre-war days there was very small demand for hostel accommodation for men, it was always the intention of the college that some should eventually be provided. It was recognized, for example, that with the post-war expansion of the college the private accommodation available to men in the Uplands and Brynmill areas, close to the college and traditional reservoirs of lodgings, would reach saturation point.

In 1944 two hostels – or halls of residence as they were already coming to be called – had been suggested for inclusion in the UGC's reconstruction programme referred to in the last chapter. Sir Percy Thomas's plan, embracing the Fulton notion of a 'complete university', had been much bolder. Yet, by 1955, with men accounting for seventy-eight per cent of the total full-time student population there was still no hostel provision for them. The enhanced capital allocations now beginning to flow from a central government committed to university expansion, focused as they were on science and technology, had not so far allowed the college to move ahead with the construction of any of the projected halls of residence at Singleton, though they were still a high priority in the development programme.

Suddenly, an opportunity to develop a hall of residence outside Singleton presented itself. In February 1952 Admiral Algernon Walker-Heneage-Vivian, the seemingly-indomitable octogenarian owner of the extensive Clyne and Parc-le-Breos estates, died and his property had to be disposed of to meet swingeing death duties. Eventually, after much obscure negotiation, part of the Clyne estate at Blackpill, including the

The south front of Clyne Castle

neo-Gothic 'castle' and some 76 acres of its immediate gardens and parkland, were acquired by the Corporation under its compulsory purchase powers. It was decided that the remarkable park and spring gardens created by the Admiral's uncle, Graham Vivian, should be preserved as a public amenity, but considerable debate attended the question of the future use of the castle itself. This had originally been envisaged as providing a prestigious official residence for the mayor or for the judges on assize. A number of other suggested uses for the castle were also actively canvassed at the time, some perhaps marginally less eccentric than others, but, in November 1952, confidential discussions began between the college and Corporation officials over the possibility of the college's leasing the castle for use as a hall of residence. With the encouragement of Trueman and the UGC, and the purposeful advocacy of Alderman Percy Morris, all seemed to be going well until, at the eleventh hour, in November 1953, the college's plans were suddenly thwarted. The Corporation suspended negotiations and decided to advertise in the press for other proposals for the future of the castle. A group on the town council, led by Alderman T.S. ('Tommy') Harris, was anxious to maximize whatever it could of the estate's commercial potential for what was seen as the financial benefit of the ratepayers – earlier there had been proposals for a hotel or a zoo and circus – while there was also the ever-continuing jealousy of 'town' towards 'gown'.

No alternative offers were forthcoming and eventually, in the spring of 1954, matters began to take a significantly more hopeful turn. At length, in April, the Corporation agreed to the college's taking a thirty-year lease of the castle with an option to purchase or to extend the lease for a further ninety-nine years. As negotiations continued, though, it became clear that in view of the capital conversion costs involved it would be to the advantage of the college to buy Clyne Castle outright. The UGC, thanks to the decisive persuasion of Sir Keith Murray,[3] its ebullient new chairman (1953–63), a fellow Scot and an Oxford contemporary of Fulton, agreed to meet both the purchase price and the cost of developing Clyne into a hall of residence from public funds. In the spring of 1955 the Corporation eventually agreed to the sale of the castle together with a surrounding three acres to the college for £12,751.

Even before the legal formalities had been completed, some £7,000 had been spent by the college on making the building 'wind and weather tight'. By July 1955 work had begun in earnest on the alteration of the castle and the construction of a new study-bedroom block at a total cost of £129,663. The nature of the house was such that it was suited to conversion and this, and the simple, somewhat Scandinavian design of the annexe, were discreetly and sympathetically carried out by Norman Thomas, son of Sir Percy. A number of the castle bedrooms could be left undisturbed and the elegant ground-floor reception rooms lent themselves readily to use as dining-room, library, and common room. Fulton's desire, too, to create an appropriate milieu for students from 'non-university' homes embraced the incidental graces of enterprising interior decoration and good furnishing. What he had already achieved at Beck Hall and, to some extent, at Singleton was therefore introduced to Clyne in what was described as a rather 'up-to-the-minute *House and Garden*' style, a 'refreshing contrast' with 'the more traditional interiors in which many students lodge' (*The Architects' Journal*, 2 January 1958). Outside, meticulous care was taken to conserve rare shrubs and mature trees and to maintain the castle's picturesque setting so lovingly created by Graham Vivian.

At last, on 1 October 1956, Clyne was ready to receive its first ninety-eight men students and on 4 June 1957 the new hall of residence was formally opened by Sir Lewis Jones as 'Neuadd Gilbertson'. It is difficult to imagine a hall of residence in a position of more exquisite beauty than Neuadd Gilbertson with the romantic backdrop of Clyne Park and its outstanding gardens reaching down to the sea. It was with justifiable pride that Sir Lewis could claim that it was one of the finest halls of residence in the country. And with Hugh Bevan as its first warden a certain style was set that has continued to this day.

Two further small plots of adjacent land were bought from the Corporation in 1964 and 1966, to enable an additional annexe to be built at Neuadd Gilbertson and, later, a second, entirely modern, hall of residence for 146 women students close by. It was a happy thought to name this 'Neuadd Martin' to commemorate both Sir Richard Martin, who had striven so much to make a university college in Swansea a reality and who, together with Gilbertson, could be regarded as one of the founders of the college, and his daughter Ethel Martin (d. 1980), the second warden of Beck Hall.

While the discussions over Clyne Castle were taking place between the college and the Corporation, the permanent development of Singleton was not being neglected. Percy Thomas's 1949 proposals had been conceived in the context of an expansion of the college to some 1,000 to 1,200 students. During the early fifties, however, as the ex-service element began to disappear from the scene, student numbers declined: from a national total of 85,421 students in 1949 to one of 80,602 in 1953. Swansea reflected this national pattern and, in terms of student numbers, the college reached its lowest point since the war in 1954 – a year later than the national trend. Paradoxically, at this

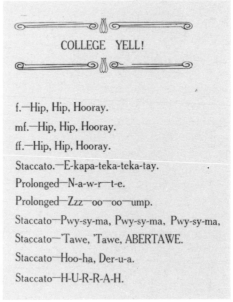

COLLEGE YELL!

f.—Hip, Hip, Hooray.

mf.—Hip, Hip, Hooray.

ff.—Hip, Hip, Hooray.

Staccato.—E-kapa-teka-teka-tay.

Prolonged—N-a-w-r—t-e.

Prolonged—Zzz—oo—oo—ump.

Staccato—Pwy-sy-ma, Pwy-sy-ma, Pwy-sy-ma,

Staccato—'Tawe, 'Tawe, ABERTAWE.

Staccato—Hoo-ha, Der-u-a.

Staccato—H-U-R-R-A-H.

The student president (Ednyfed Hudson Davies) greets the Duke of Edinburgh, Chancellor of the University of Wales, with the College Yell on 7 May 1952. It was a strict injunction of the Students' Union that the Yell should be given 'on those occasions when the enthusiasm and pride of a body of Swansea Students can show themselves in no other way, but it is usual not to use it indiscriminately as an advertisement at an impromptu gathering in town or elsewhere' time, postgraduate work increased. But, after 1955 overall recovery was rapid and within seven years student numbers at the college had doubled to reach 1,654 by 1961. This rise was a small part of what was happening throughout the national university system; between 1953 and 1956 student numbers generally rose by some 11.5 per cent, and the totality of the increase, earlier than had been expected, caused the UGC to revise its figures rapidly.

The cause of this increase – 'explosion' would be a better word – was twofold. The working through of the 1944 Education Act and the greater availability of maintenance grants were encouraging an increasing tendency of pupils to remain at school until they were seventeen or more and to qualify for university admission. It was a 'trend' that had not been foreseen: only the 'bulge' – the post-war rise in the birth-rate – had been taken into the UGC's calculations and this had not been expected to lead to increased demand for university places until the mid-1960s. These pressures from 'below' – coupled with the assumption from 'above' that Britain needed more scientists and 'high technologists' – was to lead to a relentless pursuit of university expansion. As a result, the goalposts of student targets for the universities were to be moved repeatedly over the next decade.

The reaction of the UGC to the unfolding situation, far different from the period of consolidation that it had foreseen for the later fifties, was swift. It forecast a growth in

A Singleton magnolia. It is said that if examination revision has not started when the magnolias begin to blossom then students have left it too late

student numbers to about 124,000 by the mid-sixties, with the possibility of a further increase of about ten per cent in the second half of that decade; the underlying assumption being that approximately two-thirds of the expansion would be in science and technology and the remaining third in the humanities and social sciences.

By 1956 the future seemed to be clear as far as Swansea's share of the expansion was concerned. Some 1,300 to 1,400 had been set as the student target for 1962, followed by a further fifty per cent increase to approximately 2,000 by 1967 and, conceivably, 2,500 by the early seventies. The expansion involved a doubling of the college over a decade – staff as well as students – and an enormous capital building programme to underpin it. What had been seen only a few years earlier as a progressive development, traditionally based and spread over many years, had suddenly become a pressing reality of a totally different dimension. Sir Percy Thomas's sedate development plan obviously had to be recast to take account not just of the size of the development but of new directions, academic and other, that were implicit in it.

Now something of a totally different scale was being proposed that would for ever change the character of the college not only in physical terms but in ethos too. No longer would it or could it be the intimate, somewhat paternal institution of pre-war days; and in seeking to change it, Fulton had the support of his council and most of the staff. The critical problem was how to get a quart into a pint pot and still reconcile nature and the works of man: how to create a viable and aesthetic development of the proportions required on a site of less than fifty acres when other similar schemes had two hundred or more acres available. (Such a figure, indeed, was shortly to become the minimum requirement for the new universities of the sixties.)

The new plan, undertaken by Ivan Dale Owen, who had studied and worked in American universities and was later to become senior partner of the Percy Thomas practice, continued, in the broadest terms, the concept of academic 'spheres of influence' established almost a decade before: the humanities at the eastern side of the campus extending west from the abbey precinct and encompassing the 1937 library; the applied sciences further to the west and south-west; and the sciences in the westernmost area of the site. Owen was acutely aware of the site's prominent position within a public park of great beauty. He felt that it already had some of the qualities of the academic precinct, inward-looking, and with its *genius loci* established largely by the park; if not handled sensitively, its development would be totally inimical, if not disastrous, to the romantic rusticity of Singleton. The success of Dale Owen and his colleagues in achieving this aim has been modified by the unpredictable and increasing expansion within the finite area of the college site, and, in recent years, the design and siting of individual buildings without sufficient regard to an overall concept. The result, inevitably, has been a higher density of buildings and a reduction of the spatial effect originally intended in 1958.

One of the 'North American' ideas that Fulton had encouraged Percy Thomas to incorporate in his plan was the notion of a 'College House'. This was to be central to his whole scheme: the social hub for students and staff, providing catering facilities and social amenities for the campus as a whole. Serving to bring together senior and junior members, it would be a cohesive influence in the expanding college where mere size was likely to erode old loyalties and relationships. It was also to perform the function of a students' union building, though after it had been in operation for a short time it soon became clear that there was insufficient space for all union activities and, in 1965, an extension was created at the rear of College House, ingeniously straddling the existing telephone exchange.

College House, with its large assembly hall-cum-cafeteria, dining rooms and common rooms, bars, bookshop, bank, barber's shop and medical centre, was Fulton's practical, 'social-engineering', response to his desire to create the 'complete university' at Swansea. In 1986, following his death, it was renamed 'Fulton House', a singularly appropriate gesture and a fitting memorial to the man who transformed the college.

Under the Dale Owen plan the role of College House was extended and, enlarged, it now adopted what was perhaps its most striking feature: its association with the group of three halls of residence to be built in the north-western angle of the campus and eventually, also, a fourth hall, envisaged for the site of the temporary buildings to the west of the 1949 arts building. The 'Percy Thomas' halls had been conceived of as low-rise, traditional self-contained hostels. The new 'Dale Owen' halls were to have no major catering facilities of their own and their residents were to take their breakfasts and their evening meals in dining halls in College House. Not only would this arrangement save land and avoid the economic waste of duplicating kitchens and refectories, but it was also a novel and conspicuous change in philosophy that would help to reinforce the cohesive social focus of College House without affecting the character and corporate spirit of the halls themselves. The four halls were to be for men students but women

The 'Dale Owen' development plan model (1958), showing the controversial 'chapel of unity' to the south-east of the abbey. The model was so designed that the chapel could be replaced by a tree when it was felt that the presence of the former might offend the susceptibilities of the onlooker

were not neglected. A site close by the abbey – now occupied by the social studies building – was earmarked for a women's hall, with the abbey itself being converted *à la Clyne*, when the college's administration eventually – and late in the development programme – moved to a new 'senate house' on the main entrance drive opposite the natural sciences building. By such means it was hoped that a third, at least, of the student body would in due course be in residence at Singleton, balanced by some small proportion of staff.

The order of starting of the new buildings was necessarily determined not only by academic priorities but also by the peculiarities of the site and the existence of the compact group of temporary 'pavilions' on the original college land immediately to the west of the abbey. The logistic need to retain these buildings coincided with a political concern nationally to develop scientific teaching and research and the capital funding that flowed from it. Thus, the development of the western or scientific zone of the campus naturally presented itself as the immediate priority at the short-term expense of residential accommodation.

Of all the college's disciplines, the natural sciences had been under the greatest pressure of numbers and, arguably, shared the worst accommodation in the college – the old 'College House' across the cobbled courtyard at the rear of the abbey, which had been the registrar's residence until Drew's retirement. Thus, in 1953, in the context of Percy Thomas's plan, application was made for a new complex for the natural sciences. The availability of funds meant that the building had to be constructed in two phases, but by 1956 the central block was ready and was formally opened by Sir Keith Murray on the same day as Neuadd Gilbertson. The only building at Singleton actually to be designed personally by Sir Percy Thomas, its planning had been in hand for over four years. The overall concept – costing nearly £1 million and, in its time, one of the largest capital projects funded by the UGC – was not to be completed until 1961 but even in its initial, attenuated form the natural sciences building was impressive. Its facing of buff Tondu brick – chosen as the nearest local brick available to blend with the 1937 library, its marble porch, and handsome main hall lent it an air of distinction. Such elegance, though, was criticized by some as being *too* traditional and insufficiently *avant garde* for the post-war world. As it was to turn out, ever-increasing cost restraints were to take their toll of much of the further development which as a result betrayed a more utilitarian approach to design, perhaps more 'contemporary' too, but also becoming 'dated' more rapidly.

The period of the building's planning and construction had already seen the bifurcation of the original two natural science departments into four separate elements: something which would have been unthinkable without the prospect of new accommodation. The small geography section of the department of geology and geography had become very active in the post-war years and, with a growing inflow of undergraduates, honours courses in geography had been instituted in 1953. A year later a newly autonomous department under Dr W.G.V. Balchin, then a thirty-eight-year-old lecturer at King's College, London, was created. In 1956 biology divided into the two separate departments of botany and zoology. This splitting of the old departments in no way inhibited the traditionally close working relationships of the natural sciences. In fact, as the new building was expanded and the departments diversified, even greater opportunities for interdisciplinary co-operation arose and were eagerly grasped.

Much of the planning of the botany areas of the building and of the associated botanic garden had been undertaken by Professor Mockeridge who, however, was never to work in the new building, since she retired in 1954 and was succeeded by Dr Herbert ('Bertie') Street (1912–77), a plant physiologist from Manchester. Over the next thirteen years, Street, with an infectious enthusiasm and a sometimes over-abundance of energy, built on the solid rock that Professor Mockeridge had left behind and established the reputation of the department. Throughout, he was ably assisted by a number of dedicated colleagues, like his senior lecturer, Ivor Isaac, a brilliant teacher and a down-to-earth foil to Street's occasionally hyper-exuberant character who was later (1969) to be given the college's first personal chair. To Street, too, the college owes the creation of its botanic garden, transformed over the years from waste to a haven of peace and tranquillity, replete with rare plants and shrubs – and even a snake-pit!

In 1956 Dr Wyn Knight-Jones, the deputy director of the Marine Biology Station at Bangor, was appointed Professor of Zoology on the creation of that department. Unhappily, Duncan Leitch (1904–56), T. Neville George's successor in geology, who played a major part in bringing about the new developments in the natural sciences, was denied the opportunity of moving into the new building which owed so much to his meticulous planning: he died after a long illness in January 1956. A coal-measure geologist, in the tradition of the Swansea department which he had joined from Glasgow, Leitch survived his mentor and close friend, Trueman, by only a few days. Leitch was succeeded by Professor Frank Rhodes, Associate Professor of Geology at the University of Illinois.

Hardly had the original centre block of the natural sciences building been completed than the college embarked upon the construction of a new chemistry building. Designed by Norman Thomas, this building had been projected by Sir Percy in the revision to his development plan and its start was included in the UGC's special technology programme for 1957. The year before, Professor Shoppee – Coates's successor since 1948 – had become the college's second 'in-post' FRS, but almost immediately he resigned to take up the chair of organic chemistry in the University of Sydney, New South Wales. After a short period with Ayling as acting-head of the department, Professor Cedric Hassall, an antipodean from New Zealand, arrived from the West Indies where he had been foundation Professor of Chemistry at the university college. Hassall and his senior colleagues were immediately thrown into the planning of a new building and the design of new courses. The new teaching laboratories became available in October 1960 and the first stage of the building was officially opened in May 1961 by Sir Alexander Todd (Lord Todd since 1962), then Professor of Organic Chemistry at Cambridge.

Almost exactly a year later, College House – the last of the buildings projected by Sir Percy Thomas himself – and the first two Singleton halls (Neuadd Sibly and Neuadd Lewis Jones) were opened by the pro-chancellor of the university, Lord Morris of Borth-y-Gest. Although specialist consultants had been employed initially to advise on the design of the catering, their real architect – he had to undo a number of design faults that might have proved disastrous – and author of the remarkable services that flowed from them was John Tomlin, who came to Swansea as the college's first catering officer in April 1961. The college had no previous experience of running its own catering arrangements. These had always been contracted out and on a totally different scale back to the days of 'Mother' Anderson. Virtually single-handed, but with a unique experience

The developing campus at Singleton on 3 June 1959. The first stage of the natural sciences building has been completed, the chemistry building is well under way, and the steel structure for College House has been completed. The approach to College House is fronted by a circular roundabout: this was shortly to give way to the concept of a rectilinear lawned piazza which, unhappily, never became anything more than an oblong roundabout of commercial, institutional and industrial catering and hotel management, Tomlin masterminded the commissioning of the new service and, with a deceptive ease, overcame all the difficulties that naturally arose in the practical working-out of a new concept in university catering during years of rapid expansion. With the aid of Miss Eunice Lewis, who had earlier managed the college's refectories, and a dedicated staff, he developed a service of rare quality and efficiency that coped not only with the multifarious needs of college life but also with public banquets and with the vacation conferences which were increasingly to mean so much to the financial stability of the college.

The new halls opened in very trying circumstances in October 1961. Unhappily there were building delays and they could not be completed for some months. Meanwhile, some residents had to go into temporary lodgings, while, in hall, the din, the mud and the general dislocation caused by the building operations were disruptive and intensified the 'teething troubles' that one might normally have expected. Gradually, however, the halls settled down and under the genial direction of their first masters (Professor Wilfred Fishwick and Professor Glanmor Williams) and their resident senior tutors (Garth Plowman and Robert Leaper) they began to develop a sense of community with their own separate styles and characteristics.

College House with the first two Singleton halls, Neuadd Sibly and Neuadd Lewis Jones, 1961.
Neuadd Sibly was so designed that the main stack of the college's central boilerhouse went up through the central core of the hall

The first half of the 1960s was a period of hectic building activity at Singleton. The five buildings taken over from the contractors by 1961 had cost well nigh £3,000,000 but they formed only the first part of a programme scheduled to last through the decade. It was, furthermore, an expanded programme because in 1959 the UGC had revised its estimates of future student numbers once more, on the basis of a minimum overall target for Great Britain of 170,000 to 175,000 places to be reached by the late 1960s or early 1970s. Given both the 'trend' and a continuing high birth-rate, it was thought that the potential number of students might even reach 250,000 by the late 1970s. The UGC came to the conclusion that the rate of expansion set by such targets was beyond the capacity of the existing institutions, and, believing also that the time was ripe for a broadening of regional spread and, more importantly, for further experimentation in university education and organization recommended the establishment of a number of completely new universities. The question of the criteria for their geographical spread was something that deeply interested Professor Balchin. He devised a 'county town' strategy for the UGC which embodied as balanced a regional distribution for the new institutions as the 'demand patterns' permitted and it is remarkable how closely his findings coincided with the eventual distribution pattern: moderately-sized provincial centres, with 'greenfield' sites for campus residence where, it was thought, a genuine interplay between university and local community could be speedily fostered.

The notion of a new university at Brighton had been agreed by early 1958 and over the next three years six more appeared. By 1965 all seven – variously described as the 'plate glass' universities, the 'Shakespearian Seven' or, more unkindly by Sir Maurice Dean, the head of the DES, as the 'universities of Noddyland' – had received their charters: Sussex (Brighton, 1961), East Anglia (Norwich, 1963), York (1963), Lancaster (1964), Essex (Colchester, 1964), Warwick (Coventry, 1965), and Kent (Canterbury, 1965). All seven existed as independent universities. In Fulton's phrase, they were 'born free'; they were not subject to the tutelage of another university as were the old university colleges although they were subject to the guidance of independent academic advisory committees for their first few years.

Hindsight might question whether the new universities were necessary. They were the product of the growing expansionist 'bandwagon' orchestrated by Sir Keith Murray, and supported not only by the most influential figures of the academic world but also by both sides of the political spectrum. Primarily, the concern was that the existing universities would not be able to cope with the demands of the 1970s; furthermore, the new institutions would, it was felt, provide fresh foci for innovation and experimentation. What was achieved, however, was at a higher price than might have been paid by developing the existing universities. As a result, the latter suffered, for the new creations, in Carswell's words, 'spread resources – ample though they were – much too thin [and] . . . pre-empted resources for many years ahead in order to bring the new institutions to a practical and economic size'.

It was a policy that was certainly to affect the long-term development plans of Swansea. But, for the present, the college was caught up in the general euphoria. The college readily agreed that its own target should be raised by five hundred to provide for a total student population of three thousand. In line with what were interpreted as the national 'manpower' needs of the country, and in order to hold the pattern of studies within the college in balance, it also agreed that this overall target should be broken down into places for over one thousand arts students (including education), about nine hundred pure science students and the same number of applied science students.

There were among the staff, it is true, those dissentients to whom expansion meant a lowering of academic standards, a 'scraping of the barrel'. It was, though, only the most publicly prominent of them, who, after being confronted by an English student who had never heard of metre in poetry, Jeremiah-like, prophesied, dolefully, that 'more will mean worse' and, later, was to accuse Fulton, 'an Oxford-Balliol-Lindsay-sociological-philistine man', of being 'serious about destroying the universities and turning them into vocational training centres' (Amis, *Encounter*, July 1960, p. 9; *Memoirs*, p. 123). The 'galloping' expansion predicted would, of course, alter the nature of the universities. But the die had already been cast: nationally, and years before, in the spirit of social expectation and the philosophy of increase that had emerged from the war. Grant Robertson had been a minority voice then, as Amis was now, with expansion being seen as the key to economic growth.

In 1962 the Treasury announced that the government aimed at making provision for 150,000 students in 1966–7 (instead of the 135,000 earlier forecast) and 200,000 in 1973–4 (instead of 170,000). In the meantime, the Report of the Crowther Committee, *15 to 18* (1959), had dramatically effected a public awareness of the problem of the discrepancy between the numbers of pupils qualified for university entrance and those actually selected. The Macmillan government, concerned that 'many more university places must be made available' and fretting at the apparent lack of any coherent plan for higher education overall, decided to institute a comprehensive review of the sector as a whole to establish principles for long-term development. Thus, in 1961 a committee on higher education was set up under the chairmanship of Lord Robbins (1898–1984), recently retired as Professor of Economics at the London School of Economics.[4]

Meanwhile, in 1962 following the findings of yet another investigative body, the Anderson Committee on student grants, local education authorities became obliged to make awards to first degree students, state scholarships, as such, were abandoned and the long struggle, since 1946, to standardize student grants ended. Not only that: the awards now became automatic and a student would be certain that once he had qualified and been accepted for a degree course a grant would be his 'by right'. Critical decisions affecting the rapid expansion of the university system were thus being taken even while the Robbins Committee, urged on by Philip Morris, its most potent member, was carrying out its exhaustive review of the whole gamut of higher education in Great Britain. And within twenty-four hours of the publication of the committee's Report in October 1963 the government accepted the thrust of its main argument – what came to be called the 'Robbins Principle' – that courses in higher education should be available 'for all those who are qualified by ability and attainment to pursue them and who wish to do so'.

The committee's projections showed that the number of students qualified to enter university (that is with the minimum entrance qualification of two Advanced Level passes in the GCE) was rising at twice the rate of the number of places open to them. Thus, on the basis of the 'Robbins Principle', the committee calculated that by 1967–8 a total of 328,000 full-time places would be needed in higher education as a whole, and that of this number 197,000 students should be in institutions of university status; while by 1973–4, out of a total of 390,000 places in higher education overall, 219,000 should be in the universities. To meet the perceived need, therefore, the committee proposed that six more new universities should be created together with an upgrading to technological university status of the colleges of advanced technology in England and Wales and the two analogous institutions in Scotland. Of the proposed new universities, only one – Stirling (1967) – was established, but of the former CATS ten technological universities emerged from the chrysalis of local authority control: Strathclyde (1964), Aston, Bath, Bradford, Brunel, City, Loughborough, Surrey and Heriot-Watt (1966), and Salford (1967).

The adoption by the government of the Robbins' targets of student places down to 1973–4 set an immediate task of securing the short-term expansion required by 1967–8. What was involved was a Herculean task. The expansion was far in advance of anything previously contemplated and in some universities so rapid an increase was viewed with mingled incredulity and alarm. In Swansea there was a mixed reception but, on the whole, the senate shared the view of Professor Hassall that rapid development on a large scale was both necessary in terms of national need and desirable from the viewpoint of the academic health of the college. For only by such expansion, the argument went, could high-quality research be sustained and the reputation of the college maintained in a thrusting, competitive academic world. Those, on the other hand, who had misgivings about the college's possible loss of cohesion because of its rapid growth and who predicted, through expansion, an erosion of values both in regard to teachers and taught, were few in number and subdued in voice. Nevertheless, it was becoming apparent in the early sixties that the increasing size of departments, their wider geographical spread about the campus and the cool anonymity of College House were destroying the heart-warming intimacy and simplicity of the old college. The 'airport lounge' atmosphere of the new senior common room did little to arrest the increasingly inward-looking social attitudes of departments and could not provide the companionable focus of its predecessor in the abbey.

In its original plans for the quinquennium 1962–7, drawn up in 1960, the college had considered it a reasonable and desirable academic policy to expand to about 2,500 students or more by 1966–7 in relation to a student population of 3,000 by the early 1970s. Already, by October 1963 and the publication of the Robbins Report, the full-time student population exceeded 2,000. Now it was planned to bring forward the 3,000 target from the early 1970s to the end of the current quinquennium, 1966–7, a thirty per cent increase in student numbers over a three-year period. In fact, the target figure was more than achieved and, as the following table shows, it involved a virtual doubling of the student population over six years:

Year	Student Population	Percentage Increase
1961–2	1,654	–
1962–3	1,877	13%
1963–4	2,069	25%
1964–5	2,373	43%
1965–6	2,678	62%
1966–7	2,989	81%
1967–8	3,276	98%

This rapid expansion in student numbers was matched by a more than equal expansion in the number of academic staff – and, incidentally, a marked improvement in the latter's material position.[5] Between 1962–3 – the last academic year before the Robbins Report – and 1967–8 the number of full-time students rose by 75 per cent. During the same period full-time teaching staff increased from 220 to 421, a rise of over 91 per cent, or, overall, an improvement in the ratio of full-time students to each full-time staff member from 8.53 in 1962–3 to 7.78 in 1967–8. In this the college reflected the national trend and the figures might be thought to indicate some relaxation, rather than any intensification, in the teaching load. Such figures, though, baldly taken, are misleading because they disguise the wide disparities that existed between individual departments. The expansion was supposed to be science- and technology-led – these were the days of Harold Wilson's 'white-hot technological revolution' – but the actual demand for places in non-science departments continued unabated so that while science departments were, pro rata, very generously staffed, on the arts side limitations in staffing not only exacerbated teaching pressures but, in some instances, stifled new developments.

Locally, as nationally, the increase of staff was greater in the junior grades; the percentage increase in senior teachers (professors, readers and senior lecturers) – 53 per cent – fell well below the percentage increase in full-time students, while that in the junior grades – 105 per cent – rose considerably higher. This imbalance of increase in staff between junior and senior grades contained the seeds of future difficulties. One would not necessarily agree with the sweeping generalization of Anthony Sampson that 'the new demand had attracted an inrush of second-rate teachers who could secure their coveted "tenure" more quickly and easily than their fellows in most other countries: after a few years they could not be sacked or moved or asked to adapt'. It is nevertheless true that a widely based staffing pyramid was created, which even enhanced opportunities for advancement through 'personal' promotions has not made sufficiently resilient. It cannot be denied either that in some disciplines during the post-Robbins expansion some appointments of questionable standard were made, despite the safeguards employed in staffing procedures. Of some 170 assistant lecturers or lecturers appointed to the college in the 1960s who were still in post in Swansea in 1979–80, 58 per cent had not progressed beyond the lectureship grade. Even if only a small number of this static group were of doubtful academic quality, the likelihood of the majority obtaining promotion receded daily with the passage of time. And amid the uncertainties of the harsher economic climate that set in from the late seventies and early eighties disillusion and discontent soon began to take the place of the euphoria of the heady sixties.

The time-scale of the expansion programme of the 1960s cannot be over-emphasized because it must be remembered that, while student numbers could be advanced, the building schedules for the new campus could not be so easily adjusted. New building projects – particularly bearing in mind the capital load that the college was attempting to absorb already – could not be planned and executed in time to accommodate additional students by 1967, nor was it all that easy to bring forward those buildings already planned or in course of construction. The Robbins euphoria caught Swansea in the mid-stream of its already-planned development. Yet the very existence of the 1958 plan helped the college to get rapidly into the higher gear called for by Robbins and ensured that its further physical expansion could be carried through without too great a sacrifice of architectural or landscape quality. Altogether, the substantial capital expenditure of the sixties in the circumstances was a remarkable achievement by the college.

In the fourteen years between 1956 and 1970 the college's full-time student population virtually quadrupled and Singleton itself was transformed from what was still its essentially pre-war cluster of temporary buildings nestling around the abbey and the 1937 library into a modern integrated campus. This metamorphosis involved a gross capital outlay of something approaching £12,000,000:

Completion Date	Building Project	Expenditure
1956	Natural Sciences I*	£432,000
1960	Chemistry *	£620,000
1960	Natural Sciences II*	£493,000
1961	College House/Services *	£646,000
1961	Neuaddau Lewis Jones & Sibly	£595,000
1963	Social Studies	£84,000
1964	Library Extn & Arts I	£587,000
1965	College House Extn & Alts	£500,000
1966	Applied Science	£3,800,000
1966	Neuadd Mary Williams	£420,000
1966	Physics & Mathematics	£2,026,000
1966	Chemistry Extn	£476,000
1970	Arts II	£474,000
	Site services, roads & landscaping	£620,000
		£11,773,000

* Part of the development plan devised by Sir Percy Thomas.

In addition, there were the other capital works that the college was also carrying out at this time – the refurbishment of Clyne and the building of Neuadd Martin, alterations to other college property both on and off the Singleton site, and the development of its playing fields at Sketty Lane and at Fairwood. In fact, there were a number of years when the capital grant exceeded £1 million and in 1964–5 it topped £2.7 million, a level of grant-aid that few universities would have been able to absorb administratively. It was due very much to the single-minded dedication of the registrar, John McIntyre, and his staff that so much was accomplished so smoothly, and to the active co-ordinating role of the architects that the quality of the environment at Singleton was not hopelessly spoliated.

Something has already been said about the capital schemes of the first few years of the development programme. The year 1963 saw the completion of the social studies building adjoining an attractive copse slightly to the north-east of the abbey. This site had been earmarked originally for the projected women's hall at Singleton and it was finally chosen for its new purpose only after prolonged bickering. But it was, in effect, a bonus because of the college's well-laid development plan and its flexibility of approach. As a result of 'slippage' in the development programme of another university and the readiness of Swansea to make a building start in 1964, the finance for the construction of the third 'tower block' hall could be snapped up. The third hall (Neuadd Mary Williams) was, thus, designated for women students as an alternative to the abbey site, although it meant, of course, that the eventual move of the college's administration to a purpose-built office became something of a chimera. The social studies building was intended for the new school of social studies and, in the first instance, accommodated sociology and anthropology, psychology, and, on a temporary basis, the courses in social administration. Also in 1963 came the first phase of purpose-built accommodation for the arts faculty. A new building, adjoining the new library complex, allowed the departments of history, economics, philosophy and politics to escape from the cramped quarters they had been occupying in the abbey and its outbuildings and, in turn, freed this accommodation for other arts departments and an ever-expanding registry.

Nineteen sixty-four saw the commissioning of the new library complex, much of the planning for which had been done in Miss Busby's last days as librarian. In 1959 she had been succeeded by F.J.W. Harding, and, building upon the foundations which Miss Busby had laid, Frank Harding, quietly and steadfastly, created a true university collection of teaching and research material comparable with many of the best in Britain. Like Miss Busby, Harding had come to Swansea from a London college – Birkbeck, where he had been librarian. A cautious and conservative man – though he had won the MC in 1944 – his flair for appointing colleagues of calibre gave the library one of its greatest strengths. The new library of 1964 – 'extension' was a complete misnomer – more than trebled the accommodation for books and readers, while a further extension in 1974 brought the main library storage capacity alone to well over half a million volumes with places for about 920 readers. The construction of the reading-room areas which were 'suspended' from external steel girders owed much to direct collaboration with the engineering department and the researches of the Professor of Civil Engineering, Bernard Neal, into the plastic design of structures. Harding retired in 1980, to be succeeded by the college's second female librarian, Miss Mary Cooper from Strathclyde. Unhappily, he died within the year.

Although expanding and diversifying, the arts faculty throughout this period remained the poor relation in terms of accommodation. Those disciplines that had not been able to find a home in the new building continued in cramped quarters in the old 'temporary' buildings or in the abbey. The applied sciences and physics and mathematics, it is true, were not much better off but at least they had a more immediate prospect of relief. The main thrust of capital development was still for the sciences and, now, on a scale far greater than anything that had gone before. From 1961 planning was well under way for the applied science building, at nearly £4 million the largest single scheme yet undertaken by the college. Construction work on the complex, again involving close collaboration between the architects and the engineering department on the structure of the building, began during the 1962–3 session and by 1965 the lecture rooms were ready for use. A year later the whole building was complete. It had been a vast undertaking, and although a great many individuals had been involved in its planning, the main administrative weight in co-ordinating and organizing the exercise had fallen on R.O. ('Dickie') Dunmore, a lecturer in engineering since 1961. Virtually singlehanded and totally unruffled, he had seen to all the detailed planning, from the ordering of equipment to the selection of furniture, and at the same time he had carried his full share of teaching duties. After the building was opened Dunmore was appointed permanent sub-dean of the faculty but, tragically, he died suddenly in 1968: in many ways the applied science building is his memorial.

By September 1966 the main areas of the physics and mathematics complex had been taken over with the radioactivity block following in June 1967. This £2 million development and the social studies building both secured Civic Trust awards. The latter building also earned for the architects the RIBA Architecture Bronze Medal while the physics and mathematics building brought them – by now known as the Percy Thomas Partnership, who were not only the development architects for Singleton but also the executive architects for the individual buildings on the site – the coveted award of the gold medal for architecture given in the Royal National Eisteddfod of 1970.

The academic year 1965–6 saw the completion of a further extension to the chemistry building but, at last, in 1970 came the second stage of the arts building on the opposite side of the 'mall' to its 1963 precursor. Singleton Abbey, which had been used by the registry and a succession of academic departments since the 1920s, now became almost wholly the preserve of the college's administration, although the abbey's continuous teaching link of half a century was preserved because the old orangery remained as a lecture room. It had to because the UGC had taken the decision not to provide large

The social studies building was awarded the RIBA Architecture Bronze Medal for the building of outstanding merit erected in south Wales in the years 1961–4

lecture rooms for the arts faculty: this short-sighted approach had an unfortunate effect then and afterwards. The various moves were tortuous and in them one discerns an element of 'musical chairs', for there was a redeployment of accommodation in the arts faculty as a whole based on the spatial requirements of the departments. History and economic history left the original stage of the arts building and were joined in the new stage two by romance studies, English, Welsh, German, education and social administration.

The completion of the second stage of the arts building effectively brought to an end the college's major construction programme at Singleton for a student population of three thousand although permanent accommodation for the newer life sciences and some sections of the earth sciences had yet to be provided. The programme had already cost the Exchequer nearly £12,000,000. The total development projected for Singleton in 1958 had, even at the prices obtained then, been estimated at over £10,000,000. From the outset the college had been encouraged by the UGC to make its own financial contribution to the costs involved; originally 10 per cent had been suggested but later, with the escalation of costs, a figure of 5 per cent had been agreed to help complete the programme and to finance undertakings, like the proposed chapel of unity, the cost of which would not be met from government funds.

The college had few reserves other than the original endowment fund established by David Davies during the Great War. In 1960 a development fund appeal was, therefore, launched with £500,000 as a target. At Fulton's insistence, while the detailed organization of the appeal was left to the officers of the college, a special appeal committee, wider-ranging than the council and deliberately aimed to encourage the direct interest of industry and commerce, was set up as a sponsoring body. Its members were influential figures: each was hand-picked, both to involve the interest of capital and labour and to obtain entrée, on a personal basis, to as wide a range of substantial industrial and commercial undertakings as possible. Through the personal approaches made by members of the committee, over £170,000 had been promised before the appeal was formally launched. Within six weeks of its becoming public knowledge, £250,000 had been received and almost before six months had passed three-quarters of the target had been reached, much of the support coming from industry. By 1962 the fund had topped the £450,000 mark and if the final stages to the ultimate target proved increasingly difficult in the harsher economic climate of the mid-sixties, eventually, by 1967, the total £500,000 was achieved. It was, however, to be the college's tragedy that the money was not to be put to purposeful use in good time, for when eventually the fund was tapped in the late seventies inflation had cut a swathe through its effective value. It is perhaps too easy, with hindsight, to condemn the decisions of a quarter of a century ago but one could wish that the fund had been invested in buildings rather than in equities.

The redevelopment of the college in the late 1950s and 1960s had been a sustained and intricate operation. Throughout, there had also been an intensive use of the temporary buildings of the 1920s. Indeed, it was only in 1967 during the preparatory work for the second stage of the arts building that any of the early 'pavilions' were demolished. One group of temporary buildings enjoyed its third distinct usage as a music, art and drama centre, which, together with the adjacent arts theatre, formed a focal point for cultural activities in the college until the opening of the Taliesin arts centre in 1984. Again, until the permanent sports centre was opened at Sketty Lane in 1980, part of the former engineering building was used for indoor games, and, later, as an experimental theatre-workshop. Other buildings, originally designed as chemistry laboratories and later altered for the applied sciences, afterwards provided much needed relief for geography, geology, botany, zoology, genetics and microbiology until a further major extension to the natural sciences building could be completed in the summer of 1975. This process of intensive utilization continued, for oceanography, instituted as part of the department of geology in 1967 and established as an independent department in 1976, occupied a range of former engineering buildings until its demise in 1987.

In describing the physical development of the original plans of the post-war period one has naturally had to stray beyond the Fulton era. But although so much of the detailed planning and construction of the new campus occurred after his time, the concept and the inspiration were his. Fulton's ability to seize upon and develop ideas and his powers of persuasion to obtain greater building allocations from the UGC were remarkable. He took full advantage of the climate of change after the war and the thrust to expand the universities. At the same time he was himself one of the architects of that expansion, one of that constellation of academic statesmen who consecrated the new creed. He, seemingly, knew everyone who mattered and he built up an especially close rapport with successive chairmen of the UGC, Trueman and the committed expansionist, Murray. Fulton's own expansionism, though, was not simply a devotion to size: through growth Fulton strove for the 'complete' university. He was concerned to broaden courses, to extend the range of subjects, to foster the new social sciences, and, above all, to broaden the cultural awareness of Swansea students. Both the 'freshers' essay' scheme and the courses of weekly lectures on subjects of general academic interest – often given by distinguished visitors who, more often than not, were personal friends of Fulton – owed their introduction to the college in 1949 primarily to him. Unhappily, some of this 'cultural enhancement', especially the 'freshers' essays', evoked suspicion and criticism especially from people not invited to participate in the scheme; it was said to divert attention from the really 'relevant' academic work and to smack too much of 'Oxbridge'; the principal's occasional unguarded reference to a 'freshman' rather than a 'fresher' could provoke a reactive *frisson*. Even such a staunch supporter as Henry Lewis, on whom Fulton depended a great deal in his dealings with the senate and the academic staff, was not persuadable.[7] Yet, positive though he was in his ideas, Fulton was flexible enough to take account of the views of others even when such views might not accord with his own; and, if necessary, to give way. It was not unnatural, therefore, that he should win the respect even of those who did not see eye-to-eye with him. But to put his broader ideas into action he needed the support of the college council. Here, the key was the attitude of Sir Lewis Jones, the senior vice-president of the college and a man of equally strong personality. If at times their relationship was not an easy one, Fulton's readiness to consult and to explain gained for him the essential backing he needed.

The creation of a humanistic atmosphere in the college was something that Fulton saw ranging beyond 'freshers' essays' and the weekly general lectures. It was something that he saw embracing students' everyday lives, and, as part of their cultural development, he wanted them to experience at first hand the best of modern furnishing and interior decoration arising out of post-Festival of Britain design. Hence his meticulous attention to the fitting-out of Clyne and the arts hall and of the refurbishment of Beck Hall and Maes-yr-Haf where he engaged Sadie Speight, one of the country's leading interior designers. It was an approach he was to carry through to College House and the Singleton halls, for which he secured the design services of the remarkable Professor Misha Black.[8]

To Fulton the real challenge lay more in the beginning of things and far less in the tedium of working them through. In 1959, after twelve years of setting the college on its new course, he left Swansea to become the first principal (and, before it opened, vice-chancellor) of the new University (College) of Sussex at Brighton. His labours at Singleton, he felt, were completed and he could happily leave to others the practical fulfilment of the developments he had planned. He could be freed to refine from first principles, on a much broader canvas and in a positive climate of university experimentation which he himself had done so much to influence, the academic concepts he had tentatively embarked on at Swansea. For the college his departure was a tremendous loss and, though there were some who shed few tears at his going, his like was not to be seen again at Singleton. The success of the college today owes much to his dynamism and foresight.

The college followed its time-honoured procedure of taking soundings of eminent academics and others in considering suitable persons as his successor. At first there was some difficulty in making an appointment, for some of the shortlisted candidates proved disappointing at interview but, in due course, Dr John Horace Parry, principal of the University College, Ibadan, Nigeria, was appointed to the principalship from 1 September 1960. The interregnum of a year necessitated the appointment of an acting-principal. In the normal course, E. Victor Morgan, who had been Professor of

John Horace Parry (1914–82), principal
(1960–5) and vice-chancellor of the University
of Wales (1963–5)

Economics since 1945 and who had succeeded as vice-principal for the usual two-year period in 1958, would have expected to serve in this capacity. Instead, the council decided to invite Frank Llewellyn Jones, Professor of Physics also since 1945.

Prior to going to Ibadan Dr Parry had been Professor of History at the University College of the West Indies and before that a fellow of Clare College, Cambridge, and a university lecturer in history. He soon developed a close affinity with his senate, academic colleagues generally and with the student body. He was, indeed, particularly 'good' with students, always available and ready to listen but never shirking discipline. Parry brought to his office some distinctive cultural qualities and a rare ability to 'compartmentalize' his mind. Despite the extreme pressures of his administrative load he continued very much as an active historian. Very often late at night – owing much to his wartime naval experience and habits – Parry wrote two distinguished and wide-ranging expositions, *The Age of Reconnaissance* (1963) and *The Spanish Seaborne Empire* (1966), as well as contributions on Latin American history to the *Cambridge Modern History*.

The five years of Parry's principalship will always be thought of as a vintage period of the college's development. It was during his time that most of the new buildings at Singleton were completed, the Fairwood estate was acquired, and Hendrefoilan House with a large part of its estate was bought: academically, there was an apparently never-ending stream of innovations, with new faculties, new disciplines and new chairs constantly appearing as if by some magical process. They were 'heady' days 'with financial resources flowing into the College almost faster than we knew how to deal with them' (Professor Balchin in *Newsletter*, 257, p. 3). Parry's time as principal thus coincided with a unique phase in the history of the college. But, in many ways he was fortunate as Fulton's successor, for the main lines of the college's development had already been charted. It is doubtful if, in the long term, he could have coped with the primary planning that had already been undertaken and, at the same time, maintained his other interests: the days when one could be both a committed scholar and a practical university administrator had gone; indeed, they had already passed even in the quieter days of Edwards. This was something Parry soon recognized and attempted to meet with the appointment of Professor George Kerferd, Farrington's successor in the chair of classics, as co-ordinator of academic developments.

For Parry's administrative activities were not confined to the college alone. For two years, between 1963 and 1965, he was an active vice-chancellor of the University and deftly handled the emotively difficult issue of the University Commission, even if criticism of him as a 'bird of passage' in some quarters hurt him sorely. Also during his time at Swansea Parry headed a government committee on Latin American Studies, which led to the creation of five 'Parry Centres' in London, Oxford, Cambridge, Liverpool and Glasgow, and which have become important bases for postgraduate work on Latin America.

In some respects his experience as a member of a self-governing academic community at Cambridge and in what were still colonial universities did not altogether fit him for the principalship of a civic university college, and especially a university college where the council still, even in the sixties, played a powerful role in day-to-day affairs. Cultured, urbane, sociable, and with active interests which ranged from sailing to ornithology, Parry yet lacked something of the keen political nose of a Fulton. His naval

John McIntyre (1907–76) receiving the honorary degree of MSc (Econ) from the vice-chancellor of the University of Wales (Principal Frank Llewellyn Jones) at the Jubilee Degree Congregation, 29 September 1970. On the left is Professor Balchin and seated on the right is Lord Fulton

manner and his quickness of decision were not readily assimilated by everyone. His sometimes all-too-apparent disdain for local 'parochialism' was not appreciated in quarters where it was deserved. On occasion, his very openness was suspected by those of less rigorous standards. And gradually, over the five years of his principalship, his relations with Sir Lewis Jones, in his old age increasingly under the influence of a small coterie ill-disposed to Parry, deteriorated. This and the realization that, even with his dynamic personality and immense energy, he could not combine the active pursuit of historical scholarship with the demands of the principalship of a rapidly expanding college persuaded Parry to go. When, in 1965, the offer of the Gardiner Chair of Oceanic History and Affairs at Havard came it was a temptation that he could not resist.

Within the college Parry's passage was tremendously eased, administratively, by the registrar John McIntyre. Edwin Drew had retired in 1952 after thirty-two years of unremitting, and often exacting, service. His work for the college had been distinguished and disinterested. He had made significant contributions to its smooth running at times of the utmost difficulty. And hard taskmaster as he might have been, he had seen to it that his staff were thoroughly grounded in the ways of administration. As a result, he left his successor an efficient and self-effacing office team. John McIntyre, came to Swansea from Sheffield where he had been assistant registrar since 1944. He had served his administrative apprenticeship in Glasgow, graduating in history while he was still working in the registry, and had had a wide-ranging experience of university administration. Afforded little in the way of any 'handover' by his predecessor, McIntyre was thrown headlong into the maelstrom of expansion, the difficult bargaining over Clyne and the negotiations over Singleton. Throughout, he was ably assisted by registry staff who had loyally served the college for many years: Harold Jenkins (appointed in 1931), Edward Wright (in 1924), and Harold Smale (in 1934) were only the most senior. They were very much the 'engine room' and McIntyre was dependent upon them, as were his professional assistants who, starting with Stephen Jeffreys in 1955, tended to 'leap-frog' them, though lacking their vast experience.

To them all, and to McIntyre especially, fell the onerous task of administering the physical and academic developments of the expansion. It was an undertaking of magnitude. And as McIntyre's close friend and fellow 'Swansea Town' supporter, Ivor Isaac, later stressed, three successive principals were to owe an immeasurable debt to the reliability and devoted industry of the registrar during this period. Unassuming, throughout, McIntyre never lost his humanity. Professor Charles Gittins made the point when presenting him for an honorary degree that McIntyre 'never forgot that reports, procedures, regulations and the entire mechanism of administration were a service to *persons*, not to robots. The Man was never lost in the Registrar.' McIntyre's concern for the welfare of students and his unquenchable interest in their activities were recognized by the fact that each of the student bodies in the three universities he served, conferred on him honorary life membership of their unions. He was eventually to retire in 1968, his last years darkened by ill health brought on as much by changes in administrative style in the college, as by the problems of administration itself which he had always taken in his stride.

Fulton's early years were marked by the departure of the last of the College's earliest teaching staff. Professor Coates and Professor Mary Williams were the first to retire in 1948, Edwin Drew left in 1952 as did Professor Heath, and in 1954 Professor Henry Lewis[9] and Professor Mockeridge. They were the 'last of the bunch', as 'Tee Jay' Rees (since 1950 the college's treasurer) fondly called them, since earlier in 1954, and shortly before his own retirement, Professor W.D. Thomas had died suddenly. Thomas, distinguished-looking, courteous and very much a gentleman, was a brilliant teacher; sensitive to style and alert to ideas he was perhaps more at home with the small informal group than in the formal lecture. Encouraging and generous though he was to others he was over-critical where he himself was concerned and his writings, full of grace and polish, were few and far between. As Fulton put it, 'The world that was beyond the range of his voice is the poorer for this'. Thomas's patience and clarity of thought were brought to the fore during his periods as vice-principal although administration as such was not his forte and routine departmental chores he left in the capable hands of Isabel Westcott, for forty-one years, as assistant lecturer, lecturer and senior lecturer the devoted linchpin of the department.[10] The esteem in which Thomas was held in the college was matched outside. Few members of the staff did as much to bring his department into lively contact with the town and district, whether through extra-mural work or a whole range of local cultural societies from the *Bookmen* to the *Little Theatre*. In this his interests were akin to those of Ernest Hughes who had also died a few months earlier and both were commemorated by the establishment of memorial funds.

The year 1948 had seen the retirement of F.W. Halliday from the headship of the German department which he had held since its inception in 1931. Halliday was

Registry staff at the retirement presentation to Harold Jenkins (1900–68) in September 1965. *Left to right*: Peter White, Raymond Stephens (1915–83), John McIntyre, Edward Wright, David Ambrose (1912–91), Harold Smale, Harold Jenkins, John Dermody and Albert Devonald (1910–85). For their long and distinguished service to the college both Mr Jenkins (thirty-four years) and Mr Wright (fifty years) were awarded the honorary degree of MA of the University of Wales on their retirement

Miss Isabel Westcott (d. 1992) with David J. Thomas of BBC Wales, a former student, *centre left*, and Professor Cecil Price (1915–91), *right*, after a lecture by Mr Thomas to the English department on 21 April 1966. Both Mr Thomas and Professor Price were students at the college, Mr Thomas graduating with a first in French in 1932, and Professor Price being student president in 1937–8

succeeded by the mercurial Dr Erich Heller (1911–90) from Peterhouse, Cambridge. Heller, whose independent lectureship was translated into a chair in 1950, was tall and handsome, and exuded an air of mystery and incomprehension. Born in Bohemia, a subject, as he liked to say, of the Austro-Hungarian empire, he was a distinguished literary critic, expert on Goethe, Nietzsche and Thomas Mann. Publicly, he was regarded as the most intellectual of the college's staff at the time, though in more jealous university circles he was suspected of being something of a charlatan. Certainly, through his broadcasts and literary reviews he built up an enviable reputation, crowned in 1952 by his collection of essays, *The Disinherited Mind*.

In 1946 Fred Schonell, the breezy, unobtrusively academic, Australian Professor of Education, resigned to take up the chair of education at Birmingham.[11] He was succeeded by Evan John Jones from Cardiff. A classicist and authority on Welsh heraldry, Jones, a kindly man, typified the quieter traditions of the college. Yet he ably steered the introduction of a collegiate faculty of education and of new courses in youth leadership which flowed from the McNair Report of 1944. As a consequence of its implementation the University of Wales assumed responsibility for the education and training of students in the Welsh training colleges. Collegiate faculties of education were accordingly established in 1948 at each of the four constituent colleges, bringing the training colleges and the university college departments of education into a close form of association. In 1965 Maes-yr-Haf, acquired nearly two decades earlier as a 'temporary' students' union building, was converted into a centre and library for the collegiate faculty and remained as its headquarters until both the faculty and department of education moved to Hendrefoilan in 1973. This move, while serving to bring faculty and department much more closely together, did create for the department a remoteness from the academic scene at Singleton which has continued to this day. The department of education, besides preparing students for the postgraduate certificate in education and for higher degrees in arts, has, in more recent years, undertaken responsibility for the M.Ed. degree, and, latterly, for undergraduate courses too. It has also developed a number of diploma courses in youth leadership, special education, educational psychology, and school counselling.

At the same time that the collegiate faculty of education was being fostered, a diploma course in social science was started at the college as a response to the urgent need in post-war Britain for social workers and administrators. David Marsh[12] was the first lecturer-in-charge in the subject but left for New Zealand in 1949 to be succeeded by Robin Huws Jones who came to Swansea from a background as a lecturer in social science at Liverpool and in adult education with the Oxford extra-mural delegacy. Occupying primitive accommodation left behind by builders, the success of the original course – students included Alun Richards, the writer and broadcaster, and Tom White, principal of the National Children's Home – was rapid. But the obviously distinct needs of the few students from developing countries who enrolled for it encouraged the establishment of a separate diploma course in social welfare and administration sponsored by the United Nations and the Colonial Office. This new course was intended specifically for social workers and administrators from low-income countries, which then included Japan and the oil-rich nations, as well as countries in the Commonwealth. Over the next eleven years the vision and energy of Huws Jones were to make this course well known throughout the Third World. Students went on to obtain posts of distinction in government and the voluntary services worldwide.

In 1960 a second overseas diploma course was instituted for middle-level social workers and although Huws Jones left in the following year to become founder Principal of the National Institute of Social Work he left to his successor, Andrew Lochhead, a rapidly expanding department, solidly based even if it was largely dependent financially on student fees and the generosity of charitable trusts. The generosity of the trusts, in fact, extended beyond the financing of the courses. The Rowntree Memorial Trust, for instance, funded a three-year research project into the family and social change, the results of which were published in 1965 (C. Rosser and C.C. Harris, *The Family and Social Change*) and which was the start of social research in the department.

The sixties saw changes in the coverage of the overseas courses as interest tended to concentrate more on the broader issues of the economic growth of developing countries than on the practical concerns of social welfare. Thus, the diploma course in social *welfare* became social *policy* in 1961 and the departmental teaching programme was widened. The sharpening of interest in social policy and planning led from 1973 onwards to a move into postgraduate teaching with a reorientation of the courses to equip students with more theoretical and analytical skills. While the 'overseas' developments had been taking place the 'British' component had not been neglected and in 1970 a chair in social administration was created with a particular responsibility for these courses which by 1976 included a degree course, a postgraduate diploma course in social work and one in community work as well. Indeed, so successful were the courses overall that by 1976 it was decided to transfer the 'overseas' element to an independent centre of development studies with a new chair in development policy and planning to continue and expand them, albeit, as hitherto, on a self-financing basis.

In 1957 mathematics split into two separate departments – pure and applied. Professor J.G. Oldroyd (1921–82), who had come to the foundation chair of applied mathematics from a research fellowship at Trinity College, Cambridge, in 1953, was appointed to the headship of the new department. This was a change which recognized the developments that had been taking place in the two interrelated disciplines and their increasing interaction with other subjects. Rowland ('Tug') Wilson, now the college's senior professor, continued as Head of the Pure Mathematics Department until his retirement in 1961. He had then been at Swansea for forty years and was one of the college's most devoted and colourful members. Deeply respected by his students, many of them owed him much; ex-servicemen, in particular, struggling to adjust to the rigours of academic life, had no greater advocate and friend.

Wilson was succeeded by Dr Jeffrey Weston, Reader in Mathematical Analysis at Newcastle, who took over the mantle of planning the move from the department's forty-year-old 'temporary' quarters to the new physics and mathematics complex that opened in 1965. Almost before the move occurred Professor Oldroyd resigned to take up a chair at Liverpool, his place being taken by Dr Neville Temperley, a senior principal scientific officer at the Atomic Weapons Research establishment, as Professor of Applied Mathematics. When Temperley in turn retired in 1982 pure and applied mathematics were reunited, after twenty-five years, as a department of mathematics under Weston.

In 1954 a department of political theory and government was set up, J.C. Rees (1919–80), Reader in Politics and Head of the Department of Government at Leicester, being appointed to the new chair. These were days when the study of politics on any scale was a relatively fresh academic enterprise and they were therefore crucial times in the development of the discipline. Rees was one of its most prominent figures and, through his own rigorous and exacting standards of scholarship and teaching, he rapidly established for his department a remarkable reputation for the study of political theory and ensured for it an authoritative position in the faculty of arts. His meticulous attention to detail and his unsparing concern for meaning meant that his publications were few but what did emerge from his pen sparkled with clarity and vigour. Scholarship was fundamental to him; administration an unnecessary distraction. Thus in 1962 he took the unique step for Swansea of resigning his chair and reverting to a lectureship. It was no capricious decision and although he quickly became a reader he would never allow his name to go forward for a personal chair when that avenue became available to him; the inconsistency of doing so would never have squared with his conscience.

In 1957 Glanmor Williams succeeded David Quinn in the chair of history on the latter's appointment to Liverpool. Quinn, who had followed Ernest Hughes in 1944, was an authority on European exploration and expansion, Williams on early modern Wales and the Reformation. It was a department that had always attracted staff members of distinction: now it was entering its greatest period. Professor Williams's study of the

Glanmor Williams, *left*, and Oleg Zienkiewicz, *right*. Professor Williams, a formative influence on the development of the college since the Second World War, was a vice-principal in 1975–8 and was elected an FBA in 1986. Professor Zienkiewicz, one of the most academically honoured members of the college, was elected an FRS in 1979 for his achievements in the Finite Element Method, and other contributions to Applied Mechanics

medieval Welsh Church received great acclaim and his distinction as a historian was marked shortly after his retirement from the chair in 1982 by his election to the Fellowship of the British Academy. With his colleagues a veritable constellation of historical scholarship was formed: Ieuan Jones (later to hold a chair at Aberystwyth), Walter Minchinton (later a professor at Exeter), Muriel Chamberlain (now Professor of History at Swansea), David Walker and Neville Masterman were only the most prominent. It was a nursery of scholarship, too, where young historians learnt their apprenticeship: Kenneth Morgan (later a fellow of The Queen's College, Oxford, before becoming principal of Aberystwyth, and an FBA); Rees Davies (an FBA and Professor of History at Aberystwyth); John Davies (also at Aberystwyth); Prys Morgan; and Ralph Griffiths (now Professor of Medieval History at Swansea).

In these years, too, the English department was a nursery of young scholars. James Kinsley (1922–84) had succeeded W.D. Thomas in 1954. An authority on Dryden and the Augustans he left for Nottingham in 1961 – he became an FBA in 1971 – and was in turn succeeded by Cecil Price, an old student of the college (a former president of the union) and an authority on eighteenth-century theatre. 'Jo' Bartley (d. 1967), author of *Teague, Shenkin and Sawney, being an Historical Study of the Earlier Irish, Welsh and Scottish Characters in English Plays*, joined the department after the war to be soon followed by David Sims (1922–89) and Sam Dawson, and with Willy Smyth (d. 1973) of classics, Esmond Cleary of economics and Peter Winch of philosophy, all stalwarts of college life for many years and stars of the staff dramatic performances that were such a feature of these days; a seemingly irreverent group who did much to spark the enthusiasm and imagination of the student generation of the late forties and fifties.[13] Kingsley Amis wrote *Lucky Jim* at Swansea before moving on to Cambridge. Although this first novel was based more on Leicester than on Swansea, Amis developed during these years a rare insight into the southern Welsh character which he displayed to great effect in some of his other works. Other, later, colleagues who gained distinction elsewhere included Alastair Fowler (at Oxford, Edinburgh and Virginia: an FBA in 1974), Howard Erskine-Hill (at Cambridge: an FBA in 1985) and A.J. Smith (at Southampton).

Most departments possessed a clutch of distinguished scholars and teachers over these years: D. Simon Evans and his brother Ellis Evans in Welsh (now Jesus Professor of Celtic at Oxford and an FBA since 1983), J. Gwyn Griffiths in classics, Rush Rhees (1905–89), Roy Holland and Peter Winch in philosophy, Jack Lively and Frank Stacey (d. 1977) in politics, Maurice Davidson and Granville Beynon in physics are but a few of those who enhanced the reputation of the college and ensured that the 'Amis principle' was not fulfilled as the college expanded. There *was* no falling-off of standards; the percentage of 'good' degrees was maintained and in some areas considerably increased while postgraduate research, especially at doctoral level which had been almost non-existent before the war, expanded greatly. Fulton once said that one of the marks of a successful university was its capacity for getting students into the higher civil service. This was achieved in 1960 when Donald Anderson, with a 'first' in modern history and politics, entered the foreign service.[14] In 1964 Jean Thomas achieved a 'first' in chemistry and began a distinguished academic career that has led to an FRS and a professorship at Cambridge. But Anderson and Thomas were only two of the students of these years who were to bring lustre to the college.

The mid-fifties saw a series of changes in the department of engineering. The distribution of students led in 1954 to the establishment of a separate chair of civil engineering to which Dr Bernard Neal, a fellow of Trinity Hall, Cambridge, was appointed. The following year Professor Kastner left for King's College, London, and the opportunity was taken to redesignate his chair as a chair of mechanical engineering. At the same time a new chair in electrical engineering was created and Dr Wilfred Fishwick was appointed to this, R.H. Macmillan becoming Professor of Mechanical Engineering shortly afterwards.

The college, too, reflected the major changes that were taking place in the industrial scene of south Wales at this time. In applied science, especially, it had been recognized at the outset that both teaching and research had to be linked to the reality of industry if it were not to retreat into academic isolation. By the fifties, south Wales had become a major centre for oil-refining in Britain. The growth of the associated petro-chemical industry and the increasing emphasis on the development of synthetic products and the scientific processing of raw materials encouraged, in 1954, the foundation of a department of chemical engineering. Dr Stanley Sellers (1912–88) occupied the foundation chair until 1960 when Dr J.F. Richardson succeeded him. In the same year, the creation of a second chair of metallurgy, concerned primarily with scientific problems in the fabrication of metals, resulted from a £100,000 endowment from Richard Thomas and Baldwins Limited and the Steel Company of Wales. The introduction of this new chair of physical metallurgy recognized again the changing needs of the metal industries, which was emphasized, once more, in 1973, by the

Three professors at the forefront of the developments of the fifties and sixties: Jack Richardson (Chemical Engineering – 1960–87), *top left*, Frank Rhodes (Geology – 1956–68), *top right*, and Cedric Hassall (Chemistry – 1957–71), *bottom right*. Professor Rhodes is now President of Cornell University. Professor Hassall was elected an FRS in 1985, and has played an important role advising on the development of a number of overseas universities addition of 'materials technology' to the title of the department. In 1962 the applied sciences, which for some years had been a sub-faculty of the faculty of science, became a full faculty in their own right and in 1969 the department of engineering, which had already passed through a metamorphosis of existence as the 'school of engineering', split into three independent departments.

The early sixties saw the further creation of new chairs and the introduction or development of several new disciplines: a second chair of history, a second chair of physics and a chair of industrial engineering, this last being at the same time one of only three in the country, and its tautologous title concealing its concern with the development of courses in management. Chairs in physical chemistry, applied economics and second chairs in geography, electrical engineering and pure mathematics followed, while chairs and departments of genetics and computer science were also created. The introduction of social studies into the college had had its first tentative foundations laid in Fulton's first year. Now a series of new disciplines was developed, including sociology and anthropology, psychology, and economic history. It was a development that afforded exciting possibilities for new courses in which the new subjects could combine with the college's long-established disciplines such as history, politics, economics and geography. The prospects were relished with some enthusiasm and a new faculty of economic and social studies was created in 1964 with Professor Glanmor Williams as its first dean. Unhappily, although successful in many ways, the new faculty never fully achieved the potential that many, like Williams, had hoped for it because of the eventual lukewarmness of some of those who had been its most ardent supporters. Nevertheless, the range of subjects introduced in these years allowed a new co-operative and interdisciplinary approach to schemes of study reflected in the present syllabuses of the college which would certainly have appealed to the innovatory Fulton.

In establishing the policies to be adopted in the expansion of universities the UGC appointed a number of independent committees to advise it on specialist topics. Reference has already been made to Dr Parry's committee on Latin American studies. In 1960 a similar committee under the chairmanship of Sir William Hayter was set up to review Oriental, Slavonic, East European and African studies and, as a result of its report, published in 1961, Swansea was selected as a centre for Russian and East European studies, teaching posts being established in Russian history, economics, politics and geography. As a separate venture, teaching in Russian language and literature also became available in the German department, while Italian and Spanish were introduced into the department of French, the title of the latter being changed to 'romance studies' to reflect its greater breadth of interest. Nearly twenty years earlier, it will be recalled, both Russian and Spanish had been proposed as new subjects in the post-war development plan put forward to the university in 1944.

The college is fortunate in its parkland setting on the western shore of Swansea Bay. For many generations, however, the first impact on the visitor to Swansea by rail from the east was the grim desolation of the landscape of the lower Swansea Valley. On some visitors, it is said, the effect of the scene was so awful that they returned home immediately without even venturing into the town from the station. This wasteland was all that remained of the heyday of copper-smelting and tinplate manufacture. It was an industrial inheritance spread over a thousand or more acres of derelict land with abandoned works, seven million tons of metalliferous slag and coarsely vegetated, eroded and polluted soils on the valley sides. While most Swansea people were apathetic in their attitude to the industrial spoliation and affected to ignore it – it was said that some even wanted the dereliction preserved as a memorial to nineteenth-century capitalism – there were a few to whom it was a matter of grave and urgent concern.

In 1961, inspired by Robin Huws Jones, since 1953 the director of social administration courses, the college, in partnership with the Nuffield Foundation, the Ministry of Housing and Local Government, the Swansea Borough Council and a number of other interests, embarked upon a comprehensive, multi-disciplinary survey of the area as a first step towards bringing it back into the natural stream of social and economic use. The cost of the survey – about £50,000 – was met mainly by the Nuffield Foundation, the Department of Scientific and Industrial Research, the Corporation and the ministry. The scheme captured the imagination of John Fulton. With his encouragement and subsequently that of John Parry, and, under the administrative direction of Kenneth Hilton, a former colonial service officer, a number of college disciplines – the natural sciences, chemistry, engineering, economics, history and sociology – involved themselves deeply in the work, supported by the borough, the Welsh Office, the research councils and industry. The ultimate aim of the project was nothing less than a comprehensive reclamation of the valley, and although there were nothing like enough funds to allow the college to complete this work, it was hoped that the academic study, together with a limited amount of practical action, might serve to overcome the long-standing local apathy towards the derelict area, and at least provide a detailed source of information for future developments. The removal of the slag heaps was thought to be too vast and expensive an operation to contemplate. Experimental work was, thus, undertaken in the botany department to encourage grasses, trees and shrubs to grow in the barren environment and to see whether the valley's appearance could be improved. After five years the fruits of the research were published as *The Lower Swansea Valley Project* (May 1967), with recommendations for the reclamation and revitalization of the area.

While much of the Project report was of academic interest, it did point the way forward. It was, said the Duke of Edinburgh, 'like an explorer's torch in the gloom of a cave'. There was, though, always the danger that the light of the torch would peter out and that, like the earlier report by Sylvia Crowe on the Swansea foreshore, *The Lower Swansea Valley Project* would gather dust on some forgotten shelf. The complacency of both the public and government authorities had, however, been shaken by the recent tragedy of the Aberfan disaster. Public funds for land-reclamation schemes became more readily available and, although restoration of the valley was at first slow and uncertain, the pace quickened, especially after the reorganization of local government in 1974. Much of the valley has now been acquired by the city council and, overall, some £18.5 million has so far been spent on its rehabilitation. A 'heavily landscaped' 'enterprise park' for light industry, retail outlets and office accommodation is being developed north of the railway line, while to the south a 'leisure park' is being created. The new landscape that is arising literally from the ashes of Swansea's industrial past could not have been created without the foundations laid by the project. And this, in its turn, was dependent upon fundamental inter-departmental and inter-faculty activity within the college. The work of the project would never have been completed without the whole-hearted support of the borough council and especially the enthusiasm of Percy

Ivor Isaac (1915–78), *left*, and Trevor Marchant (1905–82), *right*. The first of the college's personal professors with the last of the original college staff of 1920. Isaac, a student at the College with a 'first' in botany in 1937, was a vice-principal in 1973–7. Marchant served the geology department for fifty-three years, rising from lab. boy to chief technician

Morris and Iorwerth Watkins, the town clerk. It was a prime example of the happy relationship that by the 1960s existed between the college and the Corporation after so many earlier years of mutual suspicion and misunderstanding.

During these years there were changes in the leading personnel of the college. In 1955 Sir George Barstow retired from the presidency of the college after twenty years' service. With the expansion of the college very much uppermost in people's minds, it was decided to seek an eminent public figure as Barstow's successor, and Major Gwilym Lloyd-George (1894–1967), currently Home Secretary and Minister for Welsh Affairs in the Conservative government, agreed to accept the office. The new president played a significant role in the organization of the development appeal and throughout his ten years in office was consistent in his support of the college. In 1965, however, Lord Tenby, as he had become in 1957, was forced to retire from the presidency on grounds of ill health – he died early in 1967 – and was succeeded by Sir Edmund Davies. A native of Mountain Ash, Edmund Davies was educated at King's College, London, and Exeter College, Oxford. Called to the Bar at Grays Inn, he took silk in 1943 and as a barrister was widely known for his skilful advocacy. As a judge he presided over the Aberfan tribunal with great compassion but he was perhaps best known to the public at large as the judge who sentenced the 'train robbers'. For a number of years he had had close

Sir Lewis Jones (1884–1968), MP for Swansea West (1931–45), talking in characteristic pose, in Tabernacle Vestry, Morriston, on 'How the Government Works'. Taken from *Picture Post*, 1 January 1944

associations with Swansea and was its recorder from 1944 to 1953. In many respects the college was fortunate in the wide experience and wisdom of its new president. He involved himself much more closely in its day-to-day affairs than ever Lloyd-George had been able to do, frequently chairing council meetings, and he had thrust upon him many of the problems arising from the student troubles of the late sixties and early seventies.

A consequence of the beginnings of the expansion of the college in the fifties had been the increasing load on the president as chairman of the college council, a load which, compounded by the additional requirement of attendance at committees and working parties, would have placed an intolerable burden upon a public figure not resident in the area. When Sir George Barstow retired, therefore, it was decided to separate the chairmanship of the council from the presidency and to create a new office specifically to fulfil the former duties.

Sir Lewis Jones, the senior vice-president of the college since 1934 and a member of the court and the council since 1920, was appointed to the office. From the Amman Valley, Lewis Jones had, at considerable parental sacrifice, trained as a teacher at Reading University. Although coming from a deeply Welsh background he had gone there rather than to a Welsh college at his father's insistence; 'Go to Reading, get out of Wales and find out that there are other people in the world'. He left teaching for politics and during the Great War was secretary of the priority department of the Ministry of Munitions. This work brought him into contact with Gilbertson and in 1917 he returned to Wales and to the Siemens Steel Association. Here he became a master of negotiation and a figure of some significance in the industry, so much so that in 1931 he was successfully put up for Parliament as one of its spokesmen.

For almost as long as anyone could remember the college, Sir Lewis (he was knighted in 1944) had been a commanding personality. On countless occasions for twenty years he had chaired meetings of the college council and there is no doubt that he cherished the hope of succeeding to the presidency. Equally, there is no doubt that there was powerful opposition to such a candidacy. To some extent the formalizing of his new office was a sop, but as elected chairman of the council Sir Lewis made a contribution to the development of the college of a significance even greater than before.

For the next eleven years he was responsible for steering much of the capital development programme and had a considerable hand in a large number of critical academic appointments. Occasionally his attitude gave rise to controversy and at times was interpreted as being unduly intrusive. His relationship with successive principals was sometimes fraught but he was wont to say that he never had a cross word with any. The truth was that few worked with such zeal for the college or possessed such deep intensity of devotion to it: not merely for its physical growth and development but even more for 'the reputation which the infant College so rapidly acquired from the successful work of the students and staff, of which he was intensely proud' (Annual Report, 1968–9, p. 135). Lewis Jones's naturally warm and kindly nature was often masked by a brusque and gruff exterior while his passionate regard for the college and, no doubt, his industrial background did occasionally bring forth in him an intimidating dominance. His tragedy, also, was that he probably remained too long in office at too great an age, for, sadly, there can be little doubt that in his last years he was manipulated and his judgement was swayed by others who in no way shared his disinterested loyalty to the college. Nevertheless, it was no more than appropriate that Lewis Jones's long and devoted service to the college and especially his constant concern for the welfare of its students – there were many and staff members, as well, who had reason to be grateful to him – should be recognized by the perpetuation of his name in the title of one of the Singleton halls of residence, and in his lifetime too. His retirement in 1966 severed one of the last remaining links with the foundation of the college.

Notes

1. 1898–1990; later Lord Morris of Grasmere and Vice-chancellor of the University of Leeds, 1948–63.
2. 1901–79; Director of Education for Kent, 1938–43; Director General of Army Education, 1944–6; Vice-chancellor of the University of Bristol, 1946–66; knighted, 1946.
3. B, 1903; fellow and bursar, Lincoln College, Oxford, 1937–44, and rector, 1944–53; chairman, UGC, 1953–63; knighted, 1955; KCB, 1963; Lord Murray of Newhaven, 1964.
4. R.B. Southall (1900–65), one of the college's vice-presidents and General Manager of BP Refinery (Llandarcy) Limited, was a representative of technical education on the committee. Southall has, perhaps unfairly, been characterized by Carswell as one of the committee's 'silent minority'. Admittedly a man of few words, what he said was usually trenchant and wise, and he was a potent influence during Parry's principalship. His death was a keenly felt loss to the college.
5. The inter-war period saw £1,000 being established as the normal salary for a professor (something below the maximum salary for a principal in the civil service). By the late sixties the 'average' salary for a professor

had reached some £4,500 (rather above the scale of an assistant secretary in the civil service). Since the seventies this comparison has been considerably eroded.

6. The committee comprised the following, in addition to the president (Lord Tenby) as chairman: Sir Lincoln Evans, a former General Secretary of the Iron and Steel Trades Confederation and currently Deputy Chairman of the Iron and Steel Board; the Rt. Hon. James Griffiths, Labour MP for Llanelli, a former President of the South Wales Miners' Federation, Minister of National Insurance in the first Attlee administration (1945–50), for a short period Colonial Secretary in the 1950–1 Labour government, and, later (1964–6), to be the first Secretary of State for Wales; Harald Peake, Chairman of the Steel Company of Wales and a vice-chairman of Lloyds Bank; Sir Julian Pode, Managing Director of the Steel Company of Wales and chairman of the local south Wales board of Lloyds Bank; and the Rt. Revd J.J.A. Thomas, Bishop of Swansea and Brecon and a former vicar of Swansea. The committee's secretary was the assistant (later deputy) registrar, Stephen Jeffreys.

7. Lewis, delivering one general lecture on the 'Treason of the Blue Books' in the presence of Fulton, dilated upon the distinction of the commissioners, especially Ralph Lingen, taking great glee in pointing out that 'he was a fellow of Balliol, too'.

8. 1910–77; an international authority on industrial design Black was Professor of Industrial Design at the Royal College of Art, 1959–75; knighted, 1972;

9. Lewis maintained his connections with the college until his death, through his membership of the college council.

10. Miss Westcott, who died in 1992 aged ninety-one, was characterized by a single-minded concern for the welfare of students and colleagues. A devoted churchwoman, she was a tireless social worker in areas which were far from fashionable and required resource and personal courage. She explained her tiredness one morning by admitting that she, in Gladstonian fashion, 'had been walking the streets all night'.

11. 1900–69; knighted 1962, Schonell was Vice-chancellor of the University of Queensland from 1960 until his death.

12. 1917–83; Professor of Social Science, Victoria University College, Wellington, 1949–54; Professor of Applied Social Science at Nottingham, 1954–82.

13. Students of this period included the late John Morgan, and Geoffrey and Mavis Nicholson, and Dewi Zephaniah Phillips, Professor of Philosophy at the college since 1971, and recently appointed to the Danforth chair of the philosophy of religion at the Claremont Graduate School, California, an appointment he will hold jointly with his Swansea chair.

14. Anderson returned to the department of political theory and government as a lecturer in 1964. In 1966 he entered politics as Labour MP for Monmouth and has been Labour MP for Swansea East since 1974.

CHAPTER SIX

'THE TURNING OF THE TIDE':
REVOLT, RETRENCHMENT AND
RATIONALIZATION

Sir Lewis Jones had been a first-hand witness to the college's progress from the expectant beginnings of the twenties, through the slough of austerity and depression of the thirties and forties to the transformation, academic and physical, of the years of his chairmanship of the council. The last six had been years of surging growth. By 1967 there were over three thousand students at Singleton, about a tenth of whom were postgraduate or research students. This was almost a doubling of the numbers present only five years before and already represented the goal to which the Robbins Report had pointed; now even further development seemed imminently sustainable. But it was not to be. Robbins was to be the last euphoric expression of the attitudes that underlay the expansion of the sixties and had been increasingly dominant for so much of the period since the Second World War.

Now the tempo was to slow down considerably. The apparent prosperity of the Macmillan era was giving way to a bleaker economic climate and, with an irreversible commitment to the new universities, it was natural that the traditional university sector should be kept in greater check. In Swansea this meant that over the whole of the quinquennium 1967–72 the overall student population rose by only 172. In many respects this deceleration should have afforded some relief from the feverish activity the college had experienced over the past few years. It bred uncertainty, however, not lessened by the increasing effects of the recession in the country at large in the later sixties. It coincided, too, with a welling-up of some of the less wholesome aspects of the erosion of societal conventions and the mushrooming of 'teenage culture' and permissiveness that characterized these years and which, in universities, with large numbers of students, young, free and well away from their home environments, manifested themselves most obviously in the politicizing of student unions, confrontation with authority and disruption of campuses. Fortunately, the established nature of the college with its solid structure of traditional academic values helped to prevent the excesses that occurred in the some of the new universities. But the 'troubles' at Swansea, the sit-ins, the turbulence and, underlying them, the changing conditions and patterns of college life that in part arose out of the shifting flux of society generally and in part was a repercussion of very rapid expansion, created taxing problems which the growing complexity of other areas of university administration did not minimize.

It was into this changing and increasingly more exacting situation that in 1965 John

Frank Llewllyn Jones, principal (1965–74) and
vice-chancellor of the University of Wales
(1969–71)

Parry was succeeded as principal by Professor Frank Llewellyn Jones. Like Edwards, almost forty years before, Llewellyn Jones was an internal appointment and, again like Edwards, he was powerfully supported by influential sections of the college council. Now fifty-eight, he had joined the college in 1932 as an assistant lecturer in physics from a senior demyship at Magdalen College, Oxford. A lively and stimulating teacher with a deep commitment to his subject, over the years he also achieved a notable reputation as a research physicist, especially in ionization physics and the physics of electrical contacts, and he built up active research schools in these areas. It was symptomatic of Llewellyn Jones's commitment to the college that, while at the Royal Aircraft Establishment at Farnborough during the war, he continued to carry out a complete lecturing programme by returning to Swansea for a week each month to give intensive courses.

In 1945 it was natural that he should follow Jenkin Evans as professor of physics. For the next twenty years he presided over a growing department with great dedication and proved himself a capable administrator, latterly directing the planning of the new physics building. His heavy involvement in the policy decisions about the expansion of the college as dean of the faculty of science, vice-principal for two terms and as acting-principal in 1959–60 and 1965 confirmed his reputation as an effective administrator. But his increasing responsibilities within the college in no way diminished his outside commitments. These were many and varied, the most notable being his chairmanship, from 1961 to 1964, of the Central Advisory Committee for Education (Wales) whose

Report highlighted the problems of the scarcity of science teachers in the principality, and his role as senior scientific adviser in civil defence for Wales. With his wife, Eileen, he was – and continues to be – also a prominent and enlivening figure in a whole range of local cultural activities.

Llewellyn Jones brought to the principalship, therefore, not only scholarly standing but also a wealth of experience of the inmost workings of the college, a name for administration and a single-minded devotion to the college. Nevertheless, it was perhaps difficult for him, with a perspective forged over thirty years in an environment of differing values, to respond easily to the suddenly changing ethos of the university world of the late sixties and seventies. Within all too short a time as well he lost the invaluable counsel of John McIntyre, whose deteriorating health forced his early retirement in 1968.

The burdens on the principal were immense; the tactics of student activism created a paralysis of will even in the most dynamic but Llewellyn Jones's remarkable stamina and sense of purpose saw him through the occupations, disturbances and personal vilification. He was fortunate, too, in his vice-principals, initially Professor Balchin and then, from 1967, Charles Gittins, the Professor of Education. The new stresses, though, strained the college's traditional approach to management out of all proportion. The long-hallowed dependence on the part-time assistance of a single full-time academic, often with considerable departmental obligations, was breaking down and, in 1970, the device, already attempted elsewhere, if with limited success, was decided upon of converting the vice-principalship into a full-time office. Gittins had already temporarily given up his headship of department to be able to devote more time to college affairs but

The college officers in 1968. Left to right: His Honour Trevor Morgan (1892–1976), Sir Edmund Davies, Sir Lewis Jones, Peter Williams (the treasurer) (d. 1980), Principal Frank Llewellyn Jones, and Professor Charles Gittins (d. 1970)

his tragic death in a boating accident in August 1970 scotched any more permanent arrangement.

Gittins had succeeded Evan J. Jones as Professor of Education and Dean of the Faculty of Education in 1956, coming to Swansea from a background of educational administration – for the previous twelve years he had been Director of Education for Monmouthshire. A man of energy and flair, whose department and faculty rapidly expanded under his leadership, he was responsible for a growing crescendo of new developments, including new diploma courses, research projects and, in the wake of Robbins, the – at the time – alarming prospect of *taught* masters' degrees. One imaginatively cohesive scheme particularly dear to his heart was the conversion of Maes-yr-Haf into a faculty centre and library. From 1964 to 1967 Gittins had chaired the Central Advisory Committee for Education (Wales), the Welsh equivalent of the Plowden Committee, and emerged as a powerful advocate of bilingualism as a means of fostering the Welsh language.

For the college, however, his most important work was accomplished in the last few years of his life when as vice-principal – and with little direct experience of the main thrust of college administration hitherto – he had to confront the challenges and complexities of the later sixties. Student relationships were the burning issue, and whether they encompassed participation in college government, demands for greater 'relevance' in the curricula, the modernizing of college regulations, or insistence on new codes of conduct for the halls of residence in the climate of the Latey Report on the age of majority, Gittins made them his special concern and bore the brunt of their working out. The air of dignity and reserve that he had cultivated as a professor new to academic life was soon dissipated and his transparent integrity and patience quickly won him the respect of both staff and students. Thanks to his perseverance often apparently intractable problems, where there was seemingly no meeting of minds nor will to resolve them, were reduced to manageable proportions.

Professor Balchin stepped into the breach again following Gittins's all-too-untimely death but two years later the vice-principalship was expanded into a triumvirate of part-time vice-principals, each one specializing in a particular area of practical concern – academic, administration and student affairs – thus spreading the administrative load while retaining the honorific nature of the vice-principalship. For, despite the turning of the tide of expansion and abundant government support and quite apart from the deflection of the recurring pains of student militancy, the administrative pressures were becoming progressively heavier. Government, through the UGC, was becoming more intrusive and more questioning, as was the Committee of Vice-chancellors and Principals in its collective advocacy of the universities; moreover, the college's commitments were still growing.

Already, before the sixties were out, a fresh assessment of the college's future pattern of growth had been made necessary by the acquisition of Hendrefoilan House and 121 acres of its associated estate for some £90,000 in June 1964. Hendrefoilan, once the home of Lewis Llewelyn Dillwyn, had been bought only after a great deal of heart-searching on the part of Principal Parry and the college officers: indeed, but for what was seen as the importunate persistence of a member of the college council it might never have been acquired at all. The estate was situated over two miles to the north-west of Singleton and its possession at once raised major questions. In what was still the first flush of Robbins there was even talk of speedy expansion to eight thousand students. Proposals to effect some fundamental academic split between the two sites with the sciences remaining at Singleton and the humanities moving to Hendrefoilan were aired. They were soon put on one side, but it was not until May 1966 that there was sufficient consensus in the college to allow Sir Percy Thomas and Son to produce new development plans for both Singleton and Hendrefoilan although, even then, long-term proposals for the latter site had to be kept vague.

The essence of the new scheme, put to the UGC as part of the college's Quinquennial Submission for 1967–72, was that the future development of Singleton should be devoted entirely to academic purposes and that, while the overall nature of the development of Hendrefoilan should remain an open question, further residential accommodation for students should be concentrated there on the basis of a 'student village' concept. It was recognized that there might well be some peripheral academic activities at Hendrefoilan, for example experimental research units, though large-scale academic developments there were not foreseen unless the college embarked on further major expansion. Nevertheless, since experience had shown the undesirability of trying to control university growth within predetermined limits, bearing in mind the unpredictability of social and academic needs and fashions, it was decided to restrict the initial requirement for residential accommodation for two thousand students to one part of the site only and to keep the general layout 'sufficiently flexible to permit further expansion in a rational and economic manner'.

For Singleton there were factors to be taken into consideration now which had not been in existence when the previous development programme had been crystallized and, following publication of the Robbins Report, the college's student target increased to three thousand to be achieved by 1967–8. In the light of Robbins the question of yet further expansion had been considered by the college. While it was felt that it would be unwise to take any decision as to the ultimate student population 'attainable, it was decided that, because of the limited extent of the Singleton campus and in order to preserve its parkland, the maximum student population that could satisfactorily be accommodated there for academic purposes should be about four thousand. However, the college took pains to stress in the Quinquennial Submission that it had 'the will and vitality to meet a further expansion after the four thousand stage, to promote a natural development of existing disciplines and of new projects in the light of national needs and varying academic pressures, providing that the necessary buildings and resources are made available'. Such further growth was dependent on additional land at Singleton. If this was not forthcoming, and if Hendrefoilan had to be used for teaching and research on a large scale, a redefinition of the college's academic organizational pattern would be required 'to take into account the changed conditions which would result from . . . a split Campus'.

Another element absent in 1958 had been the question of a medical school at Swansea. The idea of such a school, attached to the local general hospital, was not a new one. The question of establishing medical education at Swansea had been mentioned, if only in passing, by John Jones Jenkins to the Aberdare Committee and it had been a contention of Sir Hussey Vivian before the arbitrators in 1883 that the principal building of the general hospital, opened in Swansea fourteen years earlier, had been designed with a medical school in mind. The building, in the 1960s, of the new

Singleton Hospital close by the college campus had strongly revived the interest in medical studies, to the extent that the borough council promised to make additional land available at Singleton for a medical school. For good reason the Robbins Committee had excluded the question of medical education from its deliberations. It therefore became the subject of a separate royal commission appointed under Lord Todd in 1965. Both the college and the local medical profession submitted cases to the commission which, when it eventually reported three years later, recommended that if national needs after 1975 made an extension of medical education desirable the claims of Swansea should be favourably considered. Unhappily, the cost implications of the Todd Commission's recommendations, coupled with the government's quite separate commitment to the Robbins Report, meant that however pious the commission's hope it would never be fulfilled in the increasingly gaunt economic climate of the seventies. It became an increasingly forlorn hope despite the active lobbying of Ifor Davies (1910–82), the MP for Gower, over the twelve years he was chairman of the college council (1970–82).

The close geographical relationship of hospital and college was an important constituent of the commission's consideration of the Swansea submissions. Furthermore, the additional land (some twelve acres) finally allocated by the Corporation for the site of the medical school itself was contiguous to the northern boundary of the hospital and little more than a hundred yards from the north-western limits of the college. Thus the

The 1966 plan for Singleton, showing the proposed medical school site (left foreground)

problems that separation and distance so often created for clinical and pre-clinical studies elsewhere would have been obviated and the medical students at Swansea could have been as immediately involved in the activities of the Singleton campus as other students. Although the notion of a medical school came to nothing, the proximity of the hospital did encourage the growth of a range of significant research-orientated science-medicine links involving medical physics, biochemistry and work on metals for internal splints and joints and artificial limbs. These areas of co-operation have been greatly expanded and, more recently, the area of health care has become focused on the establishment of an institute of health care studies and a school of postgraduate medical studies in medical and health care. In the offing, too, is a major new nursing college for mid and west Wales, set up at Swansea primarily because of the teaching and research resources already available.

Another major academic development which the college considered during these years was the introduction of a faculty of law. With the president, Sir Edmund Davies, and the chairman of the council, Judge Trevor Morgan, both lawyers and with a number of senior members of the profession on the college council it was natural that the notion should have powerful backing. Courses in law for solicitors' articled clerks had been a feature at the college since 1922, but this link with the subject had been severed in 1962 when the Law Society changed its regulations for legal education. Now, for all the enthusiasm, with degree courses in law available at Aberystwyth and Cardiff, the university was unconvinced of the need for yet more at Swansea. The bid came to nothing. A quarter of a century later, a faculty of law is to be introduced at Singleton and the first professor has been appointed. This departure, and the college of nursing, will make significant contributions to the academic expansion which the college is currently planning for the remainder of the century.

While the discussions about a medical school were taking place, the Corporation agreed to sell the college a small piece of land in the Singleton 'Boating Lake' car park. Although this land was not actually transferred to the college (for £4,000) until 1969–70, its promise facilitated the planning of the much-needed extension to the natural sciences building without the necessity of building to the south-east of the existing complex and, therefore, without any appreciable disturbance of the botanic garden. In all these discussions over land, both for the natural sciences building and the projected medical school, the backing of Percy Morris and his successor as leader of the town council, John Allison, and the town clerk, Iorwerth Watkins, was never lacking for one moment.

Any hopes the college may have had of achieving a target of four thousand students by 1972 were dashed when in the course of the quinquennial visitation in May 1966 Sir John Wolfenden (1906-85), Murray's successor as chairman of the UGC, made it clear that there could not be the same dramatic increase in the number of university students that there had been in the past and that, in any case, the bulk of any increase would have to be taken up by the new universities. This was a blow to the college's progressive development because it was already clear from the level of existing intakes that the student population was likely to rise to at least 3,150 by 1967–8, an overshoot beyond the Robbins target that merely reflected the situation in the country as a whole. Again, as nationally, the growth point in student numbers was in the humanities. Nevertheless, the proposed expansion of the arts faculty was, therefore, cut back wholly – except for the department of education – in order to allow for some increase in the other faculties. In effect, it now seemed that, at least for the time being, all the college could do was maintain its current level of student entry and consolidate, as best it could, its most recent new developments even though there was clearly potential for further growth.

As it turned out, there was a slight increase in student numbers to 3,448 by October 1971. There was also a shift in government policy towards the end of the quinquennium and, in 1971, the college was set a target of 4,700 to 4,800 full-time student places by October 1976. This new figure was, however, notional only and was not to be attained in the time. In any case, it was dependent on the earlier completion of three additional major building projects at Singleton: the extension to the natural sciences building intended, in the main, to allow the department of genetics, other parts of the school of biological sciences, and a section of the department of geography to move out of their temporary quarters; and extensions to the library and College House.

Grant-aid for a start on the extension to the natural sciences building in 1971–2 had been announced in 1968–9. Suddenly, however, at Christmas 1971, the building allocation was unexpectedly withdrawn by the UGC and only after considerable pressure did the committee agree eventually to the reinstatement of the scheme in the building programme for 1972–3. The building – now known as the natural sciences building west – on a much reduced scale and providing only about two-thirds of the accommodation originally hoped for, was eventually opened by Lord Zuckerman[1] in the summer of 1977. Despite the setback this reduction in scale represented, the overall capital picture did not appear to be too depressing, for the library extension, to provide places for an additional 327 readers and book storage for some 120,000 volumes, was also included in the programme for 1972–3 and there seemed every prospect that the major alterations contemplated for College House would follow in 1975.

It appeared, now, as if the college's building programme at Singleton, which had been very much in the doldrums and restricted to minor projects since 1970, was at last being revitalized. In the year 1972–3 the capital allocation from the UGC exceeded £1,000,000 for the first time since 1965–6 and the campus, at both its western and eastern ends, was resuming the aspect of a construction site that had been all too familiar in the sixties. However, starts on the £600,000 scheme for the natural sciences extension and the £275,000 library project heralded but an Indian summer for the college. Although these particular developments proceeded reasonably well despite the economic difficulties and industrial shortages of the early part of 1974, the public expenditure cuts of that year saw the College House project being deferred indefinitely and the completion of the library in 1974 brought government-sponsored building at Singleton virtually to a halt.

While major building activity at Singleton was running down, Hendrefoilan was becoming the scene of mounting activity throughout much of the seventies. Initially, the house itself had been used as a postgraduate student residence while thought was being given to the estate's future long-term use. The first permanent project to be started at Hendrefoilan was a 'general purpose' building, erected close by the house itself in 1970–1, and intended for the use of psychology, parts of the education department and, temporarily, for botany. The proposal had been mooted for some time, however, that the whole of the education department and the collegiate faculty – still divided

The natural sciences building west seen from the botanic garden lily pond

between Singleton and Maes-yr-Haf – should move to Hendrefoilan. At last, in 1973, and at a cost of £100,000, this was the move that took place. What was now called the 'study building' became the home for both these closely-knit academic activities as it did for the education library until its recent transfer to the refurbished stables of Hendrefoilan House. Maes-yr-Haf was freed for the South Wales Miners' Library imaginatively formed from the retrieved collections of miners' institute libraries in the south Wales coalfield until it, too, moved to Hendrefoilan with the closure of Maes-yr-Haf in the economies of the mid-eighties.

Hendrefoilan was also humming with much larger scale activity. In 1971 the site was opened up by the construction of a new entrance off the Gower Road to enable its residential development to begin and, gradually throughout the seventies, in three distinct phases, accommodation for some 725 students was provided on the estate. Since the building of the college's earlier halls of residence at Singleton and Clyne, however, the policy of the UGC in regard to grant-aiding residential accommodation for students had changed and, because of the scarcity of public funds, by 1971, the committee had restricted its financial support for such schemes to a maximum of twenty-five per cent of the capital costs. To complete the schemes at Hendrefoilan the college had therefore to borrow on a substantial scale, but by 1980 a self-catering 'student village' with its own amenities centre had been built and was already developing its own distinct life-style. Now self-catering accommodation is provided at Hendrefoilan for over 1,400 students, the majority of them undergraduates. It seems to have been a great success in many different ways and clearly to have been popular with students, while to the UGC it was 'an imaginative development at reasonable cost'. The scheme continues with houses for a further 250 students to be opened in 1992.[2]

The completion of the first three phases of residential accommodation at Hendrefoilan, the acquisition of a speculative flat development (Vivian House) at Blackpill in 1972, again through loan-finance, and additions to Beck Hall (Neuadd Beck) in 1979, meant that by 1980 the college was able to offer residential accommodation to over fifty per cent of the student body. Great strides had been made in twenty years: in 1960 only some thirteen per cent of students lived in a hall of residence – a third of women students in Beck Hall and less than a tenth of men students in Neuadd Gilbertson. By 1980 the college was getting nearer the goal set by Fulton in 1958 of being a predominantly residential college, even if the life-style envisaged at that time had changed dramatically with the emergence of a self-catering 'student village', flats and student houses. The 'formality' of the halls of residence had become a thing of the past.

Accommodation difficulties do seem to recur with unpleasant regularity at the beginning of most sessions but they tend to be of a temporary nature and the majority of students who want college accommodation are usually settled quickly. With a full-time student population now more than 5,500 and with shifting demands there are bound to be problems but the college has been able, more or less, to maintain the proportion of residential accommodation achieved ten years ago. Vivian House and a range of converted houses in the vicinity of the college provide accommodation for both single and married postgraduate students. And, since 1975, all the halls of residence, except those at Clyne, have taken in both male and female students; even Neuadd Beck, 'after more than fifty years of proud and distinguished existence as an exclusively womens' hall of residence'. It was a development viewed with considerable misgivings, indeed with consternation by some, and some bygone members of the Beck Hall Committee must have turned over in their graves. But, despite some teething troubles, it, too, seems to have been a success.

If the provision of residential accommodation for students had been a matter of concern to the college since its earliest days we have already seen how the question of sports facilities had also been regarded as important since the Sketty Lane playing fields with their pavilion and the later swimming bath were created in the thirties. These facilities could not, however, keep pace with the needs of the expanding college of the late fifties and sixties. In 1963 the eighty-acre Fairwood Lodge estate, abutting Fairwood Common in Gower and about four miles away from Singleton, was acquired for £33,750, primarily for additional playing fields. For some years, Fairwood Lodge itself was used as the principal's residence but it was somewhat remote and rambling and never proved entirely satisfactory for its purpose. In 1975 it was disposed of to provide lodgings for the assize judges.

Gradually, the extensive grounds at Fairwood were developed to provide playing fields, a rifle range, pavilion and even a fishing lake, while at Sketty part of the grounds was converted into a four-hundred-metre cinder athletics track with jumping and throwing areas. In 1980 a new sports centre was completed at Sketty Lane, at a cost of some £500,000. This prestige building with its general-purpose sports hall, five squash courts, weight-training room and climbing wall replaced, in the grandest style, the temporary indoor sports accommodation with which students had had to make do in part of the old engineering buildings at Singleton since 1969. This was a project about which the UGC was enthusiastic – as it had been over the original sports developments of the thirties – but it could meet only a limited element of the cost, most of which had to be borne from the college's own resources.

The bulk of the cost was met from the Development Appeal Fund and the Welsh Church Acts Fund which were also committed to sorely needed lecture facilities at Hendrefoilan and to the major, £1 million project of an arts centre at Singleton. After many trials and tribulations, including the distinct possibility of its having to be abandoned altogether, the Taliesin Centre was completed to the design of the Peter Moro Partnership of London and was formally opened by Sir Geraint Evans in 1984. At the heart of the campus the new centre comprises a splendidly equipped theatre (which also serves as a concert hall, cinema and lecture theatre) seating up to 365 people, a self-financing art gallery (the Ceri Richards Gallery), a bookshop and a bank; the building also accommodates the centre for development studies. The 'new' arts hall of 1949 remains: the theatre has become the Taliesin Studio Theatre, providing a second performance area seating up to 200 and flexible space for music and drama productions; while the smaller staff and lecture rooms have been converted into music practice and tuition rooms, a music library and art studios.

The Taliesin Centre, with its wide-ranging activities extending from professional and

The Taliesin Centre

student drama to dance, opera, film and concerts, classical, jazz and rock, has proved itself a cultural boon not only to the college but to the townspeople of Swansea as well. It is open to everybody and continues that close cultural relationship between the college and the local community which was given such a fillip with the opening of the 'new' arts theatre in the dark days after the war.

One cannot, of course, leave this connection without some further mention of extra-mural studies which Ernest Hughes and then P.S. Thomas fostered so successfully in the early years of the college. For it would be difficult to overestimate the influence that the department has had on the locality since its inception. The fourteen extra-mural classes of 1921 had, for example, developed into sixty-four classes by 1954 when Berwick House, in the Uplands, was bought by the college, by means of a grant of £4,500 from the UGC, to serve as a much-needed administrative centre and focal point for the already far-flung department. A driving force in the rapid growth of extra-mural studies after the war was Dr Illtyd David (1896–82) who succeeded P.S. Thomas in 1941 as senior staff tutor but who had been involved with the tutorial classes since the earliest days of the college. He was, in the fullest sense, a pioneer of the adult education movement in south-west Wales, helping to forge the strong links which existed for many years between the tinplate and steel industry and the adult education agencies in the area. In 1960, David was followed by I.M. Williams as the first director of extra-mural studies, and, by 1980, when Williams was appointed to the new chair of adult and continuing education, the total of teaching activities had grown to 209 classes, day schools and lectures, and extended throughout the borough, much of West Glamorgan, the eastern industrial part of Dyfed and south-west Powys.

Gradually over the years the nature of the classes and courses provided for the local community by the department has changed. While traditional classes and courses offering opportunities for liberal studies in both the humanities and the sciences continue, there has been an increasing emphasis on the provision of 'continuing' education designed to meet the specialized needs of professional or industrial groups. At the same time, many of the traditional activities have demanded an increasingly more intensive academic approach than was necessary in the past. In recent years the academic standing of the department has thus been enhanced considerably, a development marked by the breadth of scholarship of many of the publications of its members of staff. Over a decade ago the fundamentally changing nature of the department's work was recognized, first by the creation of the new chair in 1980 and then, in the subsequent session, by the redesignation of the department itself to 'adult and continuing education'. Now, even more meaningfully, the title of the department has become 'adult continuing education'. The problems of adjustment to the 'third age' and industrial and commercial updating come within its ambit. The desire of the arts visitors in 1919 that the college staff might be 'an influence in broadening the training and the outlook of the people of Swansea' has expanded into distance and open learning programmes for people in rural and valley communities, particularly those hit by heavy mining redundancies and where the educational resources are very poor. This is a growth area and the department's work in the community has been commended by the newly established Universities Funding Council (UFC) – which replaced the UGC in 1989 – and awarded a substantial increase in funding. As a result of this support, the college's vision of a 'community university for the valleys' might well become a reality before the century has ended. The efforts of the department have also resulted in the recent introduction of part-time degree schemes in the humanities, mathematics and computer science for 'second chance' mature students who want to return to education on a part-time basis. In this development – which it is hoped will be extended in science and technology – the college is in the forefront of the University of Wales and, to a lesser extent, among United Kingdom universities in general. These developments, the substantial research profile of the department and its strong European presence, all exemplify the transformation of adult continuing education into a mainstream college department and stress the importance the college puts on the effort. It is all something which would have excited Haldane himself.

It is, perhaps, not too fanciful to see some resemblance between the work of adult continuing education and some aspects of what was being attempted in Swansea more than a century ago at the Royal Institution of South Wales. Any significance the Royal Institution may have had as a centre of major scientific and cultural influence was comparatively short-lived. Even in later years, when it slipped into the backwater life of a middle-class provincial society, its declining membership – little encouraged by the insalubrious location of the Institution's building – and falling income made even this role difficult to maintain. As the present century advanced the Institution's museum became fossilized and the ravages of the Second World War virtually extinguished the society altogether. Somehow, it tottered on from one year to the next thanks to the dedication of its council members, honorary curators and especially the labours of its indefatigable honorary secretary from 1945 to 1955, W.H. ('Bill') Hanna, and, more recently, Miss Betty Nelmes.

In the fifties, it was rescued from complete closure through the efforts of Professor Hugh O'Neill. As Professor of Metallurgy, O'Neill had close contacts with local industry and with the support of R.B. Southall, local industry was persuaded to support the establishment and maintenance of an industrial museum within the Royal Institution, so guaranteeing the latter's survival. Unhappily, the sixties saw this financial assistance gradually dwindle as covenants fell in and were not renewed. The Institution again lurched from crisis to crisis while the fabric of its building and the condition of many of its precious objects deteriorated. Much of its fine library was sold off to provide essential capital although, despite this ill-conceived decision, many rare specialist works and the museum's virtually irreplaceable 'local' section were mercifully preserved, a number of important volumes coming to the college library.

Approaches to the borough council for help met with little response for the latter, at the time, was unable – or unwilling – to shoulder the burden of the Royal Institution as a museum. Eventually, in the mid-sixties, it was suggested that a solution to the Institution's problems might lie in a form of association with the college. There were a number of precedents for such a link and in the case of Swansea there were seen to be advantages to both sides: the Institution would have the benefit of the college's financial resources to meet the costs of an adequate and professional staff and of essential building maintenance and development while, in its turn, the college would secure a local studies centre and science museum. The negotiations, which began in 1966, were protracted but, eventually, after almost seven years, the college and the Royal Institution agreed jointly to run a museum in the building while, as a literary and philosophical society, the Royal Institution would continue to have offices there, and sponsor the lectures, 'conversaziones' and social events for which it was well known in the city and beyond.

Llewellyn Jones, who was the prime proponent of the link, expressed the hope that it would prove possible to develop the museum along lines which were worthy of the city and in keeping with the Institution's established traditions. It was no secret, however, that within the college there was some disquiet over the linkage, especially on the science side, where the Institution was viewed more as a likely drain on scarce resources than as a cultural asset to the college. Unfortunately, although it was possible to achieve much in diversifying displays and in arranging an impressive lecture and activities programme for both adults and especially children, the resources available were never sufficient to develop the museum into the research centre that had been hoped for. In the even more difficult, cost-conscious climate of the eighties and with acute financial pressures bearing on the college, it became clear that the association between college and Institution could not be prolonged indefinitely. When all seemed lost, the Swansea city council at last stepped in and accepted responsibility for the museum building and its collections. It is to be hoped that the phoenix will again rise from the ashes and justify the dedication of all those who have served the Institution and its museum over a century and a half.

The problem of meeting the financial obligations involved in the association with the Institution was but one small element in a whole scenario of difficulties that faced the college in the later seventies. In 1974 Llewellyn Jones retired after nine years as principal. It had been a difficult stewardship, perhaps not made easier for him in his early days by his tendency to personalize his approach to college government – no doubt a reflection of his long and deep absorption in his department. His need, too, to establish his position as an internal appointee, lacking the advantages of an Edwards who had been effectively a permanent vice-principal throughout Sibly's tenure of office, did not serve him well in terms of relations with some of his senate colleagues whose readiness to help was not always appreciated. But this was in the past.

In seeking Llewellyn Jones's successor the college departed from its past practice in advertising the post as well as taking soundings. The new principal was Dr Robert

Robert Steel, principal (1974–82) and vice-chancellor of the University of Wales (1979–81)

Walter Steel, John Rankin Professor of Geography at Liverpool. Like his predecessor, Steel had been an undergraduate at Oxford (Jesus College), winning the first exhibition ever awarded for geography at the university. A university lecturer from 1937 to 1956 and a fellow of Jesus College from 1954, he moved to his chair at Liverpool in 1957, his special geographical interests being concentrated on the tropics, especially Africa. In coming to the principalship he was no stranger to the *haute politique* of university administration, having served as a pro-vice-chancellor and deputy chairman of the senate at Liverpool. A man with deep religious convictions, and with an abiding interest in developing countries, overseas students, human ecology and human rights, Steel's personality was a caring one. In coming to Swansea he needed such a personality. His first few months saw the campus convulsed with yet another recrudescence of student unrest. As a colleague put it, the situation – and it was to recur in these first few years with monotonous regularity – tested to the full Steel's 'ability to stand on principle but to seek for reconciliation'.

If the recurrence of the student troubles that had erupted on the Swansea campus intermittently since 1969 were tiresome, much more serious to the long-term health of the college was the critical financial situation that greeted Steel. As part of the attempt to combat the economic dislocation and rampant inflation arising from the oil crisis, beginning in 1973, the government decided, in 1974, not to bolster universities against the full effects of inflation. Within a month of Steel's arrival in Swansea, it was estimated that the college would be in deficit to the extent of £350,000 by the end of the financial year. Significant and urgent economies clearly had to be made in the college's budget. The college was at emergency stations and an 'economies' committee was set up to achieve the cuts necessary. In the event the government did come forward with supplementation to the extent of £99,000 but the success of the committee and the co-operation it received were such that, despite the very short time available, it was able to reduce costs by some £100,000 and prune the deficit to £145,000. Between them, this committee and its twin, the 'resources and services' committee, effecting vital savings and urging the redeployment of resources, both physical and human, helped to keep the college on an even keel.

The immediate financial crisis of 1974 was, however, but the harbinger of a period of enforced financial retrenchment dictated by the government as the country's general economic position worsened. In 1975, the warning was put out to universities that a positive cut of at least four per cent in grant-aid would have to be made in the succeeding year, that 'new expenditure leading to a continuing commitment should be kept to a minimum and existing economies continued'. This was but the first of repeated cuts in public expenditure over the next four years as successive Labour administrations tried to come to grips with a seemingly intractable economic situation. Recurrent grant-aid to universities was drastically reduced while capital support became minimal. Many buildings approved for construction starts were stopped entirely, the College House extension at Swansea being but one example.

Yet this chill wind was nothing compared with what was to come after 1979 when a new Conservative government, under Mrs Thatcher, came to power pledged to adopt a totally different, radical approach to curing the nation's economic ills, by bringing down inflation and reversing Britain's welfare-state collectivism. In Lord Annan's graphic phrase, what the universities had suffered from for a decade had been merely the rack. Now followed the axe. The end had come for twenty or more years of favoured treatment for the universities and their much-prized independence was placed in question. With self-sufficiency as a theme and higher education as a significant 'cost centre', it was natural that the universities should be targeted for retrenchment. With memories of the student troubles fresh in people's minds and a growing, if unsubstantiated, belief that the universities had failed to contribute sufficiently to the national economy, this was seen by many as only just. It was all too easy to portray the universities as 'the pampered darlings of society' that had drawn too great a benefit from the state since the increased grants of Sir John Anderson and Hugh Dalton thirty-odd years before. Necessary as much of the sea-change was, the much vaunted, if unhistorical, 'return to Victorian values' smacked somewhat of the views of Alderman John Glasbrook.

Steel's last two years were, thus, even more traumatic than his first though, in the event, thanks to careful budgeting, the college suffered much less than many other institutions. The new government's first measure was to increase overseas students' fees drastically to a full economic rate. The effect of this, as far as Swansea was concerned, where overseas student numbers especially in the applied sciences had been increasing considerably in recent years, was an appreciable loss in fee-income. By September 1979 the government was putting into place the first elements of its strategy to contract the universities and proposing swingeing reductions in the recurrent grant which raised for Swansea yet again the spectre of a huge deficit of almost £500,000 by the end of the year. A 'strategy' committee was set up and contingency plans introduced to effect savings through 'freezing' vacancies and introducing short-term contracts for academic staff – the old device of the years of Depression almost half a century earlier. On the advice of the UGC student intakes were also restricted in 1979 and 1980.

It was not until July 1981 that the real blow fell and, then, suddenly if not unexpectedly. The UGC's recurrent funding to universities was cut by 17 per cent over three years. This general reduction was not applied uniformly to all universities and Swansea's share worked out at 15 per cent. The intake of 'home' students also had to be reduced slightly and the smaller total had to embrace more students in the mathematical and physical sciences and fewer on the arts side. The prognostications were dire; for, despite all the efforts that had been made to keep the college's finances sound, if no action were taken the college would be facing an annual loss of some £1.5 million and an accumulated deficit of approximately £2 million by the end of 1983–4. With salaries and wages accounting for something like three-quarters of the college's outgoings, it was inevitable that there would have to be staff reductions across the board. In terms of the academic staff this meant a shedding of some forty people and a freezing or redeployment of their posts. Through a centrally funded early retirement scheme nine members of staff retired in 1982, including five professors and the registrar, Aneurin Davies, who had succeeded John McIntyre thirteen years before and had presided over a successive restructuring of the college's administration. More went over the next year or so and it is a sad fact that among those who formally left the college at this time – though some were to continue their teaching and research links – were a number who could be ill spared: Glanmor Williams, for example, retiring early after nearly forty years at Singleton, an inspiration to generations of students and one of the formative influences on the growth and development of the college since the Second World War.

Another to retire, but at the normal age, was the principal. Student disturbances, suddenly changing government attitudes to universities and the consequently bleaker financial climate, imposed a heavy burden, and not just administrative, on Steel. Long-term planning had been replaced by a virtually permanent 'crisis management'. There had to be a greater – and almost constant – flow of information, both to the University of Wales, the Committee of Vice-chancellors and Principals and the UGC as they came to grips with the government's policy of university contraction, and to staff and students who needed to be taken into confidence in these circumstances. Reform of the college's committee system, a reshaping of its administration, the creation of the centre for development studies, the building of the sports centre, the planning of the Taliesin Centre, and the formation of academic links with the Universities of Mannheim, Ferrara and Angers, all owed much to Steel's initiative. Always accessible, one of his colleagues described Steel as 'paternalistic . . . in its widest and best sense'.

The new principal who took up office in October 1982 was Professor Brian Leonard Clarkson, Professor of Vibration Studies in the Institute of Sound and Vibration Research of the University of Southampton. Educated at Leeds as a civil engineer, his interests had turned to the effect of noise pressures on aircraft structure and acoustics and he spent some time in the aircraft industry. In addition to his scientific distinction, what Clarkson brought to Swansea was a close knowledge of, and involvement with, industry which extended back to his postgraduate days when he had worked on the dynamics of steel-frame structures. In Southampton he had strengthened industrial links through the establishment of sponsored academic posts. It was a process that he was to continue at Swansea on a much bigger scale in the face of the increasing erosion of central-government funding and the necessary shift to private sector financial support.

Brian Clarkson, principal (1982–) and vice-chancellor of the University of Wales (1987–9)

As Clarkson arrived in Swansea so the determination of the government to change the face of higher education was rapidly getting into top gear. Lower funding levels had entailed contraction and this in turn was now the spur to rationalization. An assessment by the UGC of university research strengths came as a grave disappointment to the college and the 1986 round in the continuing process of funding cuts took account of the college's relative lack of research lustre in a number of areas – though history, philosophy, mathematics, materials engineering and civil engineering were notable exceptions. And it was a squeeze that was to continue. The assessing exercise had been a crude one and what added salt to the wound was that there had been no attempt to assess universities' teaching quality. The lesson, the principal admitted, was that the college was 'trying to do too much with too few resources . . . and thus not supporting adequately the range of activities'. It was in this context that the University of Wales set up a 'rationalization' committee to plan for stronger colleges operating in a narrower range of activities. Thus some degree of stability might be achieved and the 'crisis management' of more than a decade could perhaps be replaced by a considered strategy for the future which had been hardly possible since the abandonment of the quinquennial system in the late seventies. But it all involved savings generally, further staff reductions, and the maximizing of the college's income through the recruitment of more overseas students and the exploitation of research and the college's marketable facilities.

In terms of savings, initially, drama was withdrawn from the curriculum with the staff transferring to other universities, economic history ended its separate existence and merged with the large department of history, and oceanography was closed down, its staff returning to geology – its originally sponsoring department – to form a new department of earth sciences. Oceanography had grown vigorously since its inception in the late sixties and its research vessels, *Ocean Crest*, and latterly *Venturous*, were familiar sights in the Bristol Channel where they were extensively – and intensively – used for teaching and research. Substantial savings were made from the sale of the research vessel and reductions in staff members. But hardly had the new department got off the ground when it was decided that the Swansea and Cardiff earth sciences departments should be merged at Cardiff. It meant the end of a tradition of geology teaching at Swansea since the college's earliest days. The tragic closing of what had been such a distinguished department was not to pass without the most strenuous defensive efforts, but, in the face of intense pressure from Cardiff, it was all to no avail.

Rationalization did not work wholly to the disadvantage of Swansea. Compensatory strengthening was made in physical geography and in the biological sciences, where the four separate departments were welded into one fully integrated school. Staff were transferred from Cardiff to the department of materials engineering and from Aberystwyth to the department of chemistry, while the Cardiff postgraduate centre for the study of philosophy and health care came under the wing of the Swansea philosophy department. With hindsight this last development might be regarded with some misgivings but at the time it seemed appropriate especially since the department of philosophy at Swansea was designated the main centre of the subject in Wales.

In this chapter we have been largely concerned with the main thrust of developments over recent years and too little has been said about growth of disciplines since 1970. Partly this is due to the growing complexity of the college and partly to the rapidity of change that has seen even new disciplines introduced in the sixties and seventies altering almost out of recognition. Little or nothing has been said about the growth of interdisciplinary co-operation that has been one of the distinctive features of the college since the late sixties and especially the seventies and has applied to undergraduate courses as well as to research projects; in the humanities, for instance, American, medieval and Russian studies spring immediately to mind. For the wide-ranging development of subjects that has taken place in these years has enabled a large number of new undergraduate degree courses to be established which are more truly interdisciplinary than many of the joint honours courses of earlier years. Nothing either has been said about the college's sophisticated services and teaching and research aids, its language laboratory, closed circuit television or its computer centre, which has developed, from the introduction of what must now be regarded as an antediluvian IBM 1620 electronic digital computer into the college in 1962, into a spider's web of almost unimaginable complexity, with a network of terminals throughout the college and its satellites, and links to other universities and the powerful facilities of the Manchester Computer Centre.

The links with industry which the college is constantly forging and the ultra-modern research activities of the applied science departments would be applauded by the founders of the college. The interdisciplinary Research Centre in Materials for High Performance Applications, the Institute of Numerical Methods in Engineering, the Colloid and Interface Group – all seem a world away from the traditional departments of the twenties. They are as different as the new laboratories in computer vision and high-speed industrial networking are from the 'huts', 'last word' that *they* might have been in their time.

It is difficult to survey in any depth all the varied research projects in which the college is engaged but some may be instanced because of their material impact on modern society and because they are so much in accord with the general aims of the founders of the college. In addition to research of interest to the conventional methods of steel-making and tinplate production, such as work on lattice effects in metals, brittle fracture, creep and fatigue, materials engineering – the direct but much broader descendant of metallurgy recently defined as the materials centre for the University of Wales – has pioneered new methods of producing steel strip, which are simpler and may have economic advantages over present methods. One of these is the new spray-rolling process which produces steel strip by spraying atomized steel on to substrata, and which has also been applied to other metals such as aluminium and its alloys, zinc and copper. Other methods concern the reduction of sintered high-purity iron-ore strip, thus avoiding the need for the high temperature furnaces of normal strip production methods. In carbon technology, new graphite matrix refractory metal carbide composites for rocket nozzles and other high-temperature usages have been developed and work on the corrosive attack on carbon refactories in blast furnaces has been undertaken. Through the 'RAPRA Polymer Engineering Centre' research is also being centred on new polymer alloys and blends.

The civil engineering department has contributed to the design of motorway bridges and is investigating the hydraulics of harbours to determine the effects of wave action. Research in soil engineering and rock mechanics is also carried out, often for local industry, and model experiments and theoretical investigations were undertaken for the Aberfan Tribunal Enquiry in 1966. Professor Oleg Zienkiewicz, head of the department from 1961 to 1988 and an expert on finite elements, was elected an FRS in 1979. Mechanical engineering has much to offer industry and is carrying out research in tribology, into heat transfer problems, noise in turbine blades and problems of comfort in high-speed passenger transport, and most recently into ways of improving the speed and efficiency of printing colour magazines and books. Electrical engineering has contacts with industry, too, in the field of power systems analysis, and 'adaptive' control systems and communications, while microelectronics has become one of the department's main strengths, covering silicon devices and minute integrated circuits.

The department of chemistry is carrying out research into the chemistry of life processes including investigations into the extraction and properties of new antibiotics. Other research topics include gas chromatography and photochemistry, and the development of new magnetic materials. Of major importance was the establishment within chemistry, in 1974, of the Royal Society Research Unit initially under Professor John Beynon, FRS, who had been closely associated with the department in an honorary capacity since 1964. Royal Society research chairs, such as Professor Beynon's, are rarely held outside Oxford and Cambridge and it was some indication of the reputation of chemistry in Swansea that such an appointment – the first in the University of Wales – was made in the college. The unit specializes in research in mass spectrometry and in ion kinetic energy spectrometry. The department of physics has long been a leading centre for research into the physics of electrical contacts and of electrical discharges and in the 1960s extended its research into the fields of high-temperature plasma physics and lasers. The department has close liaison with electrical industries in south Wales and elsewhere and has also carried out research for British Rail. Physics, furthermore, has for many years had a close connection with the European Centre for Nuclear Research (CERN) at Geneva, and a number of staff have spent lengthy periods working there.

The Gower peninsula and the countryside around form a natural laboratory for the earth and life scientists, the geographers, the botanists and the zoologists. The social, cultural and linguistic patterns of the district also provide material for research, often involving collaboration between many of the departments in arts and economic and social studies. An interesting inter-departmental project, involving economics and geography, was that concerned with the significance of the Severn Bridge to the social and economic life of south Wales and the south of England, which was carried out in collaboration with the University of Bath. With increasing awareness of the present-day dangers of industrial pollution, the biological sciences have been especially deeply concerned with the increasing pollution of land and water and, in particular, on the effects of oil pollution. Recently, also, the molecular genetics and cancer biology laboratory was selected by the European Commission to participate in a new project to develop methods of monitoring workers for possible exposure to toxic chemicals.

The growing links with industry have been immeasurably strengthened by the establishment, in 1986, of the innovation centre, initially in partnership with the Welsh Development Agency which funded its foundation to the extent of £1.5 million, 'to encourage entrepreneurial academics and industrialists to establish businesses'. The overall objective is to improve the college's industrial interface and to assist the transfer of technology into wealth-creating business. With help from Europe and with the centre's finances firmly established the college has been able to buy the centre from the WDA much earlier than expected.

Aerial view of the Singleton campus, *c.* 1988

Yet external links and interests are not restricted to industry alone. Linguistic studies of interest to Wales include those carried out in the department of English on dialects. Welsh matters, particularly those concerned with the social and political life of Glamorgan, are under constant study in the department of history. The Welsh department, in addition to specialist studies on the dialects of ancient Gaul and language contacts in Roman Britain, is concerned with modern studies and literary criticism and with the organization necessary for the maintenance of native Welsh culture. But perhaps the college's speciality among Welsh departments is its vigorous role in teaching Welsh to degree level to 'learners'.

Contact with industry and external authorities, of course, goes beyond involvement with departments, research contracts and use of college facilities and expertise. These have contributed to the funding of the college as have important contacts with the EEC which are adding a new dimension to the span of the college's activities, but of particular importance have been the sponsorship of a variety of academic posts such as the Chronar chair in electronic materials and the chair of tourism initiated by the Wales Tourist Board. All this is essential if the college is to thrive and grow because there is no sign that government policy which is conditioned primarily by the cash available is likely to change significantly whatever its political complexion. For a decade universities have been encouraged to give priority to the development of technological and vocational subjects and the promotion of quality research; and to do so at the cost of a lesser dependency on public funds. In this Swansea has been something of an exemplar.

Student life has changed greatly even since the early days of College House and the Singleton halls. The impact of the different life-style of today's student and the desire for accommodation freed of the restrictions of the traditional halls of residence have already been touched on. The students' union has become a different and a more important body. One limited result of the student troubles of the sixties and the 'concordat' between vice-chancellors and the National Union of Students has been the increased participation of students in the policy decision-making processes of universities. While Swansea students had been involved with certain college committees – especially those dealing with student amenities – for many years, in the seventies they began to be invited to the council and then the senate, first as observers and then as full members though doubtless the present generation finds the business of these bodies, and the committees that academic life so readily spawns, far less exciting – or sinister – than ever their predecessors dreamed.

Grumbles about food and the lack of textbooks are perennial – even as I write there is a fleeting sit-in over these issues – but facilities exist now that would hardly have been gleams in the eyes of the students of the Fulton era. The sports centre and the Taliesin Centre, owing much to Principal Steel's forward-looking attitudes, have added greatly to the quality of life. Sketty Lane and Fairwood cater for a wide variety of sporting needs and have been a tremendous success. College rugby has not quite regained the distinction of the thirties but the college 'fifteen' has reached the final of the UAU Cup on four successive occasions since 1988 and won the Welsh championship fifteen times in the last twenty years. Paul Thorburn, Mark Wyatt, Gwyn Evans and Phil May have, moreover, joined the pantheon of the great by being awarded Welsh international rugby caps. A wider range of facilities and services is now available to students than ever Kenneth Rees would have dreamed of: tutors in all departments, medical and dental services, chaplains in all the major denominations, a student counselling service and a highly professional careers advisory service. Many facilities are provided by the students themselves with a welfare department with a full-time welfare adviser, an education welfare officer and a welfare officer for overseas students. A crèche, a shop, even a campus radio station complement the entertainments, clubs and societies that the students' union has traditionally provided for.

For a long time the college has catered for students with physical disabilities and in recent years has enhanced wheelchair access to a large number of buildings and facilities. Disabled students are under-represented in universities, but Swansea's concern for them is notable. It is committed to a long-term policy of increasing its proportion of such students, especially those with visual handicaps, and is investing substantially in the creation of a suitable learning environment for them. A specially equipped resource room and study centre has been provided for the visually handicapped and the college is now embarking on further improvements for the deaf and those whose hearing is impaired.

The past decade or so has seen many changes in the lay officers of the college. Lord Edmund-Davies retired as president in 1974 following his appointment as pro-chancellor of the university and was succeeded by Sir John Habakkuk, the distinguished economic historian, then principal of Jesus College, Oxford. In 1984, Sir John in turn retired but his successor, Lord Harlech, was tragically killed little more than a month after taking office. His successor is the current president, Lord Callaghan of Cardiff,

The president of the college, Lord Callaghan

while the chairman of the council, who took office in 1982 following the death of Ifor Davies MP, is W. Emrys Evans, a former banker.

An innovation in 1985 was the establishment of honorary college fellowships intended for award either to former students of the college who have attained distinction in the arts, literature, science or public life or to persons who have rendered exceptional service to the college or have had a close connection with it. Among the very first eleven fellows were Lord Fulton and Kingsley Amis: a paradoxical juxtaposition, with their very different views about university expansion. One wonders whether there was any meeting of minds. Already fifty-nine fellowships have been awarded and it says much for the college that forty-two have been given to former students, six of them Fellows of the Royal Society and one a Fellow of the British Academy.

Fulton House affords a panoramic view to the sea. To the east can be seen not only Swansea's docks but also the mammoth steel-plant at Margam and the oil refinery at Llandarcy. This view, as well as the symbolism of the pickaxe, hammer and anchor of the college's coat of arms, are constant reminders of the technological background of the college and the extent to which it owes its creation to the efforts of local industrialists more than seventy years ago. But although science and especially technology provided the *raison d'être* of the college, it began to develop rapidly into that 'complete' institution that so exercised the Haldane Commission when it considered the claims of Swansea to be the seat of a university college. Although cripplingly small and impoverished in its first thirty years it built up a reputation of some significance, especially in metallurgy, physics and geology. The fifteen years from 1955 witnessed a growing crescendo of expansion which, owing so much to John Fulton, has resulted in a college with a spread of disciplines, degree courses and research projects of a scale and scope of which the

British universities in 1990. The picture is already changing, as from 1992–3 every polytechnic will be free to take up the title of 'university'. The number of British universities will thus increase from fifty-one to eighty-five, and the number of university students will be doubled to 566,000. By the end of the decade, the government plans to treble the present number of university students

founders would never have dreamed. Then the tide turned and, in the harsh economic climate of the seventies and early eighties, it rapidly went out; there must have been some pessimists who were concerned that Swansea, for all its efforts, might, in common with other comparatively small university institutions, be stranded. But the spirit of co-operation and the resilient character that have always marked the college helped to see it through its difficulties. Now, one glimpses a better future for the college although

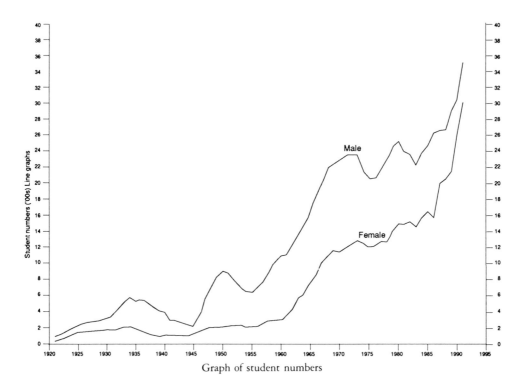

Graph of student numbers

the institution that emerges may well be as different from the college of the post-Fulton era as the college of the sixties was from that of pre-war days. And there are other unknown factors that could have an impact on Swansea, not least the uncertain future hanging over the University of Wales and the elevation of the polytechnics to university status.

In 1992 there are over 5,500 students in the college. The increase in funding that was received from the UFC for the current year (17.8 per cent) was the highest for the constituent institutions of the university and the third highest in the United Kingdom. It was based on the college's teaching standards, research ratings and overall expansion plans. For we are moving again into a period of expansion. The government has said that it expects that 'approaching one in three of all eighteen to nineteen year olds will enter higher education' by the year 2000. For Swansea that means a very swift expansion to ten thousand full- and part-time students by that year. How it will be funded, and how achievable it is, remain open questions, but funding depends on expansion and expansion, in turn, depends on funding. Yet it does really look as if the tide is on the turn again and may be coming in rapidly. Naturally there are those who are concerned about rapid expansion on such a scale. Some have argued that facilities are overstretched already and students have resorted to the 'sit-in' to protest about the implications of expansion for residential accommodation, library space and books, and lecture theatres. But much of the expansion will be taken up by the exciting new developments in nursing and in law and, in the face also of worries about a drift too far in the direction of vocational studies, assurances have been readily forthcoming about academic standards.

A rationalization of academic accommodation is also taking place so that what has become over-provision for earlier developments, as fashion changes and demand dictates, can be redirected to newer and advancing disciplines. Some of the physical developments that have taken place in recent years have been conceived in isolation and have not been subject to the rigours of an overall plan. But circumstances in the later seventies and eighties were inimical to planning, physical or academic. Now things are different and the college is actually planning with a will. There is a new spirit abroad, seen, for instance, in the introduction of modular degree study and in the collaboration with other institutions of further and higher education, especially in south Wales, which is being fostered. The funding stress on teaching and the shock over the college's perceived research standing some time ago have bred not only a willingness to broaden the scope of undergraduate studies but also a determination to enhance the college's research ratings. By the time the next congress of the universities of the Commonwealth assembles in Swansea in 1993 the new college will be taking shape. But, in all the rethinking that is taking place – from how the college will teach to where it will get its income – it behoves us to keep in mind the concern of Professor Archie Richardson half a century ago as he looked ahead with some foreboding to the post-war university world. He envisaged 'a heavy demand for routine teaching and also a materialistic outlook which bodes ill for research'. Expansion, especially in an age when public funds will be dispensed with increased rigour and selectivity, and vastly more students will be taught for less money per head, must not be allowed, in Swansea's case, to mean either a dilution of standards, academic or physical, or a crystallization of that new 'binary' division that seeks to destroy that cardinal feature of the British university system, the juxtaposition of teaching and research. The ideal of the 'complete' university envisaged by Haldane over seventy years ago must never be forgotten.

Notes

1. President of the Zoological Society of London but, more importantly, the most potent government scientific adviser since the war.
2. Part of the Hendrefoilan estate was recently sold and the proceeds are being used for general college improvements.

OFFICERS OF THE COLLEGE

PRESIDENTS

F.W. Gilbertson (1920–5, 1926–9)
Henry Folland (1925–6)
Sir George Barstow, KCB (1930–55)
The Rt. Hon. Major Gwilym Lloyd-George (1955–65; Viscount Tenby of Bulford from 1957)
The Rt. Hon. Lord Justice Edmund Davies (1965–75; Lord Edmund-Davies of Aberpennar, PC from 1974)
Sir John Habakkuk, FBA (1975–84)
The Rt. Hon. Lord Harlech, PC, KCMG (1984–5)
The Rt. Hon. James Callaghan, PC, MP (1985– ; the Rt. Hon. Lord Callaghan of Cardiff, PC, KG from 1987)

VICE-PRESIDENTS

Roger Beck (1920–3)
Ivor H. Gwynne (1920–34)
C.E. Cleeves (1923–6)
W.T. Farr (1926–7)
F.J. Rees (1927–34)
Lewis Jones (1934–68; knighted 1944)
W.T. Farr (jun.) (1935–50)
Captain Hugh Vivian (1950–6)
His Honour Sir George Clark Williams, Bt, QC (1956–8)
R.B. Southall, CBE (1959–65)
P.O. Williams, CBE (1966–74)
His Honour Trevor Morgan, MC, QC (1969–75)
D.J. Young, CBE (1974–83)
Elfed Thomas (1975–84)
The Venerable H.C. Williams, MBE (1983–9)
L.J. Drew (1984–6)
Sir Hywel Evans, KCB (1986–8)
P.A.G. Mullens, OBE (1986–)
Sir Idwal Pugh, KCB (1988–)

CHAIRMEN OF THE COUNCIL

Sir Lewis Jones (1955–66)
His Honour Trevor Morgan, MC, QC (1966–70)
Ifor Davies, MP (1970–82)
W. Emrys Evans, CBE (1982–)

TREASURERS

W.T. Farr (1920–7)
A.W.E. Wynn (1927)
H.W. Crawford (1927–32)
W.T. Farr (jun.) (1932–50)
T.J. Rees, CBE (1950–5)
P.O. Williams, CBE (1955–71)
D.J. Young, CBE (1971–80)
P.A.G. Mullens (1980–9; appointed OBE in 1985)
W.J. Franklyn (1989–)

PRINCIPALS

Dr T. Franklin Sibly (1920–6; knighted 1938, KBE 1943)
Professor C.A. Edwards, FRS (1927–47)
J.S. Fulton (1947–59; knighted 1964; Lord Fulton of Falmer from 1966)
J.H. Parry, CMG, MBE (1960–5)
Professor F. Llewellyn Jones, CBE (1965–74)
Professor R.W. Steel (1974–82; appointed CBE in 1983)
Professor B.L. Clarkson (1982–)

PROFESSORS

The following is a simplified list in terms of subject professed. No attempt has been made to embrace the changes which have taken place over the years in departmental structure and nomenclature, or to be specific over the titular form of certain chairs. While the purist may object, and some inconsistencies result, it is felt that by keeping to the basic academic affiliations of professors the list will be more generally comprehensible.

Abbreviations
L – Lecturer, IL – Independent Lecturer, T – Tutor, ST – Senior Tutor, D – Director, P – Professor

CLASSICS/CLASSICS AND ANCIENT HISTORY

D.E. Evans[1]	1921–7
S.K. Johnson	1927–33
R.B. Onians	1933–5
B. Farrington	1936–56
G.B. Kerferd	1956–67
J.P.A. Gould	1968–74
J.G. Griffiths	1973–9
C. Collard	1975–
A.B. Lloyd	1988–

ENGLISH LANGUAGE AND LITERATURE

W.D. Thomas	1921–54
J. Kinsley[2]	1954–61
C.J.L. Price	1961–80
D.L.F. Hills	1981–
T.J. Worthen	1990–

WELSH

H. Lewis	1921–54
S.J. Williams	1954–61
T.J. Morgan	1961–74
D.E. Evans[3]	1974–8
B.F. Roberts[4]	1978–85
H.T. Edwards	1989–

FRENCH

Mary Williams	1921–48
R.C. Knight	1950–74
A.H. Diverres	1974–81
Valerie Minogue	1981–8
M.J. Cardy	1991–

GERMAN

F.W. Halliday	1931–48 (IL)
E. Heller	1948–50 (IL) 1950–59 (P)
H.M. Waidson	1960–83
R.W. Williams	1984–

HISPANIC STUDIES

D.H. Gagen	1990–

ITALIAN

G.L.C. Bedani	1991–

RUSSIAN

J.B. Woodward	1979–

HISTORY

E.E. Hughes	1920–6 (IL) 1926–44 (P)
D.B. Quinn	1944–57
G. Williams[5]	1957–82
A. Davies	1961–79
R.T. Shannon	1979–
S. Anglo	1981–6
R.A. Griffiths	1982–
Muriel E. Chamberlain	1988–
D.J.V. Jones	1991–

ECONOMIC HISTORY

W.A. Cole	1966–86

ECONOMICS

K.S. Isles[6]	1937–9
S.R. Dennison[7]	1939–45
E.V. Morgan	1945–66
D.S. Lees	1965–7
E.T. Nevin	1968–85
M.J. Artis[8]	1972–6
K.D. George	1988–
H. Dixon	1991–2
S.P. Jenkins	1991–
L. Mainwaring	1991–

POLITICAL THEORY AND GOVERNMENT

J.C. Rees	1955–62
P.A. Bromhead	1963–4
J.M. Brown	1965–6
W.H. Greenleaf	1967–82
R.W. Pethybridge	1974–89
G.N. Harding	1989–
D.G. Boyce	1989–

PHILOSOPHY

A.E. Heath	1925–52
J.R. Jones	1952–70
D.Z. Phillips	1971–
H.I. Dilman	1984–

PSYCHOLOGY

C.E.M. Hansel	1965–82
J.G. Beaumont	1987–92

SOCIOLOGY AND ANTHROPOLOGY

W.M. Williams	1963–91
R.E.A. Mapes	1974–82
C.C. Harris	1985–
R.F. Byron	1991–

SOCIAL ADMINISTRATION/SOCIAL POLICY

D.C. Marsh	1947–8 (L)
R.H. Jones	1949–53 (L) 1953–61 (D)
A.V.S. Lochhead	1961–9 (D) 1969–76 (Overseas Courses D)
M. Broady	1970–82 (P)
W.M. Williams	1991–

DEVELOPMENT STUDIES

C.M. Elliott	1977–82
J.F.J. Toye	1982–7
A.W. Rew	1988–

EDUCATION

F.A. Cavenagh	1921–34
W.M. Williams	1934–42
F.J. Schonell[9]	1942–7
E.J. Jones	1947–56

C.E. Gittins	1956–70
D.G. Pritchard	1971–81
M. Chazan	1976–85
M.T. Williams	1988–
Sally Tomlinson	1991–2
R. Bolam	1992–
V.J. Furlong	1992–

MATHEMATICS

A.R. Richardson[10]	1920–41
R. Wilson	1942–61
J.G. Oldroyd	1953–65
J.D. Weston	1961–82
H.N.V. Temperley	1965–82
G.A. Dirac	1966–70
H.O. Foulkes	1970–4
D. Williams[11]	1972–85
A. Truman	1982–
D.E. Evans	1987–
J. Hawkes	1988–

COMPUTER SCIENCE

D.C. Cooper	1967–73
G.B.F. Niblett	1976–85
P. Townsend	1987–
J.V. Tucker	1989–

PHYSICS

E.J. Evans	1920–44
F. Llewellyn Jones	1945–65
P.M. Davidson	1964–8
P.C. Thonemann	1968–84
J. Dutton	1966–92
C. Grey Morgan	1970–92
D. Parker	1987–92
A.J. Davies	1990–

CHEMISTRY

J.E. Coates	1920–48
C.W. Shoppee[12]	1948–56
C.H. Hassall[13]	1957–71
J.H. Purnell	1965–92
A. Pelter	1972–
J.H. Beynon[14]	1974–86
D. Betteridge	1979–85
K. Smith	1988–
W.J. Jones	1988–

G. Williams   1988–
D.E. Games   1989–

GEOLOGY

A.E. Trueman[15]   1920–30 (IL) 1930–3 (P)
T.N. George[16]   1933–47
D. Leitch   1947–56
F.H.T. Rhodes[17]   1956–68
D.V. Ager   1969–85
T.R. Owen   1977–82
R.B. Kidd   1986–9

OCEANOGRAPHY

F.T. Banner   1976–83

GEOGRAPHY

W.G.V. Balchin   1954–78
J. Oliver   1966–70
R.H. Greenwood   1970–81
N. Stephens   1978–88
D.T. Herbert   1980–
L.J. Symons   1980–8
P.J. Curran   1990–

BOTANY

Florence
Mockeridge   1921–36 (IL) 1936–54 (P)
H.E. Street   1954–67
P.J. Syret   1967–87
I. Isaac   1969–78

BIOCHEMISTRY

E.G. Brown   1972–

GENETICS

J.A. Beardmore   1966–
J.M. Parry   1987–

ZOOLOGY

E.W. Knight-Jones 1956–81
J.S. Ryland   1976–

N.A. Ratcliffe	1984–
P.F. Brain	1987–

METALLURGY AND MATERIALS TECHNOLOGY

C.A. Edwards[18]	1920–47
H. O'Neill	1947–64
A.R.E. Singer	1956–85
J. Burke	1965–79
B. Wilshire	1982–
J.M. Marshall	1987–
R.W. Evans	1988–

ENGINEERING

F. Bacon	1920–43
R.N. Arnold	1944–7
L.J. Kastner	1948–55

CHEMICAL ENGINEERING

E.S. Sellers	1955–9
J.F. Richardson	1960–87
P.E. Preece	1989–
D.J.A. Williams	1991–

CIVIL ENGINEERING

B.G. Neal	1954–61
O.C. Zienkiewicz[19]	1961–88
D.R.J. Owen	1983–
R.W. Lewis	1984–
C. Taylor	1986–
K. Morgan	1988–
E. Hinton	1989–

ELECTRICAL AND ELECTRONIC ENGINEERING

W. Fishwick	1955–68
H.W. Gosling	1966–73
D. Aspinall	1970–8
J.V. Oldfield	1974–8
H.A. Barker	1979–
M.G. Rodd	1986–
K. Board	1986–
F. Halsall	1990–

MECHANICAL ENGINEERING

R.H. Macmillan	1956–64
F.T. Barwell	1965–78
J.M. Alexander	1978–83
W.D. Morris	1985–
R. Parker	1985–

INDUSTRIAL ENGINEERING AND MANAGEMENT SCIENCE

T.O. Jeffries	1965–8
R.B. Gravenor	1972–
S.F. Witt	1989–
B.B. Schlegelmilch	1989–

STATISTICS

A.G. Hawkes	1974–

EXTRA-MURAL STUDIES/ADULT CONTINUING EDUCATION

P.S. Thomas	1924–37 (T) 1937–41 (ST)
I. David	1941–60 (ST)
I.M. Williams	1960–80 (D) 1980–3 (P)
G.W. Roderick	1983–6 (P)
D.H. Francis	1990– (D) 1992– (P)

Notes

1. Principal, University College of North Wales, Bangor 1927–58; knighted 1952.
2. FBA 1971.
3. FBA 1983.
4. Librarian, National Library of Wales 1985–
5. FBA 1986.
6. Vice-chancellor, University of Tasmania 1957–67.
7. Vice-chancellor, University of Hull 1972–9.
8. FBA 1988.
9. Vice-chancellor, University of Queensland 1960–9; knighted 1962.
10. FRS 1946.
11. FRS 1984.
12. FRS 1956.
13. FRS 1985.
14. FRS 1971.
15. FRS 1942; Chairman, UGC 1949–53; KBE 1951.
16. FRS 1963.
17. President, Cornell University 1977–.
18. FRS 1930.
19. FRS 1979.

REGISTRARS AND LIBRARIANS

REGISTRARS

E. Drew	1920–52
J. McIntyre	1952–68
A. Davies	1969–82
V.J. Carney	1983–

LIBRARIANS

Olive M. Busby	1920–59
F.J.W. Harding	1959–80
Mary I. Cooper	1981–92
A.M.W. Green	1992–

HONORARY FELLOWS

The names of those fellows who were formerly students of the college are printed in *italic* type.

Sir Kingsley Amis, CBE
Donald Anderson, MP
Professor Bernard Atkinson
Sir Granville Beynon, CBE, FRS
Professor J.D.E. Beynon
Professor J.H. Beynon, FRS
Edward G. Bowen, CBE, FRS
Professor A.D.S. Carter
Professor Y.K. Cheung
Professor W.K.D. Davies
Professor Alan Davison
Professor D. Ellis Evans, FBA
Sir Geraint Evans, CBE
Inoke Fotu Faletau
Professor E.H. Francis
The Rt. Hon. Lord Fulton of Falmer
Professor Richard H. Gallagher
John Terence Gooding
Sir John Habakkuk, FBA
Professor Cedric Hassall, FRS
Professor Donald H. Hey, FRS
Gwynne R. Howell
Emyr Owen Humphreys
Ivor Jenkins, CBE
Daniel Jones, OBE
Sir Gordon Pearce Jones
Professor Ieuan Gwynedd Jones
Robin Huws Jones, CBE
Thomas Alun Jones

Professor F. Llewellyn Jones, CBE
Illtyd Rhys Lloyd
Sir Ieuan Maddock, CB, OBE, FRS
Terence Hedley Matthews
Professor Leonard Maunder, OBE
The Rt. Hon. Lord Molloy of Ealing, PC
John Morgan
Ernest Percival Morris
Revd William Rhys Nicholas
Geoffrey Nicholson
Mavis Nicholson
Moses Itanola Okunola
John Ormond
Rush Rhees
Alun Richards
Professor Meirion Wyn Roberts
Dato Paduka Lim Jock Seng
Shi Shao-xi
Professor Margaret Stacey
Professor R.W. Steel, CBE
Professor Robert Taylor
Professor Jean Thomas, FRS
Leslie Reginald Verney
Professor P. Wilkinson
Professor David Williams, FRS
Professor Glanmor Williams, CBE, FBA
The Venerable H.C. Williams, MBE
J. Kyffin Williams, OBE, RA
Professor Peter Winch
Professor O.C. Zienkiewicz, FRS

Presidents of the Students' Representative Council

I. Evans (1920–1)
H.C. Downes (1921–2)
H.E.G. Richards (1922–3)
J.H. Morgan (1923–4)
L.J. Cole (1924–5)
G.G. Watcyn (1925–6)
W.H. Beynon (1926–7)
S. Davies (1927–8)
E. Thomas (1928–9)
C.G. Hey (1929–30)
D.H. Thomas (1930–1)
H.C. Perry (1931–2)
A. de M. Beanland (1932–3)
I.G. Davies (1933–4)
J.B. Davies (1934–5)
J.M. Davies (1935–6)
D.A. Davies (1936–7)
C.J.L. Price (1937–8)
W.A. Rees (1938–9)
T.J. Wells/I.F. Bell (1939–40)
J.P. Owen (1940–1)
W.R. Nicholas (1941–2)
R.W. Thomas (1942–3)
G.A. Bennett (1943–4)
Revd M.W.T. Lloyd (1944–5)
Miss D.L. Jones (1945–6)
J.D.E. Jones (1946–7)
T.K.L. Nicholas (1947–8)
H.L. Ebsworth (1948–9)
J.O. Thomas (1949–50)
D.I. Turner (1950–1)
E.C. Davies (1951–2)
D. James (1952–3)
A.R. Jellings (1953–4)
E. Jones (1954–5)
P.J. Thomas (1955–6)

C. Thresher (1956–7)
G.W.A. Ellington (1957–8)
E.A. Maciver Slowe (1958–9)
J. Ford (1959–60)
W.C. Slade (1960–1)
J.P. Dawson (1961–2)
D.H. Thorpe (1962–3)
A.G.L. Macken (1963–4)
I. Norris (1964–5)
J. Phipps (1965–6)
I.R. James (1966–7)
L. Brook (1967–8)
R. Trask (1968–9)
P. Cadogan (1969–70)
D. Williams (1970–1)
M. Lewton (1971–2)
C. Proctor (1972–3)
H. Roberts (1973–4)
J.R. Barnes/H. Roberts (1974–5)
J. Davey (1975–6)
S. Tarbet (1976–7)
P. Griffiths (1977–8)
Miss G. Lewis (1978–9)
D. Griffiths (1979–80)
P. Dinwiddy (1980–1)
D. McBride (1981–2)
G. Reading (1982–3)
D.C.H. Jordan (1983–4)
C.P. Lines (1984–5)
P. Stokes (1985–6)
D.B. Moxham (1986–7)
R. Staines (1987–8)
J.R. Higgins (1988–9)
D. Pritchard (1989–90)
Ms V. Spence (1990–1)
K.J. Durham (1991–2)

BIBLIOGRAPHY

PRIMARY SOURCES

Records

Public Record Office
PRO ED119/74: Committee of Council papers relating to the proposed south Wales university college and the claims of Cardiff. These papers contain the minutes of the proceedings of the Arbitration of 1883 and many other documents relating to Swansea.
PRO ED119/78: Similar papers relating to Swansea's claim to be the seat of a south Wales university college but their scope is limited.
PRO ED119/79: Board of Education papers relating to the foundation of the University College of Swansea.

Bodleian Library, Oxford
MS SPSL 357/10, fols 218–380: Curriculum vitae, testimonials and correspondence with the Society for the Protection of Science and Learning (formerly the Academic Assistance Council).
MS SPSL 438, fols 389–97: Home Office file, 1934–6.

University College of Swansea Library (Archives)
Council, Senate and Committee minute books 1920 onwards.
College correspondence files 1920–59. (These are considerably depleted for the years before *c.* 1960 since a great deal of material was sent for salvage during the Second World War and more was destroyed at the time of the retirement of Mr Drew.)
Newspaper cuttings' files. (These are very sparse for the years before *c.* 1960.)
Minute books and other documentary material relating to the Swansea Grammar School, 1852–93.
Undergrad, 1921–5 and *Dawn*, 1925 onwards. (The magazines of the Students' Representative Council of the University College.)

University College of Swansea Registry
Annual Reports of the Council to the Court, 1920 onwards.
University College of Swansea Gazette, 1958–67.
University College of Swansea Newsletter, 1966 onwards.
College records and correspondence files, 1959 onwards.

University of Wales Registry
Court and Council minute books and correspondence files.

Swansea City Archives
TC3/1881– : Corporation council and committee minute books 1881 onwards.
TC53/6243: Town clerk's papers relating to the movement to develop the Swansea Technical College into a university college.
TC53/9156: Parliamentary committee minutes and papers relating to the university college.
TC/2468: Miscellaneous papers relating to the application for additional land at Singleton in 1949.

Official Reports

Report of the Royal Commission on Scientific Instruction and the Advancement of Science (the Devonshire Commission), 1870.
Report of the Committee Appointed to Inquire into the Condition of Intermediate and Higher Education in Wales (the Aberdare Committee), 1881.
Report of the Royal Commission on University Education in Wales (the Haldane Commission), 1916–18.

Report of the Committee on Higher Education Appointed by the Prime Minister under the Chairmanship of Lord Robbins, 1961–3, 1963.
Report of the Royal Commission on Medical Education, 1965–8 (the Todd Commission), 1968.
Miscellaneous reports and surveys of the University Grants Committee (UGC), the Department of Education and Science (DES) and the Committee of Vice-chancellors and Principals.

Newspapers

Cambria Daily Leader, Swansea Central Library.
The Cambrian, the Royal Institution of South Wales (complete original run); Swansea Central Library (microfilm); Cardiff Central Library (certain years only).
South Wales Daily Post (after 1931 *South Wales Evening Post*), Swansea Central Library.
Swansea and Glamorgan Herald, the Royal Institution of South Wales.
The Swansea Boy, Swansea Central Library.
The Swansea Journal, Swansea Central Library.
The Times, Cardiff Central Library (microfilm).
The Times Educational Supplement, Cardiff Central Library (microfilm).
Western Mail, Cardiff Central Library.

SECONDARY SOURCES

Articles and Books

Place of publication is London unless otherwise stated.

Amis, Kingsley, 'Lone Voices: Views of the Fifties', *Encounter*, July 1960, pp. 6–11.
Amis, Kingsley, *Memoirs*, 1991.
Annan, Noel, *Our Age: Portrait of a Generation*, 1990.
Archer, R.L., *Secondary Education in the Nineteenth Century*, 1966.
Argles, Michael, *South Kensington to Robbins*, 1964.
Armytage, W.H.G., *A.J. Mundella 1825–1897: The Liberal Background to the Labour Movement*, 1951.
——, *Civic Universities*, 1955.
——, *The Rise of the Technocrats*, 1965.
Arnold, Thomas, *Introductory Lectures on Modern History . . .*, 1843.
Ashby, E., *Community of Universities*, Cambridge, 1963.
——, 'Education for an Age of Technology', in Charles Singer, E.J. Holmyard, A.R. Hall, Trevor I. Williams (eds.), *A History of Technology*, vol. V, 1958, pp. 776–98.
——, *Technology and the Academics*, 1958.
Ashby, Eric and Anderson, Mary, *Portrait of Haldane*, 1974.
——, *The Rise of the Student Estate in Britain*, 1970.
Balchin, W.G.V., *Concern for Geography*, Swansea, 1981.
——, (ed.), *Swansea and its Region*, Swansea, 1971.
——, *Universities in Great Britain: A Geographical Conspectus*, Swansea, 1957.
Barker, Sir Ernest, *British Universities*, 1946.
Beanland, W.W., *The History of the Royal Institution of South Wales . . . 1835–1935*, Swansea, 1935.
Beloff, Michael, *The Plateglass Universities*, 1968.
Berdahl, R.O., *British Universities and the State*, 1959.
Caine, Sir Sidney, *British Universities: Purpose and Prospects*, 1969.
Cardwell, D.S.L., *The Organisation of Science in England*, 1972.
Carswell, John, *Government and the Universities in Britain*, Cambridge, 1985.

Chrimes, S.B., 'History of the University College, Cardiff', unpublished.
Cowley, F.G., 'Religion and Education', in Glanmor Williams (ed.), *Swansea: An Illustrated History*, Swansea, 1990.
Davie, G.E., *The Democratic Intellect*, Edinburgh, 1964.
——, *The Crisis of the Democratic Intellect*, Edinburgh, 1986.
Davies, W. Cadwaladr and Jones, W. Lewis, *The University of Wales and its Constituent Colleges*, 1905.
Dykes, D.W., *Wales in Vanity Fair*, Cardiff, 1989.
Ellis, E.L., *The University College of Wales Aberystwyth 1872–1972*, Cardiff, 1972.
Ellis, T.I., *The Development of Higher Education in Wales*, Wrexham, 1935.
Evans, D. Emrys, *The University of Wales*, Cardiff, 1953.
Evans, Leslie Wynne, *Education in Industrial Wales 1700–1900*, Cardiff, 1971.
Evans, W. Gareth, *A History of Llandovery College*, Llandovery, 1981.
Francis, Geo. Grant, *The Free Grammar School, Swansea . . .*, Swansea, 1849.
Fulton, Sir John, *Experiment in Higher Education* (The Tavistock Lecture for 1963), 1964.
Fussell, Paul, *Wartime*, New York, 1989.
Gallie, W.B., *A New University: A.D. Lindsay and the Keele Experiment*, 1960.
Gamwell, S.C., *The Official Guide and Handbook to Swansea and its District, British Association for the Advancement of Science Meeting at Swansea 1880*, Swansea, 1880.
Glascodine, Charles Henry, 'Where ought the Welsh University to be located? – The Claims of Swansea', *The Red Dragon*, I, February 1882, pp. 85–9.
Glass, D. (ed.), *Social Mobility in Britain*, 1954.
Gosden, P.H.J.H., *Education in the Second World War*, 1976.
——, *The Education System since 1944*, Oxford, 1983.
Griffiths, Ralph A. (ed.), *The City of Swansea: Challenges and Change*, Stroud, 1990.
——, *Clyne Castle, Swansea*, Swansea, 1977.
——, *Singleton Abbey and the Vivians of Swansea*, Llandysul, 1988.
Haldane, Viscount, *Universities and National Life*, 1911.
——, *The University and the Welsh Democracy*, Oxford, 1922.
Hall, A. Rupert, *Science for Industry*, 1982.
Halsey, A.H. and Trow, M., *The British Academics*, 1971.
Harrison, J.F.C., *Learning and Living, 1790–1960*, 1961.
Harte, Negley, *The University of London 1836–1986*, 1986.
Higher Education in Wales: Debate in the House of Commons on Tuesday July 1st 1879, n.d. [1879].
Hilton, K.J. (ed.), *The Lower Swansea Valley Project*, 1967.
Hudson, J.W., *The History of Adult Education*, 1851.
Hughes, Sally, *Ernest Hughes*, Llandysul, n.d.
Jones, W.H., *History of the Port of Swansea*, Carmarthen, 1922.
Kelly, Thomas, *A History of Adult Education in Great Britain*, 2nd edn, Liverpool, 1970.
Lewis, D. Gerwyn, *The University and the Colleges of Education in Wales 1925–1978*, Cardiff, 1980.
Lewis, Samuel, *A Topographical Dictionary of Wales*, 2 vols., 1833.
Livingstone, Sir Richard, *Some Thoughts on University Education*, Cambridge, 1948.
Locke, Robert R., *The End of the Practical Man: Entrepreneurship and Higher Education in Germany, France and Great Britain, 1880–1940*, Greenwich, Connecticut, 1984.
Masterman, Neville, *J. Viriamu Jones 1856–1901: Pioneer of the Modern University*, Llandybie, 1957.
Matthews, John Hobson (ed.), *Records of the County Borough of Cardiff*, 6 vols., Cardiff, 1898–1911.
Matthews, R.P. and Griffin, T.L.C., 'The Student Population of the University College of Swansea: A Statistical and Geographical Analysis', *The Swansea Geographer*, Swansea, n.d.
Minchinton, W.E. *The British Tinplate Industry*, Oxford, 1957.
——, (ed.), *Industrial South Wales 1750–1914*, 1969.
Moodie, Graeme C. and Eustace, Rowland, *Power and Authority in British Universities*, 1974.
Morgan, Kenneth O., *The People's Peace: British History 1945–1989*, Oxford, 1990.
——, *Rebirth of a Nation: Wales 1880–1980* (vol. VI, *History of Wales*, ed. Glanmor Williams), Oxford, 1981.
——, *Wales in British Politics 1868–1922*, Cardiff, 1970.
Morgan, T.J., 'The First Fifty Years – A Brief Survey', in *University College of Swansea – Fiftieth Anniversary 1920–1970*, Swansea, n.d. [1970], pp. 3–12.

Mountford, Sir James, *Keele: An Historical Critique*, 1972.
Perkin, H.J., *New Universities in the United Kingdom*, Paris, 1969.
——, *Origins of Modern English Society*, 1969.
——, *The Rise of Professional Society*, 1989.
Phillipson, Nicholas (ed.), *Universities, Society and the future*, Edinburgh, 1983.
Price, D.T.W., *A History of Saint David's College Lampeter*, 2 vols., Cardiff, 1977, 1990.
Reflections, A Departmental Tribute [to retiring members of staff of the Department of Education, University College of Swansea], Swansea, 1991.
Roberts, Glyn, *The Municipal Development of the Borough of Swansea to 1900*, Cardiff, 1940.
Robertson, Sir Charles Grant, *The British Universities*, 1944.
Roderick, G.W., 'Education in an Industrial Society', in Ralph A. Griffiths (ed.), *The City of Swansea: Challenges and Change*, Stroud, 1990, pp. 179–93.
Rogers, W.C., *A Pictorial History of Swansea*, Llandysul, 1981.
Salmon, David, *Swansea Training College*, Swansea, 1913.
Sampson, Anthony, *The Changing Anatomy of Britain*, 1982.
Sanderson, Michael, *The Universities and British Industry 1850–1970*, 1972.
Shannon, Richard, *Mr. Gladstone and Swansea, 1887*, Swansea, 1982.
Simmons, Jack, *New University*, Leicester, 1958.
Smith, Carl, 'A History of the Swansea Grammar School', in *Bishop Gore's Swansea Grammar School*, Swansea, 1982, pp. 6–14.
Sommer, Dudley, *Haldane of Cloan: His Life and Times*, 1960.
Stewart, Robert, *Henry Brougham: His Public Career 1778–1868*, 1985.
Stewart, W.A.C., *Higher Education in Postwar Britain*, Basingstoke, 1989.
Stimson, Dorothy, *Scientists and Amateurs: A History of the Royal Society*, 1949.
Sutherland, Gillian, *Elementary Education in the Nineteenth Century*, 1971.
Swansea Technical College Jubilee Brochure 1897–1947, Swansea, 1947.
Taylor, A.J.P., *English History 1914–1945*, Oxford, 1965.
Truscot, B. [Allison Peers], *Redbrick University*, 1943.
Varley, W.M., *The Swansea Technical College*, Swansea, 1913.
Venables, P.F.R., *Higher Education Developments: the Technological Universities 1956–76*, 1978.
Warnock, Mary, *Universities: Knowing Our Minds*, 1989.
Williams, D. Trevor, *The Economic Development of Swansea and of the Swansea District to 1921*, Cardiff, 1940.
Williams, Glanmor (ed.), *Swansea: An Illustrated History*, Swansea, 1990.
Williams, Iolo Wyn, 'The Western University of Great Britain', *University College of Swansea Collegiate Faculty of Education Journal*, 1966, pp. 32–40.
Williams, J. Gwynn, *The University College of North Wales: Foundations 1884–1927*, Cardiff, 1985.
Williams, Lewis, 'Where ought the Welsh University to be located? – The Claims of Cardiff', *The Red Dragon*, I, February 1882, pp. 89–94.
Wolfenden, Lord, *Memoirs*, 1976.
Wright, Leonard, *The Department of Physics, University College of Swansea 1922–1945*, unpublished.
Young, G.M., *Portrait of an Age: Victorian England*, (ed. George Kitson Clark), 1977.

Unpublished Theses and Dissertations

Davies, Hugh M., 'The Place of the Royal Institution of South Wales in the History of Scientific and General Education in the Nineteenth Century', University of Wales MA, 1940.
Dykes, D.W., 'The University College of Swansea – Its Background and Development', University of Wales Ph.D., 1982.
Evans, Thomas, 'The Mechanics' Institutes of South Wales', University of Sheffield Ph.D., 1965.
Ridd, T., 'The Development of Municipal Government in Swansea in the Nineteenth Century', University of Wales MA, 1955.
Thomas, John Peter, 'A Consideration of Technical Education in the Swansea District 1850–1900', University of Wales M.Ed., 1979.
Weaver, Jean A., 'The Development of Education in Swansea 1846–1902', University of Wales MA, 1957.
Webster, John Roger, 'The Place of Secondary Education in Welsh Society', University of Wales Ph.D., 1959.

INDEX

Page entries in *italics* refer to the captions of diagrams and illustrations.